Additional p

"Carrie Rickey has delivere
an enduring stimulus to show and watch varda's films."
—Henry K. Miller, *Sight and Sound*

"The first major biographical work dedicated to her life and craft. Like Varda herself, *A Complicated Passion* is short and to the point. Considering that Varda spent practically her whole, long life in a state of creation, Rickey's biography is surprisingly just under 300 pages but still manages to fit in everything a newcomer would want to learn, as well as everything a die-hard fan might not yet know.... With *A Complicated Passion*, she gives Varda the remembrance she deserves."
—Conor Williams, *Los Angeles Review of Books*

"This definitive biography of trailblazing French New Wave filmmaker Agnès Varda tells the engrossing story of a brilliant artist and fierce feminist who made movies and found success on her own terms."—*Millions*

"Varda mania has fully arrived—and stands to continue with this new biography from Carrie Rickey, a former film critic for the *Philadelphia Inquirer*, who shows how the French New Wave filmmaker's life inspired her deceptively light meditations on the passage of time, women's rights, and more."
—*Art in America*

"Insightful and comprehensive."
—Peter Keough, *Arts Fuse*

"*A Complicated Passion* manages, with exceptional art and without ever feeling rushed or perfunctory, to compress into a little more than two hundred pages a very long and very productive artistic life.... Rickey shows how life and work can be so thoroughly intermingled as to be inseparable."
—Geoffrey O'Brien, *Book Post*

"Supremely entertaining.... Rickey's fine biography is more than just a catalog of gossip. It's also a proper acknowledgement of cinematic greatness."
—Christopher Schobert, *Film Stage*

"Film critic Rickey delivers the definitive biography of French filmmaker Agnès Varda (1928–2019).... Rickey captures Varda's tenacity and pluck, serving up a portrait of an artist determined to succeed on her own terms. This is a must for cinephiles." —*Publishers Weekly*, starred review

"Providing colorful anecdotes from friends and luminaries in Varda's orbit ... [and] depicting her subject's trailblazing influence and unique cinematic vision embracing creativity, spontaneity, and willingness to tackle provocative issues through an uncompromising body of work. A richly documented examination of this visionary filmmaker's influential career." —*Kirkus Reviews*

"Agnès Varda possessed an almost superhuman degree of talent and hustle, and as Carrie Rickey vividly shows in *A Complicated Passion*, she would need it all to make her way in a man's world. Rickey's portrait is an enthralling blend of personal and contextual history, stylistic analysis, penetrating insights into the films, a humming awareness of the electric combination of Varda and her husband, director Jacques Demy—all during the most exciting and innovative period of French cinema. This is biography and film scholarship at their combined best—the irresistible story of an indomitable woman!" —Molly Haskell, film critic and author of *Frankly, My Dear*

"A landmark achievement, this deeply engrossing biography of Agnès Varda, the first ever in the English language, fills a major gap in film history, chronicling the life and career of one of world cinema's most gifted writer-directors. Carrie Rickey's brisk, jaunty style lends itself perfectly to her peripatetic and multitalented subject." —Noah Isenberg, film historian and best-selling author of *We'll Always Have Casablanca*

"Finally, the definitive biography of a filmmaker whose place in the cinematic pantheon keeps ascending. Carrie Rickey's writing is vivid and colorful, her judgments judicious and astute, her research impeccable, and she captures Agnès Varda's spirit, her achievement, her uniqueness in the very act of analyzing her. One could not ask for a smarter or more engaging take on the subject." —Phillip Lopate, editor of the Library of America's *American Movie Critics*

A Complicated Passion

THE LIFE AND WORK OF
AGNÈS VARDA

CARRIE RICKEY

W. W. NORTON & COMPANY

Independent Publishers Since 1923

For information about permission to reproduce selections from
this book, write to Permissions, W. W. Norton & Company, Inc.,
500 Fifth Avenue, New York, NY 10110

For information about special discounts for bulk purchases,
please contact W. W. Norton Special Sales at
specialsales@wwnorton.com or 800-233-4830

Manufacturing by Lakeside Book Company
Book design by Brooke Koven
Production manager: Louise Mattarelliano

ISBN 978-1-324-11045-3 pbk.

W. W. Norton & Company, Inc., 500 Fifth Avenue, New York, N.Y. 10110
www.wwnorton.com

W. W. Norton & Company Ltd., 15 Carlisle Street, London W1D 3BS

10 9 8 7 6 5 4 3 2 1

To Paul

For Morgan and Cora

*In memory of Ida Applebroog, Lauren Rickey Greene,
and Tom Luddy*

Talent is insignificant. . . . Beyond talent lie all the usual words: discipline, love, luck, but, most of all, endurance.

—JAMES BALDWIN

Contents

Introduction

AGNÈS VARDA MOVED ME to tears even before I'd seen one of her films.

It was 1971, I was an undergraduate at the University of California, San Diego, and the class was "A Hard Look at the Movies," an eclectic film survey taught by the painter and film critic Manny Farber. Then new to teaching, Farber had no syllabus; most weeks he just started a movie, turned down the sound, and drew our attention to how framing shaped the narrative. Sometimes he had the projectionist run the movie backward. Farber showed us 1950s film noirs like Sam Fuller's *Pickup on South Street*, 1960s experimental films like Michael Snow's *Wavelength*, and elliptical narratives lately shown at the New York Film Festival, like Robert Bresson's *Mouchette*. The week he showed Agnès Varda's *Cléo from 5 to 7* (1961), he prefaced it by telling us that the director—whom I misunderstood as "Angus Varda"—was a still photographer who had become a filmmaker. When the movie began and I saw "Script and Direction by Agnès Varda" on the screen, tears spritzed from my eyes. Who knew there was such a thing as a female filmmaker?

I was not yet aware that women directors had been there since the creation of film. Many credit French filmmaker Alice Guy-Blaché with making the first movie feature, *The Cabbage Fairy*, in

1896—although, inexplicably, she was largely absent from film history for the better part of a century. Soon I would become aware that feminist scholars had commenced the ongoing project of restoring to history female filmmakers such as Guy-Blaché, Lois Weber, Dorothy Arzner, Ida Lupino, and hundreds more who had been erased from it.

But Varda was my first, and *Cléo* . . . I had never seen anything like it! During this ninety-minute film that creates the illusion it is happening in real time, a fetching blonde pop singer accustomed to being gaped at awaits the results of a biopsy. As she waits, she has a revelation. Varda put it best in a 1975 essay: "Cléo is the cliché woman: Tall, beautiful, blonde, voluptuous. The whole dynamic of the film lies in showing the woman at the moment she doesn't want to be this cliché, the moment she doesn't want to be looked at, when she wants to do the looking herself. . . . From the object of the look, she becomes the subject who looks." Even at eighteen, I recognized that Varda had crystallized a profound instant of personal transformation and intellectual growth.

From her directorial debut *La Pointe Courte* (1954) to her posthumously released ciné-memoir *Varda by Agnès* (2019), almost all of Agnès Varda's films capture such a decisive moment in film imagery in a language all her own. She called it *cinécriture*, or film writing, bridging documentary and feature filmmaking—and revolutionizing both. Over more than sixty years and through more than forty-four shorts and feature-length films, Varda showed that a powerful, memorable film could run two minutes or two hours, depending on what it had to say; she demonstrated that documentary and fiction were not opposites, and that they could, in fact, coexist; she changed the way that movies looked by becoming an early adapter of digital technology; and, by putting women at the center of her movies, she helped expand the way filmgoers looked at men and women, at social arrangements, and the world. As Martin Scorsese put it, Varda "really open[ed] the way for filmmakers to question all the inhibitions they inherited, and all the expectations."

And yet for decades Varda was underappreciated if not unsung.

A pioneer of the French New Wave, she saw her trailblazing and probing early works—two features and five shorts between 1954 and 1961—eclipsed by what French journalist Michel Capdenac characterized as "a group of hot-headed noisy auteurs," referring to François Truffaut, Jean-Luc Godard, Alain Resnais, Jacques Demy, and their New Wave confrères, some of whom became Varda's closest friends, and one of whom—Demy—became her husband. In a conversation we had in Cannes in 1988, Varda described their marriage as "a complicated passion." The phrase equally applies, I think, to her life as a filmmaker.

Over the years, scholars and critics on this side of the Atlantic, including Kelley Conway, Manohla Dargis, Rebecca J. DeRoo, Sandy Flitterman-Lewis, Molly Haskell, Nam Lee, B. Ruby Rich, and Amy Taubin, among others, have championed her work. And with the release of *The Gleaners and I* (2000), her acclaimed film about the waste engendered by industrial farming, she gained a new following. Like so many of her films, this visual essay on the history and ecology of finding sustenance in what others reject was ahead of its time, priming audience awareness of income inequality and the "waste not, want not" zeitgeist to come. So was the fact that Varda shot it cheaply on a small, lightweight digital camera at a time when many of her peers were wringing their hands over "the end of cinema" made on costly film. Suddenly the marginalized woman in the fraternity of French filmmakers became a global icon for the green movement and a recognized advocate for recycling.

Varda's elevated profile was in no small part a product of feminist scholarship, comparable to the rediscovery of Mexican surrealist Frida Kahlo by art historian Hayden Herrera, of writer Zora Neale Hurston by author Alice Walker, of Danish storyteller Isak Dinesen by Judith Thurman, and of pioneer French filmmaker Alice Guy-Blaché by film and art historian Joan Simon.

Still, despite all the acclaim, Varda remains better known in her parts than in her whole. To film historians, she is the catalyst of the French New Wave. To feminists, she is the woman who led a 2018 march at the Cannes Film Festival—with Cate Blanchett, Ava DuVernay, Patty Jenkins, Céline Sciamma, Salma Hayek, Léa Seydoux, Kristen Stewart, and other leading actresses and filmmakers—to call attention to how few female directors had ever been invited to Cannes' main competition. To those of my daughters' generation, she is the quirky grandma of documentaries like *Faces Places* (2017). Even those who love Varda's films are often unfamiliar with the masterful photographs she shot in the 1950s, and, outside of art museums, few know her late-career work as an installation artist. And this is not even to mention the Zelig-like improbability of a woman who was chums with Susan Sontag, a political ally of Simone de Beauvoir, the discoverer of Gérard Depardieu, the director of an early Harrison Ford screen test, and a friend of Jim Morrison who kept his death under wraps for several days.

"People often speak of how [Agnès] broke new ground for women filmmakers—and she has," said Angelina Jolie when she presented Varda with an honorary Oscar in 2017. "But to discuss it that way is to limit her contribution. She broke new ground as an artist, period."

In 2019, Varda succumbed to breast cancer, the diagnosis feared by the heroine of *Cléo from 5 to 7*. When not being fêted or receiving chemotherapy treatments, Varda worked shoulder to shoulder with her daughter, Rosalie Varda, to complete *Varda by Agnès*. During her final months, "she was more loved, well known and celebrated . . . than ever before," said her close friend and collaborator Jane Birkin, the singer, actress, and screenwriter. Upon Varda's death, renowned figures from French president Emmanuel Macron to pop star Madonna celebrated Varda's films, her art, and her wit. So did the residents of Montparnasse, the Paris neighborhood where she lived for decades. As an *Irish Times* journalist who eulogized Varda put it, her family and fans "can draw consolation from the awareness that she died while part of the cultural conversation."

———

FROM MY first encounter with *Cléo* to my last with Varda four decades later, the director and her work expanded my received ideas of who a filmmaker is and what a film can be. When she died in 2019, she had directed for sixty-five years, the longest of any female filmmaker. I was curious about the internal and external forces that shaped her, how she seemed to dodge the potholes that beset so many indie and female directors and artists, and how, when she lacked the resources to make a feature, she created shorts and installation art. As an artist, she evolved from still pictures to moving pictures to three-dimensional multimedia art. The end products were, like her, boundary-blurring, erasing distinctions between documentary and fiction, film and sculpture, art and theater.

Though I'd seen, re-seen, thought about, lectured on, and written about her work, I knew precious little about how Brussels-born Arlette Varda (from the neighborhood of Ixelles, where Audrey Hepburn was born a year later), became Agnès Varda. And I knew that a director's filmography is not a biography; I wanted to understand Varda not as a timeline but in 360 degrees. I wanted to know how her studies in philosophy at the Sorbonne and art history at the École du Louvre led to her studies of photography at the École Technique de Photographie et de Cinématographie and her first career as a still photographer. I also wanted to know how an image-maker who had seen fewer than ten films in her life went from making pictures that stood still to those that moved. I wanted better to know this woman who was an artist, a filmmaker—"the first chime in the carillon that became the New Wave," as a contemporaneous critic put it—a single mother, then wife and mother, political activist, widow, grandmother, and late-life fairy godmother of independent film.

Undertaking such a project, I hope, is a contribution to keeping her work, and her memory, alive.

PART I

STILL

1

THEY HAD NAMED HER Arlette, her parents told her, because she was conceived in Arles, France, during the waning days of August 1927. Originally a Phoenician trading port that evolved into a geographically strategic city on the western edge of the Roman Empire, Arles is a vest-pocket Rome on the Rhône, a city of antiquity overlooking the mouth of a great river that threads northeast past vineyards and farms all the way to Switzerland. Arles' ancient amphitheaters, its aqueducts, and its necropolis, the Alyscamps, still stand, just a short hop from the Mediterranean. This city, where van Gogh once painted, may have particularly appealed to Varda's father, Eugène Varda, an ethnic Greek born in 1890 in Smyrna (now Izmir, Turkey). Eugène had two brothers and three sisters; their father was a medical doctor who had studied in France and was a member of the Greek diaspora's haute bourgeoisie.

Following Eugène's education at Catholic French-language schools in Smyrna, he traveled to Montpellier, France, to see his brother. In 1910, he enrolled at the University of Liège in Belgium to study engineering, receiving his diploma in 1914. Shortly after, World War I commenced. According to his son, Eugène marched with the Belgian army from Liège to Brussels, hoping to enlist. Rejected, he walked across the French border to Rennes and finally to Brest, where he enlisted in the French Foreign Legion.

At Verdun in 1916, a fragment from a grenade lodged in his gut. Subsequent surgery left him with ten fewer inches of intestine and a belt-like scar around his midsection. His service qualified Eugène to apply for French citizenship and he became a naturalized citizen in 1919. By that time, he had served first as an engineer in the design department and then as the manager of the manufacturing division of the Industrial Company of Armaments in Saint-Étienne, a town in southeast France close to the Swiss border. In May 1919, Eugène wed Antoinette Mercier, daughter of an officer friend from the Foreign Legion. It was a brief union; thirteen months later they were divorced.

By the time the divorce decree came through, Eugène likely had already met Christiane Pasquet, a striking blonde with chocolate-brown eyes. Born in 1898, she was the sixth of twelve children of Edouard Pasquet, a Protestant pastor in a French town nestled in the Jura near the Swiss border, and his Marseille-born wife, Hélène (née Fraissinet), whose family owned a prominent shipping line. According to her son, Christiane's grandparents were prosperous, but her father, Edouard, "was poor as a potter."

In 1920, when Eugène was thirty and Christiane twenty-two, they met in the nearby Swiss town of Les Brenets, near the waterfall Saut du Doubs. Christiane wasn't there for the scenery. As an adult, Varda recounted the story that Christiane was sent by her father to raise money for a Protestant mission in Africa. Her brother Jean was told that the couple met in front of Le Croix Bleu, an international temperance society that rehabilitated alcoholics. Eugène soon asked Pastor Pasquet for his permission to marry Christiane, "but the pastor was skeptical of a freethinker as a son-in-law."

It took Eugène eighteen months to persuade Pastor Pasquet to give in. Eugène Varda and Christiane Pasquet wed on December 20, 1921, in Christiane's hometown of Ferney-Voltaire. The Vardas moved to Paris, where their firstborn, Hélène, was delivered, and then to Ixelles, a Brussels neighborhood, where their son Lucien was born.

Varda was born on May 30, 1928, the third of five children, the only one with an artistic bent. She thought of herself as a fifth wheel, the singleton stuck in the middle between the elder pair of siblings, Hélène and Lucien, and the younger pair, Jean and Sylvie. Varda described herself as "the youngest of the older two and oldest of the younger two." In her 1994 memoir, Varda wondered playfully, "Did Mom, by naming me [Arlette] . . . always remember a city she loved or this conception of which my father was the director?"

What Varda did have was a mother who nurtured her creativity. She wrote of her parents that "they projected on their child to come the desire to be an artist." Christiane (known to her children as Cri-Cri) "read to me the lives of painters and also the series *Jean-Christophe* by Romain Rolland." (The latter is a ten-volume saga about the inner life of a Beethoven-like composer.) That anecdote and another about how Christiane pawned Eugène's keychain and their wedding silver because they were short on money are among the stories she later shared with Varda about her prenatal life. The money issues were resolved before Varda was born. Eugène asked Christiane to consent to his acquisition of an engineering concern, Antwerp Titan. According to a member of the family, "[Christiane] told me that when [Jean's] father took over this company, it was risky, despite everything, and she was pregnant [with Arlette]. But she told him, 'Don't worry, it will be fine.'"

When Arlette was born, Ixelles was an attractive, leafy neighborhood of Brussels. They lived at 38 avenue de la Couronne in a courtyard apartment. Christiane's father-in-law wrote to her from Athens in July, relieved that Arlette's was not a breech delivery like that of her older brother, Lucien:

> *My beloved daughter Christiane:*
> *I read with great pleasure your letter and the details of your happy childbirth. . . . All's well that ends well. . . . The name is*

*charming, Arlette from the Greek Arelaty (named by Greek
geographer, Strabo). My good son did not write to me, probably
because of his work.... According to what he wrote to me recently,
he has an overload ...*

The streets of Ixelles were studded with elegant Belle Époque
architectural gems, many of them designed by Victor Horta, father of
Art Nouveau. Varda was born eleven months before and about a mile
from the birthplace of Edda Ruston, better known as Audrey Hepburn. It is tempting to imagine the infants, both doe-eyed brunettes,
peering at each other from their prams as they passed from opposite
directions on avenue Louise, the neighborhood's main thoroughfare.

"Of my birth and my little entrance, I am only the story of others,"
Varda said in her memoir *Varda by Agnès* (1994). Both in her memoir and in her autobiographical documentary *The Beaches of Agnès*
(2008), there is scant mention of her siblings and only a little more of
her father. Her memories of Cri-Cri, though fleeting, are tender and
tactile. She remembered that her mother made her memorize their
address in Ixelles in the event that her adventurous daughter got lost.
Likewise, she remembered that Cri-Cri waved off others who coddled her, telling them, "She's old enough to tie her own laces." But as
an adult, Varda couldn't conjure a picture of the "avenue or the house
or the habitat." Examining a photo of herself at six with "a cabbage of
ribbon" atop her bob triggers memories of a comb parting her locks
"and the sliding sound of the ribbon and the feeling of hands drawing
arabesques to attach a barrette." Like her future films and writing,
her memories engage all the senses. She remembers neither "appre-
ciating nor challenging" her hairstyle. Except for an androgynous
period during her early twenties, she sported a version of that bob for
her entire life. The bangs defined a sharp line across her hexagonal
face, dramatizing eyes and cheekbones.

"The North Sea and its sand are the start for me," she announces
at the beginning of *The Beaches of Agnès*, seeming to suggest that,
like Botticelli's Venus, she emerged from the ocean. For this lifelong

explorer, the beach was primal, primeval, and elemental, a spiritual birthplace and recurring motif in her movies and art.

In another family photo there is Varda, hair topped by a brioche-scaled bow, front and center in a 1934 family snapshot on the beach at Ostend. Fists balled, she is six years old in this beach revel, running toward the camera with a mischievous grin. She looks as though she's both spoiling for a fight and about to win a race. Elder siblings Hélène and Lucien trail her on their bicycles while younger brother Jean dances on the sand nearby.

Summer holidays inevitably involved the beach. "When we were little," she remembered, "we were taken to Knokke-le-Zoute or to Ostend" on the North Sea. Beach air and exercise was good for the bones, declared Cri-Cri, who feared for her children the osteoporosis that had hastened her own father's premature death. These beaches on Belgium's forty-mile coast had diversions for Eugène as well. An inveterate gambler, he was drawn to the gaming tables at the casinos dotting the strand. While Eugène was at the roulette wheel, his children sold their handmade paper flowers on the beach, bartering blooms for seashells. The activity introduced Varda to the making and marketing of her own creations and may have helped to spark her lifelong preference for the artisanal over the mass-produced object.

Growing up in Brussels, Varda spoke French and some Flemish. In school, she studied German. As an adult, she learned Italian, some Spanish, and English. She was a lifelong lover of puns and an avid coiner of double-entendres. The granddaughter of a Protestant pastor, the adult Agnès didn't remember any formal religious training, although her brother Jean did. "My mother was a pagan," said Jean Varda, admitting that Christiane "instilled in us a few notions." Varda's daughter, Rosalie, remembers her mother telling her that "to piss off" her authoritarian and atheist father, the young Arlette received confirmation.

While the adult Varda maintained that she did not feel a strong link to her childhood, in her memoir she spoke with great warmth of the family's hand-cranked phonograph on which her mother, despite difficulty hearing, listened to Schubert's *Unfinished Symphony*.

Christiane hired au pairs from Germany to help in the house. One of them frequently played a recording of Schubert's "Erlkönig" on the family Victrola. Inspired by a Goethe poem about how the King of the Elves spirits away a boy as he and his father gallop on horseback into the roaring wind of the Black Forest, "Erlkönig" haunted young Varda. She imagined that the tale of abduction and death took place at the edge of the nearby Ixelles Ponds, through which she walked almost daily with Christiane on their way to the vegetable market. The legend left a lasting impression on her.

For one of a tender age, the abundance of linden, maple, and tulip trees and the two freshwater pools in the Ixelles Ponds resembled a fairy-tale forest. Varda would walk through this swath of green, her left hand clutching Christiane's while her right stroked "cast iron barriers of which I have a very precise memory." She loved "the spectacle of pretentious swans, with their fan-shaped tails, and seeing the ducks perching on the edges of their little huts." There were two small basins—petite versions of the Ixelles ponds—in the narrow but long garden at avenue de la Couronne, where she and her siblings made paper boats and sailed them.

Christiane, a self-taught student of art history, had a special affection for images of the Annunciation—the angel Gabriel informing the Virgin Mary of the imminent Immaculate Conception. One such painting was likely Arlette's earliest experience of visual storytelling. "Mother took us to Ghent to see and re-examine *The Adoration of the Mystic Lamb*, that large polyptych by [Hubert and Jan] van Eyck . . . poorly lit at the bottom of alveoles in a cathedral choir," she remembered. "For us children, it was a big puzzle of sketches and we giggled when we saw, again, in the upper right and upper left, a naked man and a naked woman [Adam and Eve] who hid their [privates] with their hands."

That Varda rarely spoke of her father's influence might be because she was unconscious of how his life's work, tooling devices to operate more efficiently, may have inspired her own mechanical skills. Eugène used cranes and tracks as components of lading and unlading devices. Years later, Agnès Varda used them on movie sets to take a crane shot, a perspective from above, or a tracking shot, where the camera cuts through space like a moving train.

Varda was nine or ten when she saw her first film. Christiane took her to the Cinéma Métropole, Brussels' Art Deco movie palace, to see Disney's *Snow White and the Seven Dwarfs* in 1938. It was one of the few films she saw before making one. Though she loved fairy tales and myths, and though Christiane was enchanted (and bought small felt replicas of the dwarfs for her children), Varda had little use for the Disney version.

"What is certain is that I hated Snow White," Varda remembered sixty years later. "I found her ugly and silly. I was like, 'Why does she take care of these little ones all the time? Why is she doing all this?' And, when I saw Prince Charming, I found him hideous, ridiculous, soft and insipid. . . . And then, I was very afraid of the witch, excruciating and cruel." Later Varda would tell critic Amy Taubin that what she remembered disliking about the movie was its valorization of the heroine for cleaning the house of the dwarfs without pay—a sophisticated critique for a ten-year-old.

GERMANY'S AIRBORNE attack on Belgium and the Netherlands began around dawn on May 10, 1940, coordinated with its army's motorized assault. Western Europe had lived in dread of German aggression since the prior September, when Hitler's army had invaded and partitioned Poland.

That morning, Eugène and Christiane scooped their five children into their lapis blue, seven-seat Packard to flee to France, correctly reckoning that Belgium would fall to the Nazis. What they didn't foresee was that three days later German Panzer divisions would thunder into France, ultimately occupying the country's northern half, including Paris.

Varda and her family were fortunate to have a car, as many who left on foot or bicycle sustained wounds, or died, from German bombs. Eugène was prepared to abandon his engineering concern, which during the 1930s had helped remediate the damage to the port of Antwerp, one of Europe's largest, from World War I. The Vardas were seven among the two million Belgians—fully 20 percent of the nation's population—to seek refuge in France. Hélène, the eldest of the Varda children, was seventeen; Sylvie, the youngest, was four. The bombs began raining down three weeks before Varda's twelfth birthday.

In the disruption and chaos, as Christiane hurriedly packed and Eugène loaded the car, Arlette had scant awareness of the imminent danger. "I was even happy to leave," she remembered years later. She recalled seeing one of her parents lock the door at avenue de la Couronne and thinking, "Probably, I will never see this place again."

While the valises Christiane packed had "a minimum of effects for each child," there was also a box with enough notebooks and pencils "to equip a primary school . . . but almost nothing we needed," remembered her daughter. Setting out before settling on a destination, the Vardas were in transit for at least six weeks, perhaps longer. Eventually they headed for Nice, on the southern coast of France, where Eugene had moored his 75-foot pleasure boat, the *Poppet*, purchased in 1939.

"I don't remember being scared," she recalled later, but she did remember "bad food, like rutabagas and Jerusalem artichokes." Though she blamed the vegetables for her stomachache, her unease may have been due to carsickness or anxiety.

She recalled leaving around 11 am, on a road teeming with cars and people. Over the 650 miles between Brussels and Marseille, they stopped frequently at the homes of friends, relatives, and acquaintances. "Every once in a while, we got out of the car, and hid in a ditch," she recalled. Then they resumed the drive.

It is unclear whether Eugène's objective was to use the *Poppet* to escape western Europe altogether—perhaps to Greece, as his middle daughter hoped, or to Morocco. The course they followed, to the French town of Sète, where the Vardas ultimately spent the early years of the war, did not run smooth. But the journey over land and sea had suspense and adventure enough for a World War II–era refugee movie like *Casablanca*.

Agnès Varda later recalled that when they got to Marseille, where Christiane's parents lived, Eugène and his brother-in-law set out for Nice to sail the *Poppet* back to the port city. Once moored in Marseille, which was swelling with refugees from all over Europe, the boat was hit by a bomb, conceivably because the Germans feared it might be used by the Resistance.

Varda's sister Hélène and brother Jean remembered the itinerary in finer-grained detail. It was in either Nice or nearby Monte Carlo that the seven Vardas boarded the *Poppet* bound for Morocco, setting sail before France's capitulation to Germany on June 22. Some 300 nautical miles later, they stopped to refuel in Barcelona, where Eugène learned that France and Germany had signed an armistice. As the hostilities between the two nations had ceased, he concluded that Christiane and the children would be safe in France and that he did not have to relinquish his business in Antwerp.

The *Poppet* reversed course, sailed back to Marseille and then on to Sète in the so-called French free zone administered by the Vichy government. Eugène moored the *Poppet* on a quay that was literally and figuratively a safe harbor. Christiane outfitted everyone on board with a life preserver, as she could not swim, nor did several of her children. When Eugène returned to Belgium, in his absence Lucien— who could swim—effectively became head of the family.

Varda took to picturesque Sète, known to travelers as "the Venice of the Languedoc." A tongue of land between the Mediterranean and an immense tidal lagoon, the Étang de Thau, it is crosshatched by canals, known for its shellfish, and celebrated for local rituals such as water jousting, a tradition dating back to 1666 when Louis XIV reigned. In a time of disruption, Sète was a refuge of continuity and stability.

After months of uncertainty, first crowded into the Packard on the road, bunking with friends and relatives, and then in tight quarters on the *Poppet* with precious few opportunities to stretch their legs, dropping anchor in Sète was a relief. For Varda, it was also a joy. She liked the temperate climate, where she could be outdoors year-round and enjoyed more independence than she had in Ixelles. She credited her love of nature to her discoveries in the maritime village. Christiane enrolled Arlette in the Protestant Girl Scouts, which went on group excursions twice a year, including a camping trip to the Alps. There, unknown to their charges, den mothers discreetly escorted two Jewish scouts across the border to safety in Switzerland. Come autumn, Varda returned to the structure of school.

More consequentially, in Sète, Varda struck lifelong friendships that would be fundamental to her personal and artistic development. "The real times of my youth, after adolescence, were marked by meeting the Schlegel family in Sète. Their balcony plunged above the quay where the boat, which had served as our house since the Exodus, was moored," recalled Varda in her memoir. "The parents, Éty [Étienne] and Baronne, their very daughters, Andrée, Suzou [Suzanne], and Linou [Valentine], changed my life, not only in Sète, but when we went up to Paris among the Sétois."

Andrée's future husband, the actor and theater director Jean Vilar, also from Sète, would offer Varda her first significant job. Suzanne, Varda's Girl Scout counselor, and her husband, Pierre, inspired Varda to make her first film. Valentine was her best friend, roommate, and travel companion during her first decade in Paris. The Vardas were her family of origin, the Schlegels her family of choice. Effectively, Varda was the fourth, and youngest, Schlegel sister, included at mealtimes and on family excursions.

Not only were the Schlegel girls Varda's companions and confidantes, their pursuits influenced her to become an artist. Andrée was a printer who chiseled her blocks in wood and linoleum; Suzanne persuaded Varda to listen closely to music; Valentine was a gifted ceramicist and sculptor whose organic forms may have encouraged the adult

Varda to create unique structures for film narratives. "What a godsend for me," remembered Varda, whose siblings shared neither her artistic inclinations nor her fervent desire for independence. She was most intimate with Valentine, the youngest Schlegel sister, grateful that "she saved me from the combined effects of the war and my family."

Reflecting upon her own clan during their three years in Sète, Varda later remembered, "Overall, an absent father . . . we didn't have much to eat." Unlike Étienne Schlegel, who was a furniture maker (Varda loved the smell of his workshop, associating wood with all good things), Christiane could not barter things she made for a leg of lamb. Like most people in France, the Vardas depended on ration tickets for food. Christiane sent the elder children to stand in the queues at different stores—Lucien at the butcher, Arlette at the grocer. Whoever reached the front of the line first got tickets to purchase food. Their mother dissuaded them from buying anything on the black market.

For the most part, Varda and her siblings were sheltered from the particulars of war. The *Poppet* had no radio. For news of war, the family relied on their neighbors and the village grapevine. Varda spent her time in Sète mastering skills. From the veteran Sétois fishermen she learned to mend fishing nets, while asking them questions and listening to their colorful answers. From Christiane, she learned to knit sweaters for the "prisoners," without knowing who or where exactly such prisoners were. (Presumably these were French prisoners of war.) From her elder brother Lucien, she learned how to row a boat. Her facility with rowing boats and mending nets would win Varda her first job. Her ability to ask questions of strangers would be essential for making documentaries, including her debut film.

When she was fourteen, Varda attended the wedding of Andrée, eldest of the Schlegel sisters, to Jean Vilar, the actor who became one of France's most important stage directors. Because it was wartime and because there was no money, the couple "wed around a crate of cherries," Varda would remember, evoking an image out of a Symbolist poem.

Allied forces invaded French North Africa in November; in reprisal, German soldiers crossed into the "free zone" and into Sète. The *Poppet* was requisitioned by the soldiers, who cut its masts and displaced the Vardas. The Packard came out of the garage and the family headed north, staying in an unknown village before relocating to Paris. In the village, they kept a low profile and witnessed German soldiers in retreat. For Arlette, these were rare "scenes of jubilation."

It would be a year before Parisians would experience comparable euphoria.

2

FOR THREE YEARS OF occupation, Parisians had suffered unprecedented food and fuel shortages and nightly curfews, not to mention the humiliation of being treated as foreigners in their own city. When the Vardas moved to 13 boulevard Raspail, a handsome 1920s building in the 7th arrondissement, the flags flying over Paris had swastikas. The only public place to see the French tricolor was in the Army Museum at Les Invalides—where it was locked in an exhibition case. Nearly two hundred bronze statues that once had graced the city's parks and boulevards had been seized, shipped to Germany, and melted down for use as shell casings.

The ersatz coffee served at sidewalk cafés, dubbed *café national*, was ground from acorns and chickpeas. Rutabagas, once cattle fodder and decidedly not Varda's favorite food, were by now a staple of the Parisian diet. Because there was not sufficient electricity to project a film, cinemas hired bicyclists to supply the current to generators. The Gaumont-Palace, the Parisian equivalent of Radio City Music Hall, calculated that four bicyclists pedaling at 13 miles per hour for six hours could produce enough stored electricity for two shows daily.

During the last years of the Occupation, a daily event for many Parisians was the half hour when an electric current hissed on and those with radios listened closely to cipher the forbidden BBC broadcast through the static of Germany's attempts to jam the airwaves. Now in an apartment with limited electricity, the Vardas numbered among the regular listeners, in what one eyewitness likened to a "sacred activity."

Varda was fifteen in 1943. During bombing raids, her high school classes continued in the cellars, where she "listened to a poem by Mallarmé between the sandbags." Students were allotted two vitamin cookies daily. Varda said she "didn't climb the Eiffel Tower or the towers of Notre-Dame," but hung out at the docks, where she sorely missed Sète and its seagulls. At home, she recalled, "we rarely talked about the war."

In 1943, Nazi-occupied Paris was not the beloved city of tree-lined riverbanks and bustling cafés on boulevards. The French capital was cloaked in defeat. For Varda, it was "excruciating." Accustomed to the sunshine and sea of Sète, she found Paris "grey, inhuman, and sad."

Even for born-and-bred Parisians, the city was unrecognizable. Commandeered by Nazi officers, its grand hotels were camouflaged in shades of khaki and gray. After sunset the City of Light was dark, as the occupying forces wanted to make it harder for Allied forces to identify targets. Those who survived the Occupation remember the air raids, the unremitting cold, the hunger (and ration tickets for food), the smells of urine and offal, and the hooflike clop of wooden soles on cobblestones. Lacking the materials to repair footwear, cobblers planed pieces of wood and nailed them to shoe bottoms.

Due to the strict rationing of flour and the scarcity of butter and sugar, the streets lacked the comforting aromas from bakeries. Even worse, bread had an unfamiliar texture and smell. By the end of the war allotments were down to one slice per day per person of a loaf made of two-thirds flour and one-third sawdust. Parisians would later recall how the Occupation smelled of sawdust and the fish oil the Nazis used to shine their jackboots.

Fortunately, Varda's friends from Sète, including Andrée and Jean Vilar, were among a contingent that arrived in Paris at the same time. When the Vilars attended a play (during the Occupation, theaters opened at 3 pm and closed at dusk), Varda babysat their young children. For Varda, the best part of the babysitting was when the adults returned home. In his stirring voice, Jean recited poetry. Andrée's husband was a mentor who took the young Varda's education in hand. "He would read me Gide, Mallarmé, and Valéry," she recalled, "and his wife would breastfeed their firstborn to the sound of these masterpieces."

Like many Parisians, the teenage Varda bicycled around town. French actress Leslie Caron, Varda's junior by three years, recalled that many young women avoided the Métro during wartime because older men routinely exposed themselves. (In *The Beaches of Agnès*, Varda cheekily re-creates a scene of a man exposing himself to young girls on the quays.) When Varda moved to Paris, women could not vote. (French women won that right in 1944, Belgian women in 1948, and Swiss women, astonishingly, not until 1971.)

With her Sétois friends, Varda discovered the capital, later describing it as a hotbed "of theater, painting and of craftsmen." Although she and her friends barely spoke of cinema, an exception was Marcel Carné's 1945 film *Children of Paradise*, the three-hour epic of the theater set in Paris before and after the July Revolution of 1830. Suzanne Schlegel took Varda to see it because it was written by poet (and frequent Carné screenwriter) Jacques Prévert. Another was Georges Lampin's *The Idiot*, with Prince Myshkin played by Gérard Philipe, the heart-stopping actor with tousled hair, a radiant face, and a Romantic poet's faraway gaze. Soon he would be a frequent subject for Varda in her work as a portrait photographer.

For a comparatively small provincial city (pop. 35,000 in 1940), Sète exerted an outsize influence on the culture of postwar France. Apart from Vilar and the Schlegels, other Sétois in Paris when Varda arrived included Roger Thérond, who in 1949 became the editor of *Paris Match*; Henri Colpi, a filmmaker and editor who later worked with Varda and Alain Resnais; singers Henri Serre (co-star of François Truffaut's *Jules and Jim*) and Jean-Pierre Suc; and photographer Jean Brunelin, who worked for *Paris Match* before becoming a master chef specializing in the cuisine of Sète.

The Sétois were Varda's lifeline. Not so her schoolmates at the Lycée Victor-Duruy. At the highly regarded school where she completed her secondary studies and prepared for her baccalaureate (the diploma enabling college admission), she made no connections, had no comrade or confidante her own age. She suffered from the dilemma of the newcomer: it was easy to socialize with those you already knew, and hard to get to know those with whom you were not familiar.

On August 25, 1944, when Varda was sixteen, came Liberation. Four years of occupation, hunger, and penury dissolved on a cloudless summer morning. Parisians greeted the day with unalloyed joy. Bells tolled in belfries across the city; husbands reunited with their wives, and sons with their parents. From dark cellars emerged hidden tricolors to be hoisted and bottles of champagne to be shared—even though the citizens of Paris were already drunk with happiness.

Varda wasn't in the capital to experience the great unifying event of the war. "At the moment . . . we were in the countryside," she recalled. "We saw nothing."

After Liberation, Varda plunged into both university-level and vocational studies, building her own artistic foundations as France rebuilt itself politically and culturally. Between 1944 and 1949, she matriculated at the École du Louvre, assigned herself a year of independent study, audited classes in philosophy and literature at the Sorbonne, and took night classes at the École Technique de Photographie et de Cinématographie, then on the rue de Vaugirard, to learn the fundamentals of photography. (Today it is part of the École Louis-Lumière, a center for audiovisual studies named for France's pioneer filmmaker.)

Varda's efforts to school herself coincided with France's to reconcile a nation fractured among Nazi collaborators, former Resistance fighters, and everything in between. The object was to create a shared culture. As Varda felt her way to a profession, in 1946 the Fourth Republic founded the Centre national du cinéma (CNC). Its goal was to restore the film industry back to health and generate income, via a percentage of box office receipts, to reinvest in new films. Likewise, the Théâtre national populaire (TNP), founded in 1920, was given new life in 1951 when Varda's friend Jean Vilar was named director. He was charged with decentralizing and democratizing the performing art. Rather than an outright reconstruction, France's postwar cultural rebuilding was more like an archeological excavation, where, as cultural historian Michael Kelly described, "the debris of a country in ruins was sifted for the making of a new nation."

Varda would give thousands of interviews over her career and developed the habit of telescoping events to simplify her complex chronology, leaving exact dates fuzzy. But it is certain that even before completing her baccalaureate she had already begun coursework at the École du Louvre, which nurtured nascent artists such as Louise Bourgeois and Arman. Initially her intention was to become a painter. Between 1944 and 1947, Varda completed three years of archeology, twentieth-century art history, painting, and printmaking, earning high marks in the first two.

By 1946, she found painting "too abstract." That year, an art history class with Bernard Dorival, focusing on the seventeenth-century painter Nicolas Poussin and his influence on post-Impressionist Paul Cézanne, awakened the desire to become a curator. She liked tracing how the past influences the present. Soon, though, she found that while "she was happy to listen to the teachers at school," she "tired in advance" when imagining her future as a curator, "shuffling file cards in a provincial museum."

At about this time, Varda passed the first half of her baccalaureate. Christiane bought her a special gift, which proved to be prescient. According to Varda's daughter, Cri-Cri pawned a piece of family jewelry to buy a used camera from a crime photographer at *Detective* magazine. Not just any camera, but a Rolleiflex twin-lens reflex, the Stradivarius of photo instruments, the make used by the likes of Diane Arbus, Richard Avedon, Robert Capa, Robert Doisneau, and Gordon Parks. In the hands of its new owner, the camera was no longer a tool to provide forensic evidence of a crime, but a spirit-catcher to capture the vitality of children and the inner lives of actors.

In 1946, Varda moved into an apartment in Place Pigalle, the red-light district at the foot of Montmartre, with three friends. "We were four girls in an apartment that had been lent to us, in a large studio full of books," she told an interviewer years later. The others went to work every morning, while Varda followed a program of "systematic" reading from nine until midday, while continuing her classes at the Louvre.

She read the French greats like Baudelaire, for her the "prince of poets," and she devoured "everything by Colette." She was smitten by literary modernism, from Swiss novelist Blaise Cendrars to his American and European peers John Dos Passos, William Faulkner, James Joyce, and Virginia Woolf, whom she read in translation. She was drawn to Lautréamont, the nineteenth-century poet who imagined the "chance encounter of a sewing machine and an umbrella on the operating table," and to his twentieth-century Surrealist disciples André Breton and Max Jacob. And she was fascinated by visual artists such as Picasso and the Dutch abstractionist Bram van Velde, who experimented with new forms.

"I liked the arts, the only newspaper I bought was the *Gazette des beaux-arts*. The Cubist revolution seemed to me much more important than the Russian one," she said. She was captivated by how Joyce subtly noted the passage of time, how Dos Passos layered his literary collages, and how Woolf contrasted a character's inner life and her external actions. Varda's reading rewarded her with ways to shape narratives that could convey feelings.

May 1947 marked nearly three years since the Liberation of Paris and two years since VE Day ended World War II in Europe. Though the armed conflict was over, the privations persisted. Coffee and sugar, the Parisian lifeblood, continued to be rationed. This was not top of mind for Varda. And not just because the petite brunette with the Picasso eyes and monkish haircut preferred tea. She was not thinking of libations but liberation. Happily, by her nineteenth birthday, May

30, 1947, the foul smells and interminable winters, if not the food ration tickets, were behind most Parisians. Like a blush on the city's cheek, color returned to the streets. Varda celebrated her birthday by shedding her girlish given name Arlette and began identifying herself as Agnès, a common first name among her Greek forebears.

She did not change her name legally. Her identity papers now read, "Arlette, known as Agnès, Varda." In any event, the self-christening marked a symbolic rebirth and newfound autonomy. From here on, she would be the sole author of her story.

Like most teenagers before and since, Varda was a caged bird impatient to flee her adolescence and family of origin. After two destabilizing moves during wartime, she looked forward to finding her own place and her own flock. Come September, she would continue her coursework at the Louvre. There were three interminable months until then.

Without a word to her family, she bought a third-class train ticket to Marseille. There she made her way to the wharf and booked a deck ticket on the overnight ferry to Corsica. At dawn she reached Ajaccio, inhaling the cleansing, resiny scents of eucalyptus and olive trees.

Upon arrival, she settled on a quay where there was a torn net that she began to repair. Her industry excited the attention of a fisherman looking for workers. Soon she joined his crew of three Corsican and one Sardinian fishermen for her first paying job and what she described as "unambiguous cohabitation." Her job was to row the fishermen out to sea each morning and back to port at day's end. She was expected to assist in the lowering and lifting of the nets. Proud of her self-reliance and pleasantly tired from exertion, she spent her first night of freedom on land "curled on a small coil of rope under the stars."

It no longer mattered that her mother had neglected to tell her what adults did in private. She would school herself.

As she worked and lived with the fishermen, Varda attracted the interest of a young customs officer. "One day the relationship took an unexpected turn," she recalled years later. "He was ready to drop his wife . . . to marry me. . . . I had a hard time dissuading him . . . otherwise, I might still be the wife of a Corsican customs officer!"

She liked being one of the guys, fishing with a *trémail*, a net lowered vertically like a shade or a screen. She enjoyed the "communal work and evenings on the plazas where we disembarked to build a fire, cook (and eat) broken fish and lobsters. . . . I felt good with them, it was the calm horizon, the silence, the absolute exoticism." Like the Varda siblings, they were a unit of five. As with any workplace where there is a shared objective, one need not make conversation to make friends. After three months of this rough and promiscuous life with almost silent men, she felt stronger and less fearful. A good start to her independence, she thought. But it wasn't a career. She returned to Paris and found one.

A few months after Christian Dior introduced his wasp-waisted New Look, Varda returned to the capital in fisherman's garb. Was she conscious of embodying the new look of young bohemia, the gamine? She could not have known that this waiflike fashion, soon popularized by Audrey Hepburn and Leslie Caron in Hollywood films, would be a generational style embraced internationally.

Because Varda was in Corsica in September 1947, she missed Jean Vilar's theater conclave in Avignon, later known as the Avignon Festival. Vilar would invite her to photograph the second iteration in 1948 on condition that she lend a hand.

Her coursework at the Louvre and self-assigned literary year stoked her appetite for more goal-oriented learning. Two things she knew about herself: first, she wanted to audit classes without having to suffer exams, and second, she wanted to master a manual trade.

At the Louvre, Varda had learned to look at painting and sculpture. Yet she didn't see a future as a curator. And she felt she lacked the dexterity for painting or sculpture. Still, she was attracted to the idea of being a craftswoman. Thanks to Christiane, she had a camera. Suddenly, the idea of photography introduced itself.

3

IT WAS LIKELY IN the fall of 1947 that Varda entered the Sorbonne to audit courses in philosophy and literature. There, the professor who "really blew my mind," Varda said, was Gaston Bachelard, the philosopher who influenced a generation of French thinkers including Louis Althusser, Jacques Derrida, and Michel Foucault. "The good Gaston," as Varda called him, resembled an Old Testament prophet, and wrote such imagistic works as *The Psychoanalysis of Fire* and *The Poetics of Space*. His writing had an impact on many disciplines, including psychotherapy, architecture, and, in Varda's case, film imagery and symbolism.

Bachelard, she said, "had this dream of the *material* in people; a psychoanalysis of the material world related to people, wood, rivers, sea, fire, air, all of these things. . . . He taught us to study writers not by the stories they told but the material in the things they mentioned." Bachelard would inspire the celebrated quote from Varda's narration of *The Beaches of Agnès*: "If we opened people up, we'd find landscapes; if we opened me up, we'd find beaches."

While she was too timid to introduce herself to this amiable and influential professor, she found a kindred soul. "This old man knew how to reconcile life and culture," she said. "He was the only one that captivated me." Here was a figure in another discipline who spoke of the senses in a language she could taste and touch and smell and invoked the elements in words that, to her, burned and breathed.

Paradoxically, she would later say that she didn't fully understand him, that she carried his books, *Water and Dreams* and *Air and Dreams*, pages uncut and unread, as a kind of intellectual armor to protect herself from being accused of imbecility. Perhaps she understood Bachelard more fully than she admitted, for her creative life in three different media was dedicated to imagery that engaged all the senses.

Apart from Bachelard, Varda did not speak about her time at the Sorbonne with great enthusiasm. It unnerved her that the students didn't greet one another. During her time there, the likes of Simone Veil, future president of the European Parliament, and Norman Mailer, future American novelist, matriculated at the Paris institution. Most of the courses at the Sorbonne, Varda would later complain, struck her as "stupid, antiquated, abstract, and scandalously unsuited for the needs one had at that age." Her needs were both creative and practical: she wondered, was it possible both to pursue an artistic career and support herself?

In the way that some hunger for foods that contain the nutrients they need, Varda was drawn to the vocational and artistic coursework that would help her meet her monthly expenses and nourish her creative appetite. She created her curriculum in the same way she later created her photographs, films, and art installations—through *bricolage*, the French word for tinkering. Claude Lévi-Strauss, the French anthropologist, used *bricoleur* as an antonym of "engineer." An engineer creates new tools with new materials to solve new problems. A bricoleur improvises with available tools and materials to solve such problems.

While both Varda and her father worked with cranes and tracks, her father patented improvements to these components while Varda improvised with them. Eugène was an engineer, Varda a bricoleur. The Rolleiflex was the available tool that solved her problem of which craft to pursue.

Her formal commitment to photography came after she accepted

Vilar's invitation to chronicle the second Avignon Festival in 1948, where she was the mistress of odd jobs, working as an extra, a stagehand, and a photographer. Vilar knew the importance of having Varda document his ephemeral work and using her photos for publicity purposes. While there, she felt the need for her photo credentials to be taken seriously. Varda would recall, "At the time, you needed a CAP [a certificate of professional aptitude] to have the right to practice." She embarked on an accelerated course of study, completing two years in one, to satisfy the requirements for certification, a vestige of France's medieval guilds. To support herself, she photographed life cycle events: weddings, births, christenings, communions, and bar mitzvahs. On her own, she apprenticed with those whose specialty was documenting the works of painters and sculptors. To earn her credentials, she took night classes three times a week at the École Technique de Photographie et de Cinématographie.

In 1948 and 1949, she shuttled between night school on rue de Vaugirard and a daytime internship at the Rodin Museum. There she spent countless hours hunched over a table with a minuscule brush, retouching photographs for reproduction as postcards. Varda dotted the dead spots in each image "with tiny points of gray or black gouache," dramatizing light and shadow, making the dust that had accidentally adhered to the lens disappear. She joked that "the visitor to the Rodin Museum that bought a postcard of *The Kiss* or a detail from *The Gates of Hell* also bought a little of my slime mixes with corrective gouache." While the drudgery of this work taught her patience and the critical importance of detail to the bigger picture, it may also have whetted her appetite to be the artist rather than the one who retouched photographs of the artist's work.

In this era before photocopiers, Varda took an apprenticeship in the basement of the National Library, photographing passages from books requested by readers and scholars. During Christmastime in 1948 and 1949, she donned the shopgirl uniform—a black suit, white blouse, and dark shoes—to shoot portraits of children with Santa at Galeries Lafayette on boulevard Haussmann. She described her first paid photography gig as "assembly-line work." A clerk collected the fee and the child's name and address from the parents. Another escorted the first child in line to one of two Santa Claus sets where Varda and her fellow photographer snapped pictures while silently hoping that the tot didn't scream, or worse, steal one of the toys that served as a prop. A third assistant ferried the child back to her parents. On peak days, Varda shot fifty children per hour, four hundred during an eight-hour shift—not much time to create artistic lighting or establish rapport with subjects. But in the days before through-the-lens light metering, when the photographer factored light intensity and focal distance herself, it was excellent practice for learning how to read the light and moods of her sitters on the fly.

Once she completed the coursework and passed the written test in 1949, she received her CAP on June 30, under the name of Mlle. Arlette Varda. Promptly, she registered with the Chamber of Trades and began earning a living taking photos and making albums of children—"on the streets, in their gardens, their rooms and their bathtubs," visually documenting their lives. Officially, she was a professional. Her first darkroom was anything but: "A bathroom where I rinsed photos in the bidet." In her next, there would be "real tanks and photo clips" where she could hang up photos to dry after their fixing bath. Even when she worked in other media, she incorporated photography in her films and, later, her art installations.

Varda was employed by families to photograph new babies, by artists to document new work, and by architects to chronicle the building of new structures. A favorite assignment was documenting the rebuilding of a nursery school in Le Havre on a site destroyed during the war. She photographed its regeneration and reactivation, later remembering, "What a pleasure when it was filled with children!"

WHEN THE war ended, Eugène and Christiane had returned to the avenue de la Couronne in Ixelles, with their youngest, Sylvie. Despite Varda's premonition when the family fled from Ixelles in 1940, she did in fact see the apartment there again. In 2009, it makes a poignant appearance in *The Beaches of Agnès*. Varda, her brothers, and her sister Hélène continued to live at the boulevard Raspail apartment in Paris. Anticipating the resurgence of the shipping industry, Eugène devised a crane mounted on segmented arced and linear tracks (think of a child's wooden train set) that could hoist and convey several tons of cargo—and move around corners. He filed for patents in France and the United States and by 1950 was granted them in both countries. The invention increased his prosperity to the degree that he offered to buy homes for each of his children.

By then, Varda was twenty-two. She had read Virginia Woolf and needed not just a room of her own. She needed one attached to a photo studio where she could process film, make prints, and not have to pay more rent.

At the time, Valentine Schlegel, Varda's ceramicist friend, had a studio in the 14th arrondissement: Montparnasse. Then a working-class district, it was fabled for the generations of artists and authors who had made it their home. These included Henri Rousseau, customs officer turned painter, an early twentieth-century resident, before Montparnasse became a seedbed of Dada and Surrealism. Later denizens included artists Alexander Calder, Max Ernst, and Constantin Brancusi, who drank with Picasso and Man Ray at the Café Dôme. A little later still, Simone de Beauvoir. Poet Louis Aragon and his muse, writer Elsa Triolet, also resided in the 14th. At the onset of hostilities in 1940, its population was 178,000. During wartime, the number declined precipitously to 49,000. After the war, many gravitated again to the neighborhood. It appealed to the unpretentious as well as to the tightfisted in need of generous square footage. It was exactly what Varda was looking for.

She found a place with possibilities and showed it to her father. It consisted of two adjacent properties that she hoped to consolidate. One was the abandoned shop of a picture framer outfitted with workshops—and gilding rooms!—in the rear; the other was a shuttered grocery. In between them was an alley and a courtyard equipped with what the British euphemize as "French toilets" and the French dub "Turkish toilets" (and my father called "squatting latrines"). Appalled, Eugène dismissed the set-up as a "slum" and a "stable."

"Who would want to live *there*?" demanded the man who could afford an apartment in the 7th, then one of Paris's most affluent neighborhoods. A bourgeois and technocrat, Eugène saw only two failed businesses with pissoirs in between. A bourgeois-bohemian *avant la lettre*, Varda was an artist who saw what could be: a live/work space with room for a darkroom plus a light-filled courtyard to use as a photographic backdrop, commodious living and studio spaces she could share with Valentine Schlegel, an alley to park a car if she ever had one, *and* extra room for a photo assistant, if ever she could afford it.

"[Eugène and Agnès] weren't in the same universe," observed Varda's brother Jean. He added that Eugène "would have liked Agnès to photograph cranes, but that wasn't her thing." Her father disappointed Varda because she found him dictatorial, unimaginative, and, most unforgivable, often absent. He was financially generous but emotionally stingy. Varda disappointed her father because he thought her rebellious and impractical. After all, she'd run off to Corsica and then left the École du Louvre before completing her degree. Sadly, Eugène, a lifelong Victorian and conformist, and his middle daughter, a lifelong bohemian and nonconformist, did not resolve their differences before his untimely death. Eugène would collapse and die at the roulette table in the casino of the Belgian beach town of Blankenberge in August 1952. He was sixty-one and did not live to enjoy the success of his middle daughter.

While Varda had some savings, she needed a total of 3 million old francs (roughly $6,000 in 1950 and $55,000 today) to purchase the properties. In her telling, she asked her mother for help and Christiane came through. In Jean's version, despite Eugène's preference for the *bon chic, bon genre* (safe bourgeois good taste), in the end he financed the purchase of the "stable" in the "slum."

Like the title character of *Cléo from 5 to 7*, Varda had a superstitious streak. When she noted the properties were on rue Daguerre, the street named for the father of photography, it was a good omen. As she explained to an interviewer from *France-Soir* in 1975, "When you're a photographer in need of a studio and you find one in the rue Daguerre, that's a sign, isn't it?"

In the years since she fled Ixelles, there hadn't been time or space for Varda to put down roots. When she bought 86 rue Daguerre in 1951, and later, 88, the first thing she did, even before addressing the lack of heating and sanitary plumbing, was to plant trees—a purple beech and a maple—in the courtyard. She combed the yard and the structures for treasures abandoned there by prior occupants and gave them pride of place, like the gilt frame she repurposed as a mirror and used as a prop in at least two of her films. Decades before the advent of "process art"—artworks that bear the evidence of how they are made—Varda transformed rue Daguerre into a working example of it. For the sixty-eight years she lived, worked, and died there, it would be "a work in progress," as Nathalie Obadia, her gallerist, described it.

Micheline (Mimi) Antonucci was fifteen when she met Varda in 1951. In the Antonucci apartment on the second floor (called the *première étage*, or first floor, in France) a window looked down onto Varda's courtyard. Mimi remembers that in its earliest configuration during Varda's occupancy, the offices and working spaces were to the left of the courtyard, where the framer had been, and the living spaces on the right, where the cheese store and grocery were.

Visitors to rue Daguerre entered a farm gate into a narrow corridor that opened onto the courtyard. To the left, Valentine Schlegel had her ceramics studio from 1951 to 1957. Farther down was a door to the apartment of Bienvenida Lorca, Varda's photo assistant, and her family. Behind that was Varda's photo studio and darkroom.

From 1951 to 1957, Varda and Valentine resided at rue Daguerre, working in separate studios. By then, Valentine was living openly as a lesbian. Were they lovers? In *The Beaches of Agnès*, the filmmaker/

narrator, then eighty, recalls that the two of them "sowed their wild oats together." I heard that as an acknowledgment of their emotional, and probable sexual, intimacy. The latter was confirmed by Varda's daughter in *Viva Varda*, a 2023 film documentary.

At first, there was no telephone at rue Daguerre. Phones were hard to come by. Varda arranged with Monsieur Paul, proprietor of a nearby bistro, to receive calls for her. When someone phoned, Madame Paul would yell, "*Vardaaaaa!*" and Varda would come running. To save Madame Paul the trouble, Varda rigged a buzzer from the bistro to 88 rue Daguerre, so that the bistro owner's wife need only press a button when their neighbor had a phone call. When Monsieur Paul passed away, Varda was among the contingent of neighborhood mourners who followed the casket from the bistro to a nearby church.

During her years at rue Daguerre, Varda maintained, "I don't live in Paris, I live in the 14th."

SHE MAY not have earned an academic degree, but from Jean Vilar Varda received an extensive education in theater, culture, and audience development. Concurrently at the Avignon Festival, where from 1948 she photographed the actors and documented the plays, and at the Théâtre national populaire, where in 1951 Vilar was named director and hired her as official photographer, Varda was steeped in his then-revolutionary ideas about democratizing theater. He believed that theater should be accessible and affordable to all. Like Bachelard, Varda said, "Vilar was a teacher to me without knowing." If Bachelard defined for her what artistic form was, Vilar showed her what an artist was—not an individual isolated in an atelier but one who communicated meaning and connected to a broad community that needed to be cultivated.

Jeanne Laurent, deputy director of national education, tapped Vilar for the TNP because of his commitment to theater's decentralization and democratization. He had created the Avignon event in the spirit of the former, bringing classic plays to the provinces, dispatching his troupe to perform in the banlieues and villages, and inviting young people to performances. Once the TNP was installed at the Palais de Chaillot in Paris, "he eliminated all signs of privilege," wrote theater professor Maria Shevtsova. There was neither class system nor star system in his company. Vilar jettisoned the hierarchy of good seats for the wealthy and nosebleed seats for the budget-minded. The movie stars in his company, like Gérard Philipe and María Casares, earned the same salary as those not yet established, like Philippe Noiret and Jeanne Moreau.

Believing that "theater was as necessary as gas, water, and electricity," as "indispensable as bread and wine," Vilar made certain that plays began at 8 pm (instead of 9 pm) so that those in the suburbs could be home by midnight. Reasonably priced sandwiches were sold at the theater, and audience members were not expected to tip ushers or pay cloakroom charges.

Vilar favored a stage relatively free of décor, using costumes and lighting to evoke time, place, and mood. He likewise cultivated actors, most famously Philipe and Casares, whose acting was measured rather than histrionic. He was modest about his role, believing that the director and actors were interpreters of the text and not themselves the artists. Above all, he was interested in theater that spoke to contemporary issues, especially those, like Bertolt Brecht's *Galileo* and Robert Bolt's *A Man for All Seasons*, that showed how individuals of conscience contended with forces of political authority.

Rather than photograph actors in rehearsals, a typical means of capturing a theater or movie still, Varda found that she could best interpret the spirit of Vilar's theater by distilling the drama's conflict into one potent image. To telescope the drama of Vilar's imaginative staging, she had to restage the scene so it played to the camera rather than to an imagined audience. Whether she shot at the Palais de Chaillot or at Avignon, the images she created—for instance, profiles of Vilar and Casares as the supercilious Lord and Lady Macbeth, as if stamped on a medallion—served both as official documents of Vilar's work and powerful reminders of the dramas themselves.

While collaborating with Vilar in Avignon and Paris, Varda developed and refined an array of skills. She learned to find a defining image and how to "direct" actors such as Philipe, Moreau, and Noiret. She internalized how the low-key Vilar cultivated a workplace that was interdependent and respectful. Sometimes Varda argued with Vilar, who thought her photographs of stage and screen heartthrob Philipe were too worshipful. Her portraits of the actor registered how he "smiled when sad and never forgot melancholy in moments of gaiety," as film historian David Thomson described.

The reflected light and prestige of the TNP boosted Varda's reputation as a photographer. "When Gérard Philipe came to the [Avignon] festival in 1951, there was a rush of press requests," Varda later said. "And that's how the newspapers noticed my work and asked me to do assignments. And I also started to do photo compositions for myself. I never sold any pictures back then and I never had a show." As she dryly put it, "In a matter of months I acquired one of those ready-made reputations, so common in Paris, for skill and style." She was just twenty-three.

IN 1953, Varda photographed the elephantine sculptor Alexander Calder crouching over his *Circus*. She captured the inventor of the mobile in a moment of movement, with his hands manipulating the menagerie of delicate doll-sized acrobats, animals, and clowns made of wire, wood, and found objects, bringing the imaginatively wrought creatures to life.

The prior year in Sète, Varda had met Calder through Vilar, when the theater director proposed to the sculptor that he create the sets for Henri Pichette's play *Nucléa*. (Calder did; Varda photographed them.) At the time the artist was in his mid-fifties, had just won the prize for sculpture at the Venice Biennale, and was beloved internationally for both his kinetic and still works.

Vilar and Varda took Calder on an excursion by car to see the nearby abbey of Fontfroide, noted for its medieval architecture, stopping often to enjoy the scenery. When they grew thirsty, they opened the trunk to retrieve a bottle of water. It was next to Calder's toolbox. Seeing it, Calder, who made whimsical jewelry for friends and collectors, asked Varda, "Would you like me to make you a necklace?" She did not refuse. "He took a piece of flat metal and cut it into a pattern of curves, and then he gave it to me, just like that, in the middle of the road, and we closed the trunk."

Before long, the sculptor whom Varda described as "sprightly and fat" and the photographer found that they were neighbors on rue Daguerre (Calder maintained a studio at number 22). They became fast friends. In 1954, Varda took a portrait of the laughing Calder in the middle of the street partnering a white-petaled mobile in apparent song and dance. Varda's photographs of him suggest that art is a physical emanation of the artist. She adored his sense of fun.

Clearly, Calder liked Varda's work; he invited her to photograph his sculptures and posed for a family portrait with his wife and daughters on a park bench near Place Denfert-Rochereau. When Calder came to fetch the prints, he paid her the supreme compliment of proposing that they exchange work. He got the photos and she got a mobile, the renowned artist validating the work of the budding one without monetary exchange. Varda would later describe the mobile as "all black, large flat leaves, with a single red and vertical flower, and it sways in our house."

During this period, Calder often came to visit Varda in her courtyard. "We would make paella," she recalled. "It wasn't about the eating . . . it was about being together, playing. . . . Just nattering for the sheer pleasure of it." In the courtyard, she shot a comic photo of the bearlike sculptor crouched on a child's scooter, like a surfer balanced on his board.

Since she had first met the Schlegels, the atmosphere of artists was Varda's oxygen. She took a striking photograph of Valentine, framing her from waist down to bare feet against a concrete wall, her carved wooden ladles fanned out at her feet. Valentine's graceful hands rest at the hips of her shorts, her bare legs a vertical line from carving hand to the implements it made.

Valentine likewise worked at the TNP, where she reported to Léon Gischia, former student of Fernand Léger and keeper of the Cubist flame in postwar Paris. Gischia designed or commissioned the minimalist sets Vilar preferred. He was fond of Varda, whose youthful spirits may have been mistaken for flirtation. He volunteered to introduce her to the legendary photographer Brassaï, known for his Paris nocturnes of cobblestoned streets lit by a single moonbeam and of mist-shrouded lampposts haloing the Seine. Seeking career advice, Varda made an appointment with the photographer, who lived nearby.

At their first meeting, probably in 1953, she was struck by his kindness and patience as he answered her many questions. Brassaï showed her volumes of his published photography, explaining how he achieved his effects. Then—mischievously, Varda thought—he took out a box of naughty photographs shot in brothels. For her, "they were less erotic than pedestrian." Still, she felt, it was provocative for him to have shared "these images of bare-bottomed girls" with her.

At the time, Brassaï was photographing graffiti painted or etched onto the plaster walls of Paris, especially those of hearts. Varda paid tribute to him by making a "portrait" of a shriveled, sprouting, heart-shaped potato, ancestor of those she would collect and use later in her career, when the root-fringed tuber would become her avatar. Against the graffitied walls of the 14th arrondissement, she made portraits of Brassaï, framing him with his latest motif.

By 1954, between the Avignon and TNP photos reproduced in French newspapers and magazines and her growing popularity as a portraitist of artists and their work—all developed and printed in her rue Daguerre lab—Varda had photographs enough for a solo exhibition. But she didn't know how to approach a gallery for representation. So, she glued about fifty onto a stiff backing, hanging them on the walls and shutters of her courtyard, and held her own exhibition. She got the word out by circulating flyers to local groceries and bakeries. She didn't know enough to invite newspapers to come, but her neighbors—Brassaï among them—dropped in.

That same year, she made her movie debut in front of the camera in a short for French television. In the six-minute silent film with touches of 1920s slapstick comedy, she plays herself, a photographer taking a portrait of Brassaï. The film begins with Varda, wearing a bucket hat on this rainy December day, as she leaves her courtyard juggling a tripod, a suitcase with camera and equipment, and a stool. She strides purposefully down the street, searching for a mottled wall where she can pose Brassaï. Jauntily swinging his umbrella, smoking a cigarette, and wearing a Buster Keatonish porkpie hat, Brassaï greets her. The director of the vignette contrasts the small woman whose equipment outweighs her with her unencumbered subject. Then comes the comic reveal: though she's not the director of the short, Varda immediately assumes directorial authority, repeatedly gesturing to Brassaï to move to the right so she can frame her shot. At first, he resists. But with this determined young woman, resistance is futile. He accepts her direction and moves. Whether behind her own camera and/or in front of another's motion picture lens, Varda had the gift of unselfconsciousness.

At first glance, this untitled short would look positively prophetic but for the fact that earlier in 1954, Varda had already made the kind of film that she wanted to see. In the courtyard of rue Daguerre, she spent weekends storyboarding and writing the script. She shot it in August and September. By the time she appeared in the six-minute short, her directorial debut was being edited.

PART II

MOVING

4

VARDA FREELY ADMITTED THAT her "total ignorance of beautiful films, very old or recent, allowed me to be naïve and cheeky when I launched into the profession of image and sound." When planning the film that became *La Pointe Courte*, she was twenty-five years old and hadn't yet seen twenty-five films, as she often said. She had no knowledge of film history, and thus was unaware that she was one in an illustrious line of still photographers drawn to make pictures that moved, a line extending from Man Ray and Stanley Kubrick to Gordon Parks and Mira Nair. Nor was she aware that at the dawn of filmmaking, many directors were women, and that women were in the vanguard of experimental filmmaking, like Germaine Dulac in France during the 1920s and Maya Deren in the United States during the 1940s.

At the time she made her film, Varda anticipated that her experiment would be a one-off. "I was struck by how literature had made extraordinary leaps and bounds, painting too, but cinema, people said, wasn't evolving that much." During the postwar period there were few female directors in France. Most prominent among them were Jacqueline Audry, who adapted Colette's novels to make *Gigi* (1949) and

Minne (1950); and Andrée Feix, who confected the comedies *Once Is Enough* (1946) and *Captain Blomet* (1947).

But it was a propitious time in France to be getting into the business of making films. While Varda attended to the bureaucratic process of getting a movie made, François Truffaut, a twenty-one-year-old cinephile, published his incendiary manifesto, "A Certain Tendency of French Cinema," in *Cahiers du cinéma.* He blasted postwar French filmmakers for their script-dependent movies, disengaged and bloodless adaptations of great books that were true to neither the letter nor the spirit of the novels. Even worse, they were not cinematic. Truffaut argued for the cinema of the *auteur* (author), that of the engaged filmmaker who goes beyond merely illustrating a screenplay to create a unified vision for his movie. Truffaut excoriated films that had a literary pedigree but no personality, lauding those with a distinct directorial signature and eye. "A Certain Tendency" introduced readers to what became known as the auteur theory, a director-centric organizing principle for making films as well as writing about them. Seventy-five years later, the essay's impact on how movies are made and how they are written about is immeasurable.

While preparing her movie, Varda knew nothing of the influential film journals *Cahiers du cinéma* and *Positif.* Nor did she know of the culture of ciné-clubs, which since 1935 had enriched the social and intellectual life of France by screening movies and fostering lively discussions around them, creating a generation of movie lovers and a near-religion known as cinephilia. While she wrote her two-tiered narrative set in Sète, Truffaut, Jean-Luc Godard, and the other "*Cahiers* boys"—as she would soon dub them—spent their waking hours either at the movies or polishing their theories of cinema.

The "*Cahiers* boys" dreamed of becoming directors; Varda just did it. "In the beginning," she recalled of the genesis of *La Pointe Courte,* "there was almost nothing, no idea about cinephiles or films and no even vague aspiration to enter the world of cinema." Its creation, she said, "was a mystery . . . or an incomprehensible combination of luck or larval desires."

There was another, more urgent, desire. Varda's friend Suzanne Schlegel-Fournier, Valentine's elder sister, was married to the cellist Pierre Fournier, and he had recently been diagnosed with terminal brain cancer. She and Suzanne suggested "charming projects to occupy Pierre's mind, including driving down to Sète and filming him for fun." Varda had three agendas: distracting Pierre; preparing Suzanne to become a photo apprentice so that, in the event of Pierre's death, she had a marketable skill; and making a movie.

The prior year, Varda had been under the spell of William Faulkner's *The Wild Palms*, which, in alternating chapters, tells two parallel stories. She was inspired to construct a like-minded modernist narrative. What emerged was the idea of two stories that occur in the same place, Sète. One featured a community of fishermen whose livelihoods are threatened by polluted waters; the other, an urban couple negotiating a troubled marriage. Fishermen and couple occupy the same spaces yet exist in entirely different worlds. She named the film *La Pointe Courte* (The Short Tip), after Sète's fishermen's enclave surrounded by a tidal pool. Varda returned from Sète with photographs and used them to create a storyboard annotated with drawings and dialogue.

Like professional photography, filmmaking was regulated in France, thus Varda created her own company, Tamaris Films, and registered it with the CNC as a producer of shorts. While *La Pointe Courte* was feature-length, she could afford only the price of a "short" authorization. At the time, an aspiring director was expected to make shorts, then become an assistant director, and then, after a long apprenticeship, a director of features. Varda asked the CNC for waivers. Thus, *La Pointe Courte* was considered an amateur production and could not be screened in a commercial cinema.

Before Varda commenced production, she had second thoughts. She stowed the storyboards and script in a drawer, "like stashing away notebooks of poems that no one, we believe, will ever read." Then she made the acquaintance of Carlos Vilardebó, a Portuguese director of shorts, and his wife, Jeanne, a writer and script supervisor. They advised her how to make a film on the cheap and rounded up a crew who were between movies and ready to rise to the challenge of making a truly independent film.

Varda was forever grateful to the Vilardebós for their confidence in the project, especially when her own wavered. Her first film would be informed by the compositions of classical painting, symbolically rich forms championed by Bachelard, the experimental strategies of modernist literature, and the real-life residents of La Pointe Courte.

Her father had left Varda a modest bequest of 2 million old francs; her mother loaned her 3 million more; and she also borrowed 1.5 million against rue Daguerre. She created a cooperative worth 3.5 million old francs to pay the cast and crew, who deferred payments until the film made money. Historian Richard Neupert estimates the film's final cost of 7 million old francs was roughly $14,000 in 1954 dollars. As the average French film at the time cost 70 million old francs, Varda said, "We therefore had more than ten times less money and ten times more nerve because, at that time, nobody directed at my age."

A seasoned still photographer, Varda knew instinctively when to ditch the plan and shoot the serendipitous moment. Since she couldn't afford to make the film with synchronous sound, she did not have to worry that seagull squawks or other intrusive sounds would interrupt a take and require reshooting. Dialogue would be recorded and added after the film was edited.

When Varda took her first, uncertain, step into filmmaking, she was among supportive friends. No longer the employee, she was the artist employing others. She cast Philippe Noiret and Silvia Monfort as the troubled couple, and real-life fishermen and their families as themselves. Actors and crew stayed in a rented house in Frontignan, near Sète. Varda slept in the garage, next to two rusty bicycles and a used Citroën 2CV bought to transport cast and crew to Sète and film to the lab. She swathed her bed and person in mosquito netting to protect against the scorpions that had staked their claim on the garage.

The documentary component of the film chronicles the real community of fishermen defying agents of the health department by plying their trade without permits. The scripted drama tells the story of a Parisian couple questioning their future. Together, the fishermen fight for survival; estranged, the husband and wife fight each other.

The contrapuntal film toggles between natural light and long shadow, civic victories and personal losses, straightforward documentation and oblique symbolism. When Varda frames a close-up of the couple, heads touching, their faces are at right angles to each other, contemplating different vistas and, perhaps, different futures. Varda's experimental film could not be compared to other movies. It could be spoken of in terms of the New Novel, abstract painting, and concrete music, as a revolutionary form challenging viewers, readers, and listeners. The film critic Pierre Billard observed that "[Varda's] first film had all the markings of the avant-garde, but she was the only one who didn't recognize them. She thought that was how one made movies."

What binds the dual narratives in the film is the deep-focus photography, with the foreground, middle ground, and background all equally sharp, which draws viewers into the tale of two conflicts. The fishermen's story was written with the locals, whose performances are naturalistic. The fictional couple's story, scripted by Varda, is stylized, with verbal exchanges as opaque as those in the *nouveaux roman* then so popular in Parisian literary circles. The stories do not intersect but superimpose on each other in the way that right and left eyes perceive visual information and integrate the two views into one stereoscopic view.

By the end of the shoot Varda had ten hours of footage, with ambient sound of squawking seagulls, train engines, and motorboats—and a reputation among residents of La Pointe Courte as a cat whisperer. For one sequence, Varda wanted a feline to emerge from a hole, walk along a fence, and then down to the dock. The cat didn't take direction. So, the director brushed the fence with sausage, but, instead of walking along the fence, the cat licked it. According to Varda, as wide-eyed as her four-pawed actor, she looked deep into the creature's eyes, promising it mullet for supper if it complied. The next take, she said, was perfect.

When Varda screened the silent footage for her nonprofessional actors, they immediately adopted the film as their own—with one exception. "If it weren't for those two donkeys," blurted one fisherman, referring to Monfort and Noiret. "It was clear to those of La Pointe Courte that the film was a chronicle of their neighborhood, their film," Varda reflected later.

Varda returned to Paris with a stack of film cans almost as tall as herself. Where could she find a film editor who would work for shares in the cooperative, deferring pay like the rest of the crew? The Vilardebós suggested she contact Alain Resnais, a documentary filmmaker and editor for hire, who had made several well-received shorts about artists such as Gauguin, van Gogh, and Picasso.

When Varda approached Resnais for help, he asked to see her screenplay. Immediately she delivered one to him at his place on rue des Plantes, a fifteen-minute stroll from rue Daguerre. After reading it, the future director of the classic drama *Hiroshima Mon Amour* (1959) declined politely by letter. "Your research is too close to mine," he wrote.

But Varda did not take no for an answer. By phone, she entreated Resnais to look at the rushes (unedited footage). Her persistence paid off. They met at the Éclair laboratory in Épinay-sur-Seine, north of Paris, where she could screen the footage free of charge. Given that she had ten hours of footage, Varda expected that Resnais, a laconic figure known affectionately as the Sphinx, would watch three or so. Varda sat four rows behind him in anxious silence.

About ninety minutes into the screening, where the only sounds were the dull buzz of the projector lamp and the metallic whirring of film reels, he stood up and announced, "I think I've seen enough." Varda's heart nearly stopped. The Sphinx strode to the door in silence. At six foot three, he towered over Varda. Before taking his leave, he said something to the effect that the rushes were very interesting, but that it was too big a job. "I won't be able to do it," he said politely. Varda recalled, "He left. I collapsed."

Resnais surprised Varda with a call the next morning, offering friendly advice. "While I can't do it, maybe I can help get you started," he said. For the sake of determining continuity, he explained, "you need to number the rushes." In the analog age, every foot of processed film had to be manually marked with scene number and take number. Resnais lent her two synchronizers, which track the length of a segment or reel of film, to help with the job. One had a crank, the other a toothed wheel; one crank advanced a foot of film at a time so the negative could be numbered in one-foot increments. Resnais explained that she should start at zero, crank once, and write the data at the frame's edge. The first frame of scene 25, take one, should be 25–1–1. One foot later, 25–1–2, etc. For the second take, 25–2–1, 25–2–2, etc. He instructed her to buy white India ink and a pen with a fine nib. He indicated where to write the numbers. It was a foreign language, but she attended carefully to his tutorial. Soon she would be fluent.

Varda spent mornings, afternoons, and evenings hunched over the synchronizers, like a medieval manuscript illuminator, carefully numbering footage with her fine-gauge pen, cross-eyed from fatigue. "This is a monk's job," she thought. It was not unlike retouching the Rodin photos, but this time it was her own work. On the eleventh morning, she phoned Resnais and informed him, "I did what you said. What now?"

"You numbered 10,000 meters in ten days!" he exclaimed. Impressed by her patience and concentration, Resnais agreed to edit *La Pointe Courte*. He would defer his salary for shares in the cooperative. But, he insisted, she would pay for his lunch and his shift would end by 5 pm daily. Of his terms of service, Varda joked, "Free, yes. Overtime, no."

He bicycled from his place to rue Daguerre every morning, arriving promptly at 9 am. He parked his bike in the courtyard, removed the clips from his pant legs, and worked until noon, when he took his hourlong lunch break. After lunch he returned and worked until 4:55. His commitment matched Varda's own. Through him, she learned not just the fundamentals of editing but also its poetry. When he needed an assistant to complete the task, Varda suggested that he hire her photo assistant, Anne Sarraute, who would, in 1959, become Resnais' editor. Initially, Varda did not realize that his assistant was the daughter of Nathalie Sarraute, a leading French writer associated with the *nouveau roman*. She was well acquainted with the works of the elder Sarraute and became friends with both mother and daughter. Three decades later, she dedicated her 1985 film *Vagabond* to Nathalie Sarraute.

As he edited Varda's footage, Resnais remarked, "These fishermen, they remind me of the fishermen in *La Terra Trema* by Luchino Visconti." The woman who claimed she had seen fewer than twenty-five films before she made one had never heard of the gifted Italian neorealist filmmaker, nor of neorealism, a film movement focusing on the working class that had emerged in postwar Italy. (Neorealism was likewise a movement in postwar photography, which Varda may have unconsciously internalized.) When Resnais compared her textured shots of characters before plaster walls to those by filmmaker Michelangelo Antonioni (later famous for his films of modern anomie, like *Blow-Up*), Varda looked at him blankly and asked, "Antonioni who?" Such episodes moved Resnais to educate her in film history. "I would really discover cinema at twenty-six," Varda said, "while editing my film."

"He taught me something tremendous," she recalled. "He wouldn't try to straighten out this awkward film. He saw that I had laid out a shooting schedule and that I had filmed it without any B roll, with nothing to cut away to ... no alternatives. It was a radical movie that needed to be radically edited, but with finesse. Which is what he did."

The film was composed of smooth tracking shots, all the better for the audience to understand the landscape, with just as many abrupt cuts that suggest the unease between husband and wife. Resnais showed Varda how each edit conveyed, or emphasized, a mood. "By scrupulously editing my film, he allowed me to clarify my thoughts," Varda observed later.

In 1954, female filmmakers were as rare as volcanic lightning. In the U.S., Ida Lupino had directed seven features over the past five years and would direct many TV episodes, but she wouldn't make another feature film until 1966. In the Soviet Union, Kira Muratova co-directed films with her husband from 1958 to 1967, when she would make her first solo film. Her countrywoman Larisa Shepitko didn't direct until the 1960s. In Latin America, Venezuelan filmmaker Margot Benacerraf made two striking documentaries, *Reveron* in 1952 and *Araya* in 1960. In Japan, actress Kinuyo Tanaka directed six films between 1953 and 1962, coincidentally the same number as Varda between 1954 and 1962. For all women, the barriers to becoming a director were high, usually requiring a diploma from a film program, as Benacerraf and Muratova had earned. Lupino and Tanaka were well-known actresses who had the respect and support of established film directors in their respective countries (and Lupino's husband was also her producer). Varda had a small inheritance and property, so she could self-finance a film.

Despite her ignorance of cinema history and practice, Varda had much in common with Resnais, including a passion for painting, especially Surrealism, and a liking for *Nadja*, André Breton's dreamlike 1928 novel of a man's affair with a young woman.

Resnais introduced Varda to the Cinémathèque française, the Notre Dame of cinephilia. He encouraged her to see films by F. W. Murnau (*Sunrise*), Jean Renoir (*The Rules of the Game*), and Joseph Mankiewicz (*All About Eve*). Afterward, they would discuss them. When Resnais learned that Mankiewicz's *The Barefoot Contessa* was to open in Belgium before France, he persuaded Varda's brother Jean to drive them to Brussels to see it before anyone in Paris. Varda had been under the impression that film exhibition was like that of art, traveling from museum to museum, rather than like that of magazines, simultaneously distributed to multiple outlets. Resnais explained how film distribution worked and showed her how to track box office returns.

"Besides having me go from raw filmmaker to beginner filmmaker," Varda said of Resnais, "it was through him that Paris became exotic. Its Chinese restaurants, its Jewish quarter, the green ribbon of the former circular train, and the Parc des Buttes-Chaumont" in Paris's northeast corner. There was also a trip to Venice, where the elder filmmaker introduced the newbie to the colors and atmospheres of Tintoretto's paintings. Resnais accompanied her to the Cinémathèque française on an outing she described in her memoir as a "double baptism." It was her first time at that cathedral of cinema. The film was *Vampyr*, by Carl Theodor Dreyer.

Varda would later admit to Jean-Luc Douin, a French journalist and author of a 2013 book on Resnais, that she was "half in love" with the Sphinx. And he was equally fond of her, according to Varda's daughter. Their mutual regard was more than platonic. They had a non-exclusive relationship of roughly two years, suggesting that Valentine Schlegel and Varda also had an open arrangement. She and Resnais remained close friends—and Resnais her cultural consigliere—but saw each other less frequently after 1959, when he released *Hiroshima Mon Amour* and Jacques Demy moved into rue Daguerre.

One evening in late 1954 or early 1955—Varda remembered it as cold and wintry—Resnais invited her over. In her telling it isn't clear whether she was expecting a soirée or an assignation. Dressed for the season, she walked to rue des Plantes in the bitter cold.

If she expected to find him alone, she was disappointed. When she arrived at the book-filled apartment festooned with *Dick Tracy* and *Li'l Abner* comic strips, Resnais was holding court on his bed in a cloud of smoke from unfiltered cigarettes. Six or so men unknown to her were clustered around him, sitting on chairs or cross-legged on the floor. Between drags on cigarettes, they talked to and over one another about movies, trying to impress Resnais.

He introduced her around, but it would take Varda time to distinguish Claude Chabrol from Jean-Claude Brialy, Jean-Marie

---

Scherer—known as Éric Rohmer—from Jean-Luc Godard, and François Truffaut from Jacques Doniol-Valcroze. They were editors and writers from *Cahiers du cinéma*, the influential film journal. Unlike her, they had an encyclopedic knowledge of film history. Listening to them talk about lighting, editing, and camera movement, Varda was uncharacteristically mute.

"They quoted thousands of films and suggested all sorts of things to Resnais, talking so fast that they lost me," she recalled. "I was an anomaly, feeling small, ignorant, the only girl among the *Cahiers* boys." When she knew the men a little better she realized that "their influences were movies." Hers, she said, were, "paintings, books . . . life."

The depth and breadth of their film knowledge intimidated her. A year later, when her debut film had a limited run in Paris, her formidable intellect—and, no doubt, the fact that she had completed a feature before any in their brotherhood—would have a similar effect on them.

WHILE RESNAIS and Sarraute condensed six hundred minutes of footage down to ninety, Varda dealt with the challenge of distributing her film, as she was still registered as a producer of shorts and lacked the capital to change her status to that of producer of features. And she thought her unusual film lacked the commercial potential to attract an outside distributor. Theatrical distribution of *La Pointe Courte* was not in the cards.

Resnais recommended that Varda screen the film for André Bazin, the founding editor of *Cahiers du cinéma* and an eloquent proponent of cinema as art. Bazin wrote favorably of *La Pointe Courte* in several outlets, praising its realism and artisanal mode of production. He also provided Varda with a road map of self-distribution. She should organize a private screening of the film at the Cannes Film Festival, advertise the screening in the trade paper *Le film français*, and then invite critics and industry figures to see it.

A few weeks before her twenty-seventh birthday in May 1955, Varda borrowed money from her mother so that she could rent a theater in Cannes and screen *La Pointe Courte* at the festival market (as opposed to the competition, where Delbert Mann's *Marty* won the top prize). She took a third-class train from Paris to Cannes, carrying the film reels in a suitcase.

The first review was unpromising. "Main aspect of this film is that it was made for $25,000 by a 25-year-old girl," wrote a reporter from *Variety*, the Hollywood trade paper. But Varda's birthday gift would arrive, if a little late, on June 5, in the form of an extended piece by Jean de Baroncelli in *Le Monde*, the center-left Paris daily. It was not a review, but a thoughtful reflection on cinema that hailed the film as

> the first work of a talented young woman. . . . [*La Pointe Courte*] is also the first chime of a huge carillon. . . . [It] proves to us that for the generation to which Miss Varda belongs, cinema has become a means of expression just like the pen and the brush. This means of expression is unfortunately very expensive and this is why, with rare exceptions, it remains the business of specialists. We are still in the time of the mandarins. However, it is not forbidden to hope that, with the help of television, all these young talents reduced to silence will one day find the opportunity to come forward. We will then have the poems, essays, stories, cinematographic memories. The cinema will no longer be a heavy machine for making entertainment, but a mirror in which the most diverse temperaments and styles will be reflected. . . . We are not there yet! But I thought about that future as Miss Varda's film unfolded.

A week later, *La Pointe Courte* screened at the Cinéma du Panthéon, the storied art house in the Latin Quarter. Its owner, Pierre Braunberger, producer of several Resnais shorts, had seen the film with Bazin and was an admirer. By the following January, Varda's film played daily at the movie theater Studio Parnasse. An early screening was followed by a public discussion. Like a theater ingenue

in the wings watching the audience arrive, Varda holed up in the projection booth that first Tuesday, perched on a stool, peeping out the
tiny window to see, one by one, "the cream of the intellectual set" file
in. Novelist Marguerite Duras, filmmaker Chris Marker, Nathalie
Sarraute, and François Truffaut were among them.

Varda had stage fright. During the discussion, she stayed in the
booth, eavesdropping. She heard Truffaut express his surprise that
she wasn't among them. "I'm sure she's hiding somewhere, listening to us," he guessed shrewdly. Then Marker, whom Varda knew
through Resnais, piped up, "Did anyone notice that there is one element associated with him and another with her?" He told the audience that when Noiret was on-screen, there were objects and sounds
of wood. And when Monfort was on-screen, there were metal objects
seen and metallic sounds heard. Varda was stunned. Marker understood that these materials and sounds were her way of personifying
the characters without dialogue. Noiret, playing a man born in Sète,
was connected with the material used in pre-industrial times; Monfort, whose character was from Paris, was linked to steel, the material
of the Industrial Revolution.

Varda felt understood by Marker and de Baroncelli. Creating her
own film felt more personal than interpreting Vilar's theater productions in photographs. It was heartening to be called the first bell of a
generational carillon. To paraphrase a 1957 Jean-Luc Godard review
of a Roger Vadim film, substituting Varda's name for his, perhaps it
is pointless to compliment Varda on being ahead of her time when
she was on time and everyone else was late. Still, for years she was not
considered a forerunner of French New Wave cinema, never mind
one in the rising generation redefining French films.

Not everyone was enthusiastic about *La Pointe Courte*. Truffaut,
whose often harsh reviews earned him the epithet of "the gravedig-
ger," gave the film a mixed critique. He admired Varda's "earnest and
intelligent work," but criticized the self-consciousness of the actors
and the film's "too-composed" framing. In an ad hominem crack,
Truffaut noted the director's resemblance to her leading man (both

had bowl haircuts) and characterized Varda as a "very cerebral film-maker." Neither was a compliment. Five years later, Truffaut recanted, admitting that *La Pointe Courte* "is an admirable film which we were very unfair to at the time."

University of Wisconsin film scholar Kelley Conway, who wrote a 2015 study of Varda's work, later noted that "for a film that never received a traditional theatrical release, *La Pointe Courte* generated an extraordinary amount of attention, largely positive."

Initially, the term "New Wave" was demographic. In 1957, Françoise Giroud, a founding editor of *L'Express*, a newsweekly like *Time* magazine, sent a series of questionnaires targeting the generation between eighteen and thirty years old. This was the cohort that had not finished high school by the end of World War II. The answers indicated that the respondents were "more inward-looking and hedonistic, less political and collective" than their elders, foretelling a significant social and cultural shift. In her summary of the findings, Giroud called this generation the New Wave.

France saw the political clout of this rising generation in 1958 with the election of Charles de Gaulle as the first president of the Fifth Republic. With de Gaulle's victory came his appointment of the novelist André Malraux as minister of culture. Malraux called for a "rejuvenation" of the film industry and sought, as film historian Richard Neupert observed, "to drop the notion of guaranteed subsidies based on box-office results of completed films in favor of loans, or 'advances on receipts,' to producers," which would be reimbursed to the CNC before producers could earn profits. The new system would become a popular financing instrument for New Wave films.

La Pointe Courte had its brief run in 1955, four years before the 1959 releases of Truffaut's *The 400 Blows* and Resnais' *Hiroshima Mon Amour*, widely considered the first New Wave films. The exclusion of Varda as a filmmaker of the movement was one of her first erasures from film history. In 1959, when *Cahiers du cinéma* held a roundtable with Resnais and *Hiroshima* screenwriter Marguerite Duras, many critics who participated credited Resnais with *La Pointe Courte*, even though he was its editor. This was Varda's second erasure.

Some maintained that a New Wave filmmaker had to have started his career at *Cahiers du cinéma* and evolved into a writer-director, like Chabrol, Godard, and Truffaut. Others allowed that there was a relation between "the *Cahiers* boys" and the "Left Bank group" of Marker, Resnais, and Varda, who were more overtly experimental, political, and, well, lived on the Left Bank.

It wasn't until 1965 that French film historian Georges Sadoul corrected the record by stating that *La Pointe Courte* was "certainly the first film of the New Wave." Though she was roughly the same age as most New Wave filmmakers, writers variously called Varda its mother, godmother, or grandmother. Her cost-saving strategies— filming on location in natural light, not adding sound and dialogue until postproduction—were adopted by others in the New Wave.

5

CONVENTIONAL WISDOM IS THAT the most significant challenge of a director's career is the financing and completion of a second film. Varda would achieve this three years after shooting her first, in 1957. Yet filming her sophomore effort would not be the most life-changing episode in that eventful year.

Varda and Valentine were no longer living together. Nor was Varda keeping company with Resnais. Still, she was on friendly terms with both former lovers. Resnais advised her that to be accepted in the cinema world, it was helpful to accept a commission or two. He himself had worked on many, including one the prior year for *Night and Fog*, an important essay film about Nazi concentration camps. Resnais reminded her that Pierre Braunberger, owner of the Cinéma du Panthéon, had commissioned several films from him. Thus she wasn't surprised when Braunberger approached her to make a film about the châteaux of the Loire for the National Office of Tourism. She didn't know whether to accept or to be annoyed that two years after her film debut, "the only proposition I had was a commission for a film short" for which she had scant enthusiasm. She accepted, largely keeping her annoyance to herself.

Varda, whose architectural tastes were more aligned with the medieval Romanesque, found the Renaissance-era châteaux of the Loire "decadent." But Sandy Flitterman-Lewis, a Rutgers film scholar and one of the first Americans to write about the director in depth, has observed that she was enough of a pragmatist to understand "that this might be a way to obtain recognition and financial backing from producers wary of the experimental nature of *La Pointe Courte*." Potential investors need assurance that a director can tell a story and keep to a budget. As proof she could, Varda agreed to shoot in the fall of 1957, when there would be fewer tourists than in the summer months.

While she and Braunberger were in negotiations, Varda was getting to know Antoine Bourseiller, whom she had first met in 1951 when he was a young actor at the TNP. Soon he would establish himself as a prominent director of theater and opera. In the coming decade, he would also appear as an actor in films by Resnais (*The War Is Over*) and Godard (*Masculine/Feminine*). Yet Varda was the first to cast him in a movie. His is the voice reciting poetry in what would become her playful Loire travelogue, *Ô saisons, ô châteaux* (1958). And he is unforgettable as the gentle, empathetic soldier who encounters the title character in *Cléo from 5 to 7* (1962), accompanying her through Paris.

As Varda continued her work with the TNP and the Avignon Festival, her friend Chris Marker facilitated her invitation to tour China with a group of French dignitaries. She looked forward to chronicling a place that, since the Communist revolution in 1949, was closed to most foreigners. She packed her Rolleiflex, her Leica, an array of lenses, and many rolls of both black-and-white and color film. Either because it was too heavy, too expensive, or not allowed, she did not bring a 16mm camera. She asked Bourseiller to house-sit in her absence. He watered her plants; in red pen, she wrote him long letters about the sights and, often, her insights into China.

In 1957, the People's Republic of China was not recognized by the United Nations and would not be until 1971. As her official occupation was photographer for the TNP, she told her Chinese hosts that she was most interested in seeing popular entertainment. She photographed street circuses and stick puppets, marionettes and the all-female "theater of cats" in Shanghai.

During her two months in China, she traveled from Manchuria in the north to Sichuan in the south, went by boat down the Yangtze River from Chongqing to Shanghai, and visited Yunnan, on the border with Vietnam, where there was a sizeable Muslim community. She ended her tour of mainland China in Guanzhou. Hong Kong was her last stop in Asia. While on the mainland, she was very much impressed by the "collective behavior" of adults dressed in blue and exhilarated by the "class justice and civic sharing."

From the evidence of her photographs, she was charmed by the children. Many of her photos are of babies—in their parents' laps, in whimsical headgear, and in vibrant colors quite different from the uniform blue worn by adults. Another recurrent visual theme is figures of people dwarfed by epic mountains and industrial sites. These photos simultaneously show both landscape and human scale, emphasizing the vastness of the former.

Recalling the trip forty years later, Varda rhapsodized over the "sublime juxtaposition of Tyrian pink [magenta-purple] and vermilion red . . . forever linked to a revolution that gave everyone their chances." She took thousands of images for the purpose of collecting them for a book about the new China. But when she returned to France, she learned that two of the country's most gifted photojournalists, Henri Cartier-Bresson and his protégé, Marc Riboud, had preceded her in China by two months. Their images were all over the French periodicals, making hers redundant.

Varda brought home four thousand negatives and what would become a lifelong habit of drinking hot water. And lots of mementos, including sandalwood fans, hand puppets, dragon slippers, and a hat with cat ears. Years later she added a postscript to this inventory: "in short, everything one finds 40 years later in the import stores installed between a supermarket and a bank in the middle of shopping malls." In 2012, Beijing's Central Academy of Fine Arts mounted a retrospective of her China photographs.

On Varda's return to Paris, as Bourseiller wrote in his memoir, their "tender friendship grew," soon blooming into romance. For the August holidays, they went to Sardinia. His account of "the island where sand is blue, sea green, sky yellow and sun red" is as striking as the colors of a Fauve painting. Equally striking, but in a different sense, are his vignettes of their emotional friction. Every couple has growing pains but, as Bourseiller remembers, theirs were particularly acute. When she has a bout of postcoital insecurity and worries aloud that he will betray her, he thinks she's joking, which compounds her self-doubt. When she takes portraits of the actor, two years her junior and not yet as established in his profession as she is in hers, he experiences feelings of violation: "I watched the Leica lens grab something from my ego, the click of each take like the bark of a nasty dog."

In October 1957, a month after their return from Sardinia, armed with her Rolleiflex and Hachette Blue Guide, the uncharacteristically fatigued Varda headed to the Loire to scout locations for *Ô saisons, ô châteaux*. There is a photograph of her trudging by one of the castles, eyes downcast, looking as though she is weighed down by her camera. While Varda's body language lacks her customary vivacity, the resulting short brims with vitality and wit.

When she arrived in the Loire to prepare the promotional film to which she would bring her singular vision, Varda was besotted by the landscape. "I stumbled into a sublime late fall, all golden, bathed in sunlight. I was taken with the gentleness of the Loire Valley, and the film was instilled with the melancholy of bygone epochs." It is likely that her melancholy was magnified by a heightened sensory receptivity. Beset by nausea, Varda began to shoot the short so vital to her future as a filmmaker. She soon realized that she was pregnant but waited until her return to Paris to share the news with Bourseiller in person.

Her film took its title from a Rimbaud poem. It is the first of a trio of shorts made just before and after the birth of Varda's first child, Rosalie. It is also the first of her films shot in color. While *Ô saisons* opens with groundskeepers sweeping autumn leaves from the gardens, the narration begins in the year 1000 AD and promises to share several centuries of château architecture and history. Varda promptly subverts the theme with entertaining, often anachronistic, digressions. They include spotlights on those who for generations cultivated and maintained the magnificent gardens of the region; a Sunday painter whose goal is to paint every château on the Loire; and models in jewel-tone chapeaus and gowns designed by Jacques Heim representing the aristocrats who once lived in these elegant structures. And since it is a Varda film, there are also cats.

In between the entertaining digressions and Bourseiller's recitation of sixteenth-century poems, the narrator, stage and screen actress Danièle Delorme, explains the incremental evolution of Loire Valley architecture. What was once built as a fortress became embellished with turrets and, ultimately, inspired the enchanted splendor of Chambord and Chenonceaux, castles fit for real-life queens and their fairy-tale versions.

The short ends with the Folies Sifflait, a garden of "false ruins" built to resemble historical artifacts. At a time when almost all documentaries were narrated by men, Delorme's gleeful reading is the rare voice of female authority. She delivers a choice example of Varda's polished wordplay: "Sifflait bought the land on the Loire to build the ruins, and it ruined him."

WHEN VARDA returned to Paris in December, she shared the news of the pregnancy with Bourseiller. Years later, the actor wrote an acrimonious account of the affair in his memoir. Although Varda remained unnamed, he alleged that a paramour, pregnant with his child, had ended their liaison after complaining that his temperament was too gloomy. He likewise alleged that she intentionally did not legally register him as the father of their daughter, effectively denying him paternity rights, a "fact" that Varda denied, according to Rosalie. On one point, Bourseiller's and Varda's accounts agree: Varda told Rosalie that she had initiated the break with her daughter's biological father.

Despite the estrangement of her parents, when Rosalie was a toddler, Bourseiller frequently spent Sundays with her at the Luxembourg Gardens. And the rupture between Varda and Bourseiller did not keep her from offering—or him from accepting—the important role in *Cléo from 5 to 7*. According to a 1962 interview with Bourseiller in *Le Monde*, at the time he and Varda had considered collaborating on a joint film/theater adaptation of the 1851 novel *The Last Mistress*. That project was never realized—Varda prided herself on her original ideas and avoided adapting plays or novels.

BY THE end of 1957, Varda had completed postproduction on *Ô saisons, ô châteaux*, which would be shown at Cannes and at the annual Festival of Film Shorts in Tours the next year. This would be another eventful year for Varda—and because of the general election in October, a momentous one for France.

Early in the year, Jacques Ledoux, curator of the Royal Belgian Cinémathèque, wrote Varda to tell her that EXPRMNTL, his annual program of avant-garde films usually held in the seaside resort of Knokke-le-Zoute, had a change of venue and would take place in April in Brussels as part of Expo 58, the Brussels World Fair. There would be a place for a Varda film, he said encouragingly. Nothing concentrates the mind like a deadline. As she had just completed her first commissioned film, the time was right for another personal one.

During the harsh winter, she headed for the 5th arrondissement and rue Mouffetard. Since medieval days, the street named for the *mouffet*, or skunk—because its cobbled thoroughfare was where animal skinners plied their trade—had been a pedestrian market street. From the days of François Rabelais to those of George Orwell, the neighborhood had been home to the up-and-coming and the down-and-out. Varda knew this sliver of Paris well. She had worked with Pierre Suc and Henri Serre, friends from Sète, on an unpublished book about the neighborhood, taking photos to accompany their poems. She repurposed some of those still images for the short *L'opéra-mouffe* (known in English as *Diary of a Pregnant Woman*).

While the area's history dates back to Roman times, Varda wasn't interested in its past. It was fascinating to her as a market, one that nourished the quarter and attracted the poor of Paris. In the 1950s, the Ministry of Health declared rue Mouffetard an "unsanitary slum."

When she commenced the shoot, Varda was in her fifth month of pregnancy and deliriously happy. She borrowed a 16mm film camera from Gérard Philipe, carrying it and a folding chair to the market street. As she stood on the chair capturing the faces of the drunk, the hungry, and the indigent, she felt the contradiction of being full of hope and belly amid the hopelessness and hunger of so many in a winter so cold that three of her subjects froze to death.

L'opéra-mouffe opens with a naked human back underneath a drawing of a proscenium, cutting to the human's front. She is pregnant, with pendulous breasts and a rounded belly. In eight more brief chapters, the seventeen-minute short indicates how she came to be with child and takes the viewer from the joys of conception to the attendant fears of expectant motherhood.

Varda shows us the woman's engorged belly, quickly cutting away to a ripe pumpkin, halved by a knife that scrapes out its seeds. She cuts away to a shot of tender lovemaking and the moment of conception. This is followed by two montages. One suggests how the expectant mother sees new life blooming everywhere, even in a halved cabbage sprouting a baby cabbage. The joy soon turns to anxiety when she looks at a parade of lost souls on rue Mouffetard, of the homeless, drunk, and lonely, some who perished that winter, hoping that her child will not share their fate. In her ambitious experiment, Varda connects her subjective experience with her camera's omniscient eye.

L'opéra-mouffe premiered at EXPRMNTL in Brussels, where it won both the prize of the International Federation of Cinema Clubs at the Brussels World Fair as well as the prize for avant-garde film short. It was the first Varda film distributed in the U.S. "The film won some notoriety because of its casual nudity—then still rare on American screens—and it was booked in film societies around the country, seeding the bed for later Varda appreciation," wrote Laurence Kardish, longtime curator of film at New York's Museum of Modern Art.

Although *Ô saisons, ô châteaux* was an official selection at the Cannes Film Festival that May, Varda would spend the month—and the last weeks of her pregnancy—at rue Daguerre. On May 28, 1958, she gave birth to Rosalie Félicité Justine Varda. As Rosalie remembers, "Justine" was Resnais' contribution. Both Varda's mother and Valentine Schlegel were present to welcome the new member of the family.

Over the past five months, Varda had delivered a baby and two movies. At thirty, she was old enough to know how rare it was for personal and professional happiness to coincide. She was already full of joy about Rosalie. And when she picked up the June 1958 edition of *Cahiers du cinéma* to read a rave review of her film about the châteaux of the Loire Valley, she was positively buoyant.

"THE MORE I see [*Ô saisons, ô châteaux*] by Agnès Varda, the more I like it," wrote François Truffaut. "In Cannes, she was acclaimed by the public, and that is just. There is fantasy, taste, intelligence, intuition, and sensitivity, five virtues which should never be lacking in films. Thanks to Agnès Varda, we can measure the contribution to cinema of some women endowed with certain qualities that men could not have."

Anatole Dauman, producer of the Resnais short *Night and Fog* and of features by Resnais, Jean-Luc Godard, Volker Schlondorff, and Wim Wenders, was another admirer of the film. Dauman was charmed by Varda's wit, her able handling of location shooting, and by the "irritated impatience"—by which he meant edge—that she brought to what otherwise might have been a routine travelogue. Both Dauman and the Office of National Tourism, his production partner, wanted her to bring that edge to the Côte d'Azur. He told Varda that the Riviera documentary they looked to commission from her "would outwit the stereotypes of the post-card documentary . . . with a completely free style."

He wasn't prepared for her reluctance. When he recalled their exchanges, Dauman congratulated himself for appealing "to the part of her that identified with the camera as 'superman.'" Only a woman like you, he said, "can revitalize herself after having a baby by brandishing a camera!" For Varda, the camera was not a phallus substitute; it was an instrument for capturing life. His appeal may have given her pause, but she had other reasons for reticence.

First off, her recent experience on *L'opéra-mouffe* had convinced her that she didn't want another commission; she wanted to make her own films. Second, Dauman reached out late in her pregnancy, suggesting an August start date, knowing that by then the baby would be two months old. Varda didn't know if she would be ready for a two-month shoot eight weeks after delivering a baby.

Dauman knew that Varda's father had bequeathed her mother an apartment in Roquebrune-Cap-Martin, near Monaco, which Varda had never visited. He sweetened the deal. The producer offered to rent the apartment from Christiane to install her daughter and granddaughter there. Varda's younger sister, Sylvie, would be Rosalie's nanny. Varda could begin and end each day with her newborn and make the film in the hours in between. She agreed to his terms.

While scouting locations, Varda counter-proposed that Dauman also produce a satiric companion short about the kept women of the Côte d'Azur and their consorts, to be titled *La cocotte d'azur* (Riviera Hooker). The commission would have a happier outcome than its complement.

The shoot was eight weeks, mid-August to mid-October, reuniting Varda with the gifted cinematographer Quinto Albicocco, her collaborator on *Ô saisons*. The rich colors of his camerawork nicely complemented her acute wit. Add to this a Georges Delerue score that ran the gamut from madcap to melancholy, and it made for an amusing and thoughtful introduction to the Riviera, where even ancient statues use their upraised hands to shade their eyes from the summer sun. The completed film was considerably more substantial than tourist-office eye candy.

Varda dedicated the film to André Bazin, her early champion. Satirizing picture-postcard versions of travelogues, Varda introduces the Riviera sites with Art Nouveau postcards. Anne Olivier, the film's narrator, advises us that the film's focus will not be on the locals but on the tourists responsible for the fivefold increase in population every summer. They are depicted as benevolent invading armies, covering the beaches like human wall-to-wall carpet.

One of the film's running jokes is that the Riviera has been colonized by outlanders. The first might have been Roman princess Cornelia Salonina, who came to Cimiez, near Nice, in the third century to take the waters and calm her shattered nerves. On the Riviera coast, Varda finds Japanese pagodas, Sudanese mosques, and *hôtels anglaise*. From luxury hotels to modest campsites, there are dozens named Eden, a popular term for the Riviera.

Varda's angle is that the Riviera is a false Eden. While historically it was a magnet for famous artists (Picasso, Matisse), writers (Colette, Dante, Nietzsche), and movie stars (Bardot, Loren), who came there to paint, to write, and to screen their films, tourists can engage only in a kind of compensatory encounter. They can't buy a Matisse, so they make a pilgrimage to his grave at a Cimiez monastery; they can't see Bardot, so they go to the Saint-Tropez eatery that her character frequented in Roger Vadim's 1956 film *And God Created Woman*. Varda's drollest shot is that of the tourist throng at a botanical garden. The narrator observes, "They long for the silence of the plant kingdom, but they never remember the plant's name; they prefer the plant to remember theirs." Cut to a close-up of cacti and succulents with the names of visitors carved into their hardy spears.

Despite its hurly-burly, the Riviera does possess some Edenic spots, but these tend to be lushly landscaped private villas off-limits to tourists. After Varda's inventory of the sights, eccentricities, and "faux Eves and ersatz Adams" in their counterfeit Edens, Varda finds the real deal. Her film takes us to an undeveloped island (Porquerolles, unidentified) where Eden is a beach, some pine cones, and two horses frolicking in the surf. When first I saw the short, I took it as a subversive anti-tourist film, critical of what the travel industry sells vacationers. Watching it years later suggested an alternative read: the undeveloped and undiscovered Riviera is where Eden can be found. In other words, find paradise before developers pave it into a parking lot.

VARDA RETURNED to Paris in October. According to Dauman, she did not take his editing suggestions "with grace." Nonetheless, with editor Henri Colpi, she rapidly assembled a cut of *Along the Coast* in time to receive an invitation to the fourth Tours International Short Film Days in December. Tours had a reputation as a fringe Cannes. The prior year, François Truffaut had made a splash there with his short *The Mischief-Makers*. Dauman was pleased with *Ô saisons*. "Except for 30 seconds, he said, "I thought the film was flawless." Varda's Loire Valley château film would likewise screen in Tours, but not in competition. Film shorts were hugely popular and profitable in France. In most commercial cinemas, they were shown before the feature.

Dauman wrote that he was "appalled" by *La cocotte d'azur*, but didn't share why. Perhaps he thought it vulgar. He screened it for Marker, who was enthusiastic. Then he showed it to Resnais, whose first feature, *Hiroshima Mon Amour*, he was producing. This put the Sphinx in a no-win situation of affronting either his producer or his onetime lover and close friend. After Resnais saw the short, he huddled privately with Varda, who emerged from their tête-à-tête to tell Dauman she would take her name off it, allowing him to edit and distribute it as he saw fit. When Dauman was done editing it, even he admitted that it "lacked any fizz." In her memoir, Varda avoided the subject by saying only, "I claim that [the film] does not exist." While it was no longer her film, her residual annoyance toward Dauman lingered, as did his toward her, because of some mischief at Tours.

Along the Coast screened on opening night, often a good omen at a competitive film festival. Another opening-night offering was *Living* by Carlos Vilardebó, assistant director of *La Pointe Courte*. Many of the directors whose films were shown, including Varda, Dušan Makavejev from Yugoslavia, and Norman McLaren from Canada, were on the cusp of international success. Out of competition, Marker showed *Letter from Siberia*, Resnais had *The Song of Styrene*, and Jacques Rozier had *Blue Jeans*.

It was another Jacques, however—filmmaker Jacques Demy— who caught her eye, and Varda his. He was at the festival with *Le bel indifférent*, an adaptation of a Jean Cocteau playlet about a woman frustrated by her younger lover's inattention.

Born in 1931 on France's Atlantic coast, Demy was a son of the working class. In Nantes, where he was raised, his father was a garage mechanic and his mother a hairdresser. He was three years Varda's junior. At the insistence of his father, the younger Demy attended vocational school to train as a mechanic. Ultimately, filmmaker Christian-Jaque, an admirer of the young man's work, convinced Demy's father to permit him to attend the École Technique de Photographie et de Cinématographie, which Varda had attended. Unlike her, Demy had been a cinephile since childhood, buying himself a movie camera at fourteen. Like her, he was an inveterate punster.

After earning his professional certificate and completing his military service, Demy worked as assistant to animator Paul Grimault and documentary filmmaker Georges Rouquier. By the time he and Varda met, he had already made several shorts, including *Le Sabotier du Val de Loire*, a spare chronicle of the vanishing craft that was also a portrait of the man who sheltered Demy and his younger brother during the war.

In 1956, Demy met Resnais and Godard at Tours, where he joked that earlier that year he had directed Grace Kelly's last movie. In truth, he had assisted in making the newsreel of Kelly's wedding to

Prince Rainier of Monaco. Godard invited Demy to come to *Cahiers* screenings in Paris and to film discussions at the journal's offices, where he met Truffaut and others.

At Tours, Varda recalled, Demy "invited me to the local café." He drank a plume (beer and lemonade) and she a half-verbena infusion. There was mutual appreciation, attraction, and wordplay. "We enjoyed ourselves."

As to the Tours competition, Dauman said that a juror told him that *Along the Coast* was on the brink of receiving the top prize when Silvia Monfort (who played the lead in *La Pointe Courte*) delivered to her fellow jurors a message from Varda herself: "She personally requested me to ask you not to vote for her film which is merely a commissioned work." When Dauman learned this, he was not happy.

As the producer told it, years later he was sunbathing on the beach at the Deauville Film Festival and saw Varda heading out for a swim. "I gently called to her: 'Dear lady, thinking of coasts, won't you tell me why you refused the first prize at Tours?'" She replied, "Because it would have given you too much pleasure, my dear Dauman!" Four years after Tours, Richard Roud, then director of the London Film Festival, recalled traveling with Varda from London to Paris, stopping in Boulogne to watch Resnais shoot *Muriel*. When the day's shoot ended, Resnais and actress Delphine Seyrig joined Varda and Roud in the dining car on the Paris-bound train. There, Varda, in what Roud (who adored her movies) called "her usual aggressive manner," complained about Dauman, producer of *Muriel*, for much of the journey.

While it seems like self-sabotage for a director to refuse a prize that might elevate her standing, Varda considered commissioned work not fully her own.

On Christmas Eve in 1958, Varda was on her own at rue Daguerre, embroidering felt slippers for Rosalie, nearly seven months old, who was "chirping from her baby basket." There was a knock on the door. It was Demy, bringing a Varda a single rose. Taken aback because she had neither card nor gift for her gentleman caller, she fetched a small jar of rose confiture to give him in return. She was ashamed of her "housewife's response," she recalled, "when in my heart a thousand rosebuds opened." Not long after, they had another rendezvous. "After a walk along the Loire . . . we got to know each other biblically," she said.

At the beginning of the new year, Demy moved to rue Daguerre to live with Varda and baby Rosalie.

IN 1957, TRUFFAUT HAD attended the Cannes Film Festival as a critic for *Arts*, trashing the event in his reportage. The following year, 1958, he was banned from Cannes. In 1959, his debut feature, *The 400 Blows*, Resnais' first feature, *Hiroshima Mon Amour*, and Marcel Camus' *Black Orpheus*, a French-Brazilian coproduction, were official French entries at Cannes; Truffaut won the prize for best director and *Black Orpheus* the Palme d'or for best film. It was a remarkable cultural shift.

That year, the term "New Wave" was first applied to film. French filmmakers roughly thirty and under, including Demy, Godard, Truffaut, and Varda (who was thirty-one), positioned themselves to catch the wave, knowing two things: that under Malraux, de Gaulle's minister of culture, the financing structure of French film was about to change, and that Truffaut's triumph at Cannes would open doors—and checkbooks—for young French filmmakers.

Malraux wanted to end direct grants to producers based on prior productions, which effectively rewarded them for the box office of a past film. On June 16, he announced that the CNC would support projects that had the best scripts, instead rewarding quality.

Between 1957 and 1958, the number of television sets in France rose by 44 percent, while the number of movie tickets sold declined by nearly 10 percent. "Cinema and its function had changed," wrote film critic Richard Brody. "Malraux recognized that, in order to remain viable, the French cinema would need to become art of the . . . cultural patrimony, and to be exported like Bordeaux wine or Camembert cheese."

This put Malraux at odds with the minister of finance, Antoine Pinay. "I do not subsidize groceries," he groused. "Why should I subsidize films?" When de Gaulle removed Pinay in 1960—not for his opinion of film subsidies—some claimed the victory of culture over finance.

In 1960, Truffaut wrote *Breathless*, a feature based on a news item that had caught his attention, with his *Cahiers* colleague Claude Chabrol. The latter had had a modest hit with his 1958 debut, *Le Beau Serge*. When Godard took over the project as his debut feature, René Pignières, financier of the film's producer Georges de Beauregard, applied to the CNC, correctly guessing that a project with the involvement of Truffaut and Chabrol was a good bet. *Breathless*, shot for $60,000 over four weeks in 1959, became a surprise hit the following year. De Beauregard asked Godard about other directors he knew who could shoot on the cheap and make him profits. Soon he would produce features by Demy and Varda.

Earlier in 1959, in different rooms of rue Daguerre, they were both working on the screenplay for a feature film. Demy had just completed *Ars*, an austere documentary short summoning the piety of a saintly nineteenth-century parish priest in the titular city, and turned his attention to a decidedly unsaintly tale of a cabaret singer (ultimately played by Anouk Aimée) and the men in her orbit. He showed the script to Varda, who was at first "perplexed."

"When Jacques made me read a script called *A Ticket to Johannesburg* [he later changed the title to *Lola*] it was to me like the summary of a popular novel," she wrote in her memoir *Varda par Agnès*. She did not share her misgivings with him. Only when on the set of the film in 1960, as Demy directed Aimée, did she recognize his camera skills and able direction of actors. The screenplay she was working on was *La mélangite*.

At this early point in their careers (she was thirty, he twenty-seven), Varda's star was rising while Demy's was on the horizon. Having made one feature and three shorts, Varda was commanding critical attention. In the February edition of *Cahiers du cinéma*, Godard published an admiring appreciation of her as a colorist. He admired the golden autumn she captured in *Ô saisons, ô châteaux*, the monochrome winter of rue Mouffetard in *L'opéra-mouffe*, and the bold primary colors of *Along the Coast*. He invoked painters like Matisse and writers like Proust, declaring that the shorts "are to cinema what drawing is to painting and the road guide is to the novel." He concluded, "Agnès Varda's shorts shine like real little gems."

A few months later, Dauman chose *Along the Coast* to precede Resnais' *Hiroshima Mon Amour* in theaters, having produced both. Though her early shorts likewise were distributed in commercial cinemas, when *Hiroshima Mon Amour* became an international art-house sensation, Varda's work reached her widest audience to date.

Three days after her thirty-first birthday, Varda had her first retrospective. *La Pointe Courte* and her three shorts were on an evening program at the Palais de Chaillot, attracting an audience of two thousand, a figure deemed "astonishing" by film historian Richard Neupert. Even though there was no publicity other than a few leaflets distributed here and there, the evening attracted this impressive crowd to what critic Jean Douchet described in an article the following week as "a triumph . . . intended to repair an injustice." It was unjust, he wrote, that at a moment celebrating the victory of a new, young generation of filmmakers, "the name of Agnès Varda is not even whispered." It was even more unfair, he said, since she was the true precursor and promoter of the current cinematic renewal. "Now we realize, Agnès Varda has innovated in everything."

While Varda did not come to filmmaking with any sort of unified theory—cinematic, feminist, or otherwise—she would come to describe the director's role as *cinécriture*, her own coinage, which translates as "film writing." For her, *cinécriture* encompassed framing, camera movement, sound, image, acting, editing rhythms, both still and moving images, visual composition, spoken dialogue—the intentional, the accidental, and the improvisational.

Not long after her triumph at the Palais de Chaillot, she heard from Truffaut. After his own triumph at Cannes, he continued to work closely with *Cahiers du cinéma*. He asked Varda if she could assemble a photographic chronicle of *La Pointe Courte* to publish in the journal. Replying from Sète in August 1959, she declined, explaining that time spent creating the photo essay would be time needed for completing the screenplay she was writing. Almost certainly that script was *La mélangite*, which would soon interest several producers, including Truffaut himself. Its title, a Varda neologism of "mélange" and "meningitis," would translate into English as "mixitis." Its protagonist mixes up time and place.

Varda synopsized the project as a chronicle of the romantic evolution of Valentin, a dreamer raised in Sète. The character with the masculine version of the name of Varda's former roommate and lover would be played by five different actors. Varda hoped to cast Bourseiller, Claude Brasseur, and Jean-Claude Brialy, among others. Each would embody a different emotional aspect, and age, of Valentin. At the outset, Valentin is twenty, with a girlfriend the same age. Along the way he meets Stella, a femme fatale, in Venice. After a cosmic night of love, during which their gondola surreally morphs into fourposter bed, Stella disappears.

Valentin returns to Sète and spends his next decade trying to recapture Stella and their magical time together. He will dream of her, think of her, go mad looking for her, mentally confusing the canals of Venice with those of Sète and his dreams with reality. He grows older, gets a job and a mistress, Agathe, who wants to marry. When Valentin asks himself whether he should, all the Valentins inside him answer differently. Varda described the film as "a psychological western."

She described it more fully in a 1961 interview with Jean Michaud and Raymond Bellour as "the story of a man who mixes up not only his past, his present and his future, but his lived life and his dream life. He is someone who becomes blurry." Her screenplay dramatized a psychological truism close to Varda's heart: "When we become, we do not cancel what we have been before."

Dauman and his company, Argos Films, were interested in producing. Yet either because of the bad feelings on her side about *La cocotte d'azur* or his about Tours—or both—he withdrew. In 1960, Varda approached Truffaut, soliciting his support as a producer. Truffaut's company, Les Films du Carosse, and Pierre Braunberger's Les Films de la Pleiade provisionally agreed. But this ambitious film, which Varda envisioned shooting in color on location in Venice and Sète, needed more capital than these companies could shoulder. Truffaut suggested that Varda find an Italian coproducer, which would be expedient for both financial and practical reasons. She received contracts from Truffaut and Braunberger that set deadlines for a work plan, shooting script, and compensation.

In 1960, color film was costly, and in France, risky. Fewer than 10 percent of the features shot there that year were in color because available film stocks were still in an experimental phase. To prove that she could shoot color on a budget, Varda traveled to Sète in September with Rosalie, her nanny, and an assistant, to film a prelude to *La mélangite*. The expense wasn't in the agreed-upon work plan, but Varda prevailed, thinking that this footage—what filmmakers today would call a sizzle reel—might attract other investors. While in Sète, Varda, who liked to improvise, filmed a dream sequence that was not in the script.

Because financing for the picture was not completely in hand, Truffaut and Braunberger felt that she was spending capital they didn't want to commit until funding was secure. Both wrote Varda letters of annoyance. Privately, Truffaut was pleased with the footage. He confided to his friend Helen Scott: "Agnès Varda has shot a sequence of *La mélangite*, it's rather beautiful. . . . [But] the film can't really get under way until we've found an Italian co-producer, which won't be easy, believe me, given the screenplay, which is first-rate, but terrifying."

Varda shot off a reasoned reply to Truffaut. "I wanted to try, in the planned estimate, in the planned time, with the planned film, to do more than planned. Not to impose on you whatever it is but to show you that I was able—and the others too—to shoot quickly and well and not too expensively."

Committed to securing an Italian coproducer, Varda approached Rome-Paris Films, then producing Demy's *Lola*. Rome–Paris was a partnership between Carlo Ponti, producer of *Two Women* and husband of its star, Sophia Loren, and Georges de Beauregard, producer of *Breathless*. They were interested.

Once in Rome, however, Varda was annoyed when a representative from Rome–Paris interrupted her pitch and asked why a woman like her dressed in a way that didn't show her body. She promptly turned the tables, asking why a man like him, with such a large belly, wore a vest. The decisionmakers at Rome–Paris didn't care how Varda dressed and signed on. When they came aboard, Truffaut and de Beauregard disembarked. It's unclear whether they jumped, were pushed away by the new partners, or whether there were other mitigating factors.

While Varda waited for Rome–Paris to commit fully to *La mélangite*, de Beauregard cautioned her that it would be too expensive. He advised her to instead "make a little film in black-and-white that doesn't cost more than $64,000." (She did, and that little black-and-white film became *Cléo from 5 to 7*, one of her best and most beloved films.) For the time being, *La mélangite* was set aside.

WHEN DEMY moved to rue Daguerre in 1959, two filmmakers under one roof was a comparatively rare phenomenon, perhaps because movies were a comparatively new art form. Except for experimental filmmakers Maya Deren and Alexander Hammid (wed from 1942 to 1947), there had not been a pair of cohabiting filmmakers since Lois Weber and Phillips Smalley began making movies in 1911.

Not long after Varda and Demy became a couple, more women began working behind the camera and two-director households grew more common, if not exactly commonplace. Like Varda and Demy, such couples navigated togetherness and separate careers through the hazardous waters of competition, cross-currents, long periods of separation, and unequal compensation.

Varda and Demy shared love—for each other, for Rosalie, for their son Mathieu (born in 1972), and for filmmaking. To a great degree, their professional and personal lives overlapped. While on the surface their films look and feel radically different, *Lola* and *Cléo from 5 to 7* touch upon similar themes: coincidence, the search for happiness, and being surprised by joy. Theirs are films in which characters and camera are like dance partners. Theirs are films with an appreciative eye for landscape.

Their differences are also telling. Demy's films are fables and fantasies, peopled with fictional characters whose paths cross in consecutive films, many of them musicals. Varda's films, as Martin Scorsese observed, are "beautifully balanced between documentary and fiction." With some exceptions, all are rooted in reality. Demy created his own world; Varda was inspired by the real world.

Artistically speaking, the filmmakers were not roped to each other but functioned more like trees in an ecosystem, unique but interdependent.

This is what that interdependence looked like. When Demy needed a song for his feature debut, *Lola*, Varda wrote the lyrics. When Demy asked Michel Legrand to write the score for *Lola* and the composer demurred because he had committed to write music for veteran filmmaker Marcel Carné, Varda demanded, "How could you refuse a Demy for a Carné? He's yesterday's cinema!" Her insistence persuaded Legrand to reconsider. When Varda faced a deadline to complete the screenplay for her 1965 feature *Le Bonheur*, Demy volunteered to stay in bed with her all weekend to help frame the first draft and polish the final one. With its separate offices and common areas, the structure of rue Daguerre made possible both their self-sufficiency and their mutual support. Rosalie had a nanny and had care when both parents were absent.

"Agnès was the pragmatist, Jacques the dreamer," observed their friend Tom Luddy, cofounder of the Telluride Film Festival. He characterized Varda as having "assumed the traditional male duties of [looking] after the business end of things" while Demy was "more of the nurturer." Rosalie concurred. "Jacques really raised me," she remembered, adding that when he was writing he kept more of a nine-to-five schedule, while "Agnès wrote whenever."

The creation of *Cléo from 5 to 7* began with the strict budget that de Beauregard had stipulated. To minimize travel expenses, it would be made in Paris over the cinematic time frame of ninety minutes. It would be shot mostly outdoors, so as to not require sets. In France, a *cinq à sept*, or five to seven, refers to the hours of a tryst. But that is not the subject of this film.

An image-maker sensitive to the resonances of place, Varda asked herself, "What did Paris evoke for me?" It represented "a vague fear of the big city and its dangers, of getting lost in it alone and misunderstood, and even brushed aside."

Gradually surfacing in her mind was the image of a hero awaiting a critical piece of news that would either compound or allay his fears. When she envisioned a pop singer, her hero became a heroine. What could sustain the movie's suspense? A legal verdict? The public's reaction to her songs? Perhaps the results of a cancer biopsy? Varda chose the third option, and the outcome was *Cléo*, powerfully dramatizing a passive woman whose brush with mortality spurs her to claim her agency. Varda accurately described it as "a portrait of a woman painted onto a documentary about Paris." It would have a brief color prologue, but to keep costs in line, it would be principally in black and white.

To research the personal effects of cancer, Varda visited clinics and met with more than a hundred patients. The experience made her realize that she "risked making a movie that was medical reportage." She wanted the focus to be on one woman. Rather than the large cast she had in mind for *La mélangite*, there are just two principals in *Cléo*—Corinne Marchand and Antoine Bourseiller—and a handful of speaking parts.

Cléo's loop around Paris has been compared to Leopold Bloom's through Dublin in James Joyce's *Ulysses* and to Clarissa Dalloway's through London in Virginia Woolf's *Mrs. Dalloway*. Each is a death-haunted odyssey in which the principal character lives a lifetime in a day, meandering through a hectic city that is sometimes a mirror of and at other times a diversion from his or her interior disquiet.

Cléo is a real-time odyssey through a newsreel Paris. It is a platitude of film writing to say that the city in which a movie was shot is a character in the film. With *Cléo*, it happens to be true. Varda documents 1961 Paris as a lively three-ring circus. Its sideshows include the street performers who swallow frogs and the fortune teller who reads Cléo's tarot cards to predict her fate. In the center ring is Cléo herself. For Molly Haskell, film critic and author of the feminist landmark *From Reverence to Rape*, Varda "turns Paris into a hall of mirrors—windows and faces that reflect the heroine back to herself." Often, Cléo sees a distorted image.

Though it covers six arrondissements and probably as many miles, most of the locations where Varda shot, such as Parc Montsouris and Café Dôme, are close to rue Daguerre. During the shoot, it wasn't unusual for Demy to drop by and give Varda a smooch, or for Rosalie's nanny to push the three-year-old in her stroller to watch *maman* at work.

Varda films often are simultaneously about two things. *Cléo from 5 to 7* is narratively about a pop star waiting for a biopsy result but formally about time: how it drags when one feels immobilized or passive, and how it speeds by when one is actively engaged.

On the first day of summer, Cléo, a striking blonde played by Corinne Marchand, worries that her cancer is terminal and that before she arrives at that last station, she will lose her looks. The latter, for Cléo, is a fate worse than death. For the film's first half, she is coddled and condescended to—by her maid, her songwriters, and her older lover. She hears clocks ticking down the minutes. In shop windows she sees African sculptures and thinks of death masks. When her songwriters ask her to rehearse, they give her a song about loss. Terrified, she rips off her wig, dons black, and flees from those who would define her and their premonitions of death.

Cléo decides to take time into her own hands. Contemplating a negative prognosis makes Cléo not want to be another's trophy but her own woman. And so, she evolves from a human object, both admired and leered at by observers, and becomes the film's subject, a woman capable of emotional connection. In particular, she befriends a French soldier (played by Antoine Bourseiller) on furlough from fighting in Algeria. Like Cléo, the soldier feels his mortality. Their wide-ranging conversation about life and death and love comprises the film's final act.

For Martin Scorsese, then nineteen and an undergraduate at New York University, *Cléo* was "quite a shock," one that "opened my thinking in many ways."

"I felt that I was seeing the world and experiencing time from a woman's point of view for the first time in movies," he recalled. He didn't understand those who criticized it for being insufficiently somber. "There is a remarkable sense of freedom and poignancy at those moments she looks in the mirror. Is it just a pop star obsessed with her looks?" he wondered. He experienced it as a woman confronting her mortality. "No male director would ever have dared that kind of lyricism under those dramatic circumstances."

With Demy's first feature, *Lola*, released in 1961, and Varda's second, *Cléo from 5 to 7*, released in 1962, the filmmakers officially entered the ranks of New Wave directors. The his-and-her films have noteworthy consonances. Their eponymous heroines are both entertainers, one waiting for her lover's return, the other for a medical diagnosis. Cléo meets a soldier while passing the time until she hears from her oncologist; Lola entertains American sailors while awaiting

the return of her son's father. The films' differences are likewise notable. Cléo evolves from a "woman seen to a woman seeing," as film
professor Alison Smith observed. Lola is happy to be a woman seen.

With its homages to classic films like *The Blue Angel* and *Lola
Montès* and a mesmerizing performance by Aimée, Demy's debut feature was a critical success. Varda later reflected that "it was one of
those films, like Jean Renoir's *Rules of the Game*, that had no commercial success . . . but a marvelous reputation."

Cléo, happily, was a hit on arrival. It was an official selection at
the Cannes Film Festival, where Marchand, a statuesque blonde,
was greeted like a Hollywood starlet. Varda, who thought her film
was "intimate and whispering," was pleased that it "caused quite a
stir." For its premiere, Varda wore what she called "a circus dress"
beneath a transparent spangled cape. She had a hearty laugh when
TV presenter Léon Zitrone introduced her onstage as "Agnès
Varga," confusing her surname with that of the costumer at the
Casino de Paris.

Both as a photographer and as a subject of media features, Varda
understood how newspaper culture pages operated, and worked
them to her advantage. While shooting the film in the summer of
1961, she invited journalists to the set to write advance features. Its
release was greeted with rapturous headlines, for example, above
Jean-Louis Bory's review in *Arts* magazine, "*Cléo from 5 to 7* Is a
Masterpiece." Truffaut, himself a former critic for *Arts*, saw the film
before release and also liked it, writing to a friend, "Varda's [film]
is excellent, very influenced by *Lola* and Godard, yet of unrivaled
visual beauty."

Although Varda had known nothing about ciné-clubs while making *La Pointe Courte*, with *Cléo* she allowed Bory and André Pari-
naud, an editor at *Arts*, to show the film at their new "preview clubs"
in Paris and the provinces. Varda herself wrote the queries to a post-
screening questionnaire designed to assess whether viewers "got" her
nontraditional film. The process was like that of a test screening or
focus group except that the film, questions, and audience were more

sophisticated. Example: "Do you see a greater meaning in the film that goes beyond the storyline itself?" In Paris alone, 2,000 attended previews and 1,000 returned the questionnaire, enabling *Arts* to report that 97 percent of its respondents endorsed the film. Varda was gratified to learn that many respondents connected with her brand of modernism.

The film did well at the box office—over 500,000 admissions in France, where it performed as well in the provinces as it did in Paris. While *Cléo* received its fair share of criticism on both sides of the Atlantic, the reviews were mostly in the positive to rhapsodic range. It won the Prix Méliès from the association of French critics, international recognition, and, as the critic Kelley Conway observed, earned Varda full membership, however belated, in the French New Wave.

In the 1980s Madonna, the American pop singer whose mother died of breast cancer when the singer was five, contacted Varda. She was interested in doing a *Cléo* remake with Varda. In the reboot, Cléo would be HIV-positive. Varda was interested, but the project was never realized. The two women appeared together on French television in 1993, on an entertainment show celebrating the recording artist and occasional actress. Madonna confessed that she backed out of the *Cléo* reboot because studio funding demanded a completed script and Varda wanted the shoot to be more avant-garde.

Cléo has become a classic of modernist cinema. Sixty years on, its reputation continues to grow. Varda's chronicle of how women are looked at and how they look at the world themselves is as timely as the day it was made.

7

ON A MONDAY IN January 1962, three months before the release of *Cléo*, Varda and Demy slipped into the town hall of the 14th arrondissement to be married. Her witness was Chris Marker, the movie maker of *La Jetee*—the film that inspired the futuristic *12 Monkeys*. His was Bernard Toublanc-Michel, the assistant director on *Lola* and *Cléo*. Also present was Rosalie, then three and a half years old, who, according to her mother, "was ecstatic."

"Jacques and I weren't particularly keen on getting married," recalled Varda, "but we were tired of the . . . inconveniences of this 'cohabiting' situation"—such as the time they went on a pleasure cruise and couldn't share a cabin because they weren't wed. At their low-key ceremony, there was no bouquet, but there was rice. She remembered, "Toublanc vaguely threw a handful over our heads and the matter was settled." On the return to rue Daguerre, they called their mothers to give them the news. Both cried.

Not long after the ceremony, the newlyweds vacationed in Noirmoutier, a geographical curiosity on the Atlantic coast about an hour's drive from Nantes. At low tide, Noirmoutier is a peninsula. At high tide, the Passage du Gois, the causeway connection from the mainland, is submerged and Noirmoutier is an island. As a teenager, Demy had hitchhiked there to camp in its dunes.

In 1962, while walking on the windswept shore, they were charmed by the sight of an abandoned mill that once upon a time might have inspired a fairy tale. It had both views of and direct access to La Guérinière beach. Its proprietor, "Adam the miller," had died in 1959 and it was for sale, broken windows and all. Varda always had a tender spot for orphaned buildings, people, and cats, and she and Demy were enchanted. They bought it, and made the tower and outbuildings habitable. What was to be a retreat "became a place of inspiration," where both wrote screenplays and Varda would make a film.

The two years immediately following the wedding would be the most professionally productive and hectic stretch of their lives. They were often apart—on location, in transit, or attending a film festival with a newly released movie.

They had gotten married a little less than a year after their close friends Jean-Luc Godard and Anna Karina. The director and his actress wife had two weddings. The first took place in Godard's native Switzerland, in March 1961. The second was three weeks later in Paris, where Rosalie was their flower girl and Varda and Demy their witnesses. For some time, the two couples spent Sundays together playing games like liar's poker.

When Varda accompanied *Cléo* to the Venice Film Festival in August 1962, she met filmmaker Bernardo Bertolucci, there with his debut film, *The Grim Reaper*. The Italian moviemaker became close to his French counterpart. In the early 1970s, when Bertolucci started keeping company with the director Claire Peploe (whom he later married), the Bertolucci/Peploes and Demy/Vardas vacationed together. When socializing with other filmmakers, Varda, a natural-born comic known to remove the dome from her dinner plate and arrange it on her head like the latest in millinery fashion, was not one for shop talk. She preferred games, swimming, or going to museums. Of the down time she and Demy spent with the Bertoluccis, she observed, "I am surprised that three, then four, makers of rather serious films had in common such a desire to have fun."

Demy accompanied Varda to Cannes in May 1962, both to support her and to pitch investors for his passion project, *The Umbrellas of Cherbourg*, which now had a completed script. Always helpful to fellow filmmakers, Truffaut told a young producer, Mag Bodard, about the trouble Demy was having raising money, and she signed on. Alas, no financiers at Cannes that year expressed any interest for a sung-through movie musical. As a diversion, Bodard took Demy to the municipal casino in nearby Nice. Inside the gaming palace, which Demy found otherworldly, he also found inspiration for his next film, *The Bay of Angels* (1963). He wrote the script in a week and shot it that fall on the Riviera. Demy's second feature, a romance starring a bewitching Jeanne Moreau, opened in March 1963. Most reviewers liked Moreau better than the film, which equates risking one's chips on the roulette table with gambling on love.

Varda still had high hopes for *La mélangite*. Before she left for Cannes in 1962, Rome-Paris Films sent her a contract acknowledging receipt of a completed screenplay, scheduling an eight-to-ten-week shoot beginning in September, and stipulating July 1963 as the due date for the edited film. Her hopes were dashed in August when Rome-Paris said her budget was too high and they would not proceed. According to Varda's account, she offered the part of Stella, the Venetian beauty, to Sophia Loren, but Loren demurred. She had just won a best actress Oscar for *Two Women*, and considered Stella a supporting role. In the Hollywood of that era, that would be a step down.

In one of the many interviews Varda gave in 1962, she mentioned that she was in discussions to direct *The Life of George Sand*, a film biography of the scandalous nineteenth-century novelist. She was enthusiastic about researching the life of the nonconformist writer, in many ways a precursor of Colette and Varda herself. But neither *La mélangite* nor *George Sand* were realized.

Nevertheless, Varda was pragmatic. There were passion projects and there were the films made while waiting to make passion projects. And for Varda, who left the TNP when her directorial career took off, there were always photos to take. She accepted an invitation from the Cuban Institute of Cinema and Industry (ICAIC) to visit the island and document the changes there since the revolution that had unseated Fulgencio Batista in 1959. Chris Marker had visited there in 1961 to make his documentary *¡Cuba, Sí!*, and recommended Varda to ICAIC executive Alfredo Guevara, brother of Che, as a prominent photographer and filmmaker. She traveled there in 1962.

While in Cuba, Varda shot 2,500 photographs of cane field workers, popular musicians, and revolutionary leaders Fidel Castro and Che Guevara. These still images, duplicated and edited to suggest cinematic movement, came alive when synced to the rhythms of the music she recorded for her 1964 documentary *Salut les cubains* (Hello, Cubans). It's a time capsule of the optimistic moment in which she visited, when literacy rates were soaring and the island's diversity was an international model. Hers is a collective portrait more interested in ordinary Cubans than in Castro, likening her view to a conga line through history. One of its most striking portraits is of a smiling Castro sitting in front of stone extrusions suggestive of wings. At the time, the picture might have been interpreted as an image of an angel in repose. In 1964, the thirty-minute film was distributed in Paris theaters and went on to win prizes at the Leipzig Festival and the International Exposition of Documentary Films at Venice. In 2015, her photographs were on view at the Centre Pompidou in Paris in the show "Varda/Cuba."

By the time Varda returned home in early 1963, Bodard had pieced together a deal for *The Umbrellas of Cherbourg*. Although new to producing, the onetime reporter for *France-Soir* had connections, and used them. Pierre Lazareff, *France-Soir*'s proprietor and Bodard's romantic partner, was developing an entertainment news show for

French television. To get the final chunk of money for *Umbrellas*, she persuaded him to produce a segment on the 20th Century–Fox film *The Longest Day* for the show in exchange for Fox taking U.S. distribution rights to *Umbrellas*. For $75,000, which would complete funding needed for *Umbrellas*, Darryl F. Zanuck, head of Fox, could get publicity for *his* passion project. It turned out to be an excellent deal for all involved. It was a masterstroke for Bodard, who would produce three films for Demy and two for Varda.

THERE ARE times that the movies of Jacques Demy and Agnès Varda seem to speak to each other. In Demy's *Umbrellas* (1964), a musical melodrama of young love, Madame Emery tells her love-sick daughter that "people only die of love in movies." Is it possible that this line could have influenced a sequence in Varda's 1965 film *Le Bonheur* (Happiness), a sun-dappled pastoral of married-with-children bliss interrupted by an unexpected tragedy? Both are stories of first love. Both were produced by Bodard. Still, even when Demy's and Varda's films share a theme, or a producer, they share little else, especially when it came to process.

"They had totally different ways of working," said Rosalie, who as an adult assisted Demy as a costumer and Varda as assistant and producer. "Jacques really prepared everything in advance—the film, the script, the editing, everything was in his head. . . . Everything was prepared. With Varda, everything was fluid. She would always say, 'Chance is my best assistant.'" With Demy, Rosalie said, "when the first day of shooting would arrive, we had practically already done the film, in a way." But with Varda, "when we did the first day of shoot-ing, we were throwing ourselves into the swimming pool."

Their differing approaches make sense when one considers that Varda came to film from photography, where ditching the prear-ranged plan and capitalizing on happy accidents is common. Demy, on the other hand, came from film school immediately after World War II, when careful planning was emphasized so that neither time nor costly film stock would be wasted. Moreover, as Rosalie noted, in his two most famous musicals—*Umbrellas* and *The Young Girls of Rochefort*—the dialogue of Demy's movies was song lyrics that had to be timed precisely.

Bodard met Varda for the first time in 1963 at rue Daguerre, when she came to check in with Demy and Legrand. The producer's first impression of Varda was as a "*bricoleuse*, making her own little films and documentaries." At the time, *bricoleuse* (tinkerer, female) had a specific valence due to Claude Lévi-Strauss's *The Savage Mind*, published the previous year, in which he distinguished engineers from *bricoleurs*, who improvise new objects from preexisting ones. *Bricoleurs* were, in effect, recyclers, before recycling was recognized as a way of saving resources.

At rue Daguerre, while Demy focused on the preparation and filming of *Umbrellas*, Varda spent much of 1963 editing *Salut les cubains* and writing the screenplay for her next project, *The Creatures*. Bodard committed to producing *The Creatures* if it received support from the CNC.

In February 1963, Demy and Varda took Rosalie and a friend to Nantes for the solemn declaration of faith of Hélène, Demy's sister, goddaughter, and junior by twenty years. The sisters-in-law became very close. Varda brought a camera to the church to photograph Hélène on her special day, afterward creating a photo album to celebrate the freckled eleven-year-old. Every shot focused on Hélène, who glowed like a movie star in the foreground as friends, family, and clergy were a blur of figures in the background.

In their fifth year as a couple, Demy's and Varda's professional and personal lives took on the rhythms of a familiar dance. On the professional side, they would write their movies, procure financing, shoot, edit, open in Paris, and if lucky, show at Cannes or another major film conclave. If the film was well received, there would be a festival circuit that might include Venice, Berlin, London, San Sebastián, and Tokyo. Later, New York and Toronto would be added to the dance card. On the personal side, there were vacations and extended visits to Noirmoutier to recharge and begin the dance again.

The period that Demy and Legrand spent polishing the words and music for *Umbrellas* was a particularly lighthearted time at rue Daguerre. They worked in a room off the courtyard furnished with an upright piano and an electric train set. If they hit a wall while composing, they turned from work to play. As Varda saw it, they turned their work *into* play. On the pretext of bringing them coffee, she crept into their sanctum to watch Demy dance to Legrand's music as the cat played with her kittens and Rosalie with her dolls.

The Demy and Legrand households relocated to Cherbourg for the shoot, where the two couples, each with one child, effectively became one family of six. Demy was in his element while directing his tale of a mechanic (Nino Castelnuovo) and a shopgirl (Catherine Deneuve) whose intense affair is interrupted by his war service in Algeria and her unplanned pregnancy.

When the film was completed, 20th Century–Fox chose not to release it. Bodard previewed it for the Paris exhibitors Jo and Sammy Siritsky, who were "very hesitant." Bodard enlisted Lazareff to help close the deal. The publisher came to the screening and, afterward, brought the brothers for supper at rue Daguerre, where he hinted at the coverage *France-Soir* and his TV show might give them. Demy and Varda watched quietly as the Siritskys agreed to a distribution and exhibition deal. It was their first exposure to soft persuasion and the business side of moviemaking. It would be a lesson Varda never forgot.

An immediate critical and commercial success, *Umbrellas* ultimately sold 1.4 million tickets in France, exceeding Demy's and Varda's dreams. At Cannes, it won the top prize, the Palme d'or. Of the thousands of media photos of the couple, the most tender is one taken that night of Demy and Varda dancing next to Legrand and his wife, Christine. Demy holds Varda close, looking down at her with adoration as his wife looks straight at the lens as if signaling the photographer not to trespass on this private moment. "We are floating on a little cloud," said Legrand of the months that took them to Tokyo that autumn, New York at Christmas, and, ultimately, to Hollywood and the Oscars.

Varda liked floating on that cloud with Demy. But soon after Cannes, she received news that plummeted her back to earth.

SETTLING BACK into work in June after the exhilaration of Cannes, Varda expected to hear that her screenplay for *The Creatures* would receive a CNC advance.

On the Friday when the panel voted, Bodard came to rue Daguerre. Seeing her at the door, Varda thought that the script had received a green light. Instead, the producer wanted to tell Varda in person that it had been rejected. Varda was distraught. Tears filled her eyes. As Bodard and Demy tried to soothe her, she demanded that they stop. "Don't calm me down! Leave me my anger against this commission of decision-makers." Whether her feelings were anger, humiliation, disappointment, or a combination of all three, they were not immobilizing. They were a spur. Regaining her self-control, Varda sprang into action, demanding to know the last possible day to submit another screenplay for this funding round.

When Bodard told her it was the following Tuesday, Varda instructed her producer to tell the commission that they would receive another screenplay. Indeed, they would.

"I never started to think about this movie until that angry day," recalled Varda. Immediately, she began scribbling a script she titled *Le Bonheur*. The story, about a carpenter happily wed to a dressmaker who becomes even happier when he commences an affair with a postal clerk and has intimate relations with wife and mistress, was written in seventy two hours over that weekend. For most of Friday and Saturday Varda wrote fast, then remembered that, since the script was due on Tuesday, "Someone would have to type it Monday morning." Her hand-scrawled draft was illegible to everyone except her and Demy. On Sunday, they didn't leave bed. In fountain pen, in his neat and minuscule handwriting, he copied her drafts, "tidying up the cross references, adding and changing words." Varda remembered that Rosalie came and went, munching biscuits and cheese with her parents while they worked together. Sometimes, Demy would pour himself a few fingers of wine.

"On Monday morning everything was typed on a stencil" (presumably for a ditto machine), Varda wrote. In the evening they duplicated thirty pages for each of the thirty copies on the hand-cranked machine while Varda, a nondrinker, got tipsy inhaling the spirits of methanol used in the ditto process. Within the month, *Le Bonheur* was approved for the CNC advance and by Bastille Day, July 14, Varda was shooting on location in the woods near Verrières-le-Buisson, in the suburbs south of Paris. At the same time, Demy began planning *The Young Girls of Rochefort*, a sunny homage to Hollywood musicals, featuring Gene Kelly.

Varda's first color feature is ravishing to look at. In the vivid hues of post-Impressionists such as van Gogh and Cézanne, it begins as an ode to the nuclear family, set to Mozart. A husband and wife and their son and daughter walk through nature while the screen positively explodes with the warm cadmium yellows of sunflowers, the cool viridian greens of conifers, and flashes of cerulean blue wildflowers. The overall lushness is so intoxicating that it's startling when the story takes a darker turn and, instead of fading to black, the screen bleeds to red or blinds to white.

After seeing television star Jean-Claude Drouot on the cover of *Marie-Claire* with his family, Varda approached the popular figure. She persuaded him to act in her film, adding that she also would like to hire his wife and young children, who were nonprofessionals. She had a hunch that their family relationship would register realistically on-screen, and she was right.

"A ripe summer peach with a worm inside" is how Varda summed up *Le Bonheur*. She was surprised that the scenario had "lurked" inside of her, gushing forth as she wrote. Yet it is unsurprising that she was drawn to a story of marriage or marital crisis. *La Pointe*

Courte, her first film, addressed the latter, and in the mid-sixties, *Le Bonheur* was one of three Varda projects exploring marriages fictional and nonfictional. The others were *The Creatures* and *Elsa la rose*, a documentary short about novelist and translator Elsa Triolet and her union with fellow poet Louis Aragon. What *is* surprising about *Le Bonheur* is its darkly comic tone. Also surprising is how Thérèse (Claire Drouot), a dressmaker, loving wife, and doting mother of two devoted to the happiness of her family, responds to some family news.

Her husband, François Chevalier (Jean-Claude Drouot), is a cheerful carpenter besotted with Thérèse and their children. When he tells Thérèse that he has a mistress, Émilie (Marie-France Boyer), who "increases" his happiness, François fails to notice his wife's crestfallen reaction. He is slow to recognize, if he does at all, that his increased happiness has destroyed hers. The film is one of Varda's most hotly debated, and one of her finest. (Given Varda's penchant for wordplay, "François Chevalier" suggests "French knight." Like the film's title, his name appears to be used for ironic effect, for there is nothing courtly about this Chevalier.)

In a provocative essay on the film, the critic Amy Taubin wonders if Varda "intended to make a pastoral? A social satire? A slap-down of De Gaulle Family Values? A lyrical evocation of an open marriage?" All of these possibilities resonate. Others have suggested that the film satirizes how popular advertising markets unattainable images of connubial bliss.

The film is an Edenic idyll disrupted by a snake in the garden, and leaves it to the viewer to decide whether Chevalier or his mistress is the reptile. In Varda's allegory, the sexually liberated Émilie may also represent Lilith's return to Adam. Biblical interpretations seem apt because, on one of their outings, François invokes an apple tree to justify his affair. "You and I and the kids," he says, "we're like an apple orchard, a square field. Then I notice an apple tree that grows outside the field and blooms with us. More flowers, more apples."

When François awakes from their customary Sunday postcoital nap while the children sleep nearby, his wife is no longer beside him.

He and the children find her nearby, drowned in a lake. Has she died intentionally, like Ophelia, as a vengeful act? Or accidentally, while gathering flowers? When François scoops up Thérèse to cradle her limp, wet body, the film's staccato repeat of the gesture underscores the shock. A brief flashback to Thérèse's plunge into the lake is ambiguous. Did she trip or was her fall intentional? Ultimately, *Le Bonheur* is a mordant social satire and cinematic Rorschach blot that teases out the viewer's feelings about marriage, fidelity, and male prerogative.

Because she wanted to capture the change of seasons, Varda shot the film discontinuously, between July and November, editing it in time to accompany Demy to New York for the premiere of *The Umbrellas of Cherbourg*. In February, *Le Bonheur* debuted in Paris, immediately igniting controversy, which in turn created interest. In March, it won the Prix Delluc, as had *Umbrellas* the previous year.

"When we presented the film, people were horrified," recalled Marie-France Boyer, who played Émilie. Some were shocked by its seeming immorality. "The real scandal," wrote critic and film historian Georges Sadoul, "is that happiness is not considered by Agnès Varda . . . as a bonus granted to highly deserving people." The *New York Times* reviewer A. H. Weiler compared Varda to Colette, and added, "perhaps with tongue in cheek, [Varda] has fashioned a simple fable for our time, that is highly unlikely and blithely flouts moral values and Hollywood conventions but, nevertheless, constantly captures the eye and mind, if not the heart." The feminist film historian Claire Johnston deplored the film's "unforgivably cruel" treatment of its married heroine, branding it "reactionary" and a "retrograde step in women's cinema." For Chantal Akerman, the radical filmmaker and feminist, *Le Bonheur* was a revelation. "The idea is extraordinary: One love is worth the same as another, a person can be replaced by another. For me, *Le Bonheur* is the most anti-romantic film there is."

More recently, film historians Sandy Flitterman-Lewis and Richard Neupert have written about it as Varda's most misunderstood film, with Flitterman-Lewis insisting that it is "profoundly feminist."

Varda shrugged off the critics, telling interviewer Jacqueline Levitan, "I can say that I am a feminist, but for other feminists, I am not feminist enough." The film was a success, selling 86,000 tickets in Paris (15,000 fewer than *Cléo*) and performing very well overseas. It was in theaters for eight weeks in New York, nine months in Buenos Aires, a year in Tokyo, and fifty-four weeks in Montreal. In July, it won the Silver Bear—second place, behind Godard's *Alphaville*—at the Berlin Film Festival.

Forty years later, in 2006, Rosalie Varda interviewed actresses Claire Drouot and Marie-France Boyer for a DVD extra. She posed a question that may explain why the film struck such a nerve: "Can we accept something painful in order to make another happy?"

EARLY IN 1965, with both *Le Bonheur* and *The Umbrellas of Cherbourg* making a strong impression on filmgoers and critics, *Paris Match* celebrated Varda and Demy in an article prominently featuring a posed photo of them in mid-embrace, gazing into each other's eyes. Despite the layout, the piece by Georges Reyer focused mostly on Varda and her new film. The subhead and text identified them as the first spousal filmmakers ever (though Alice Guy and Herbert Blaché, as well as Lois Weber and Phillips Smalley, had preceded them by fifty years). Given the prominence of the photo, the headline—"A 'Happiness' That Makes You Grind Your Teeth"—is confusing. Does it refer to the couple or to Varda's film?

They were young (Varda was thirty-six and Demy thirty-three, though they claimed to be thirty-four and thirty-one), photogenic, and bohemian. Their artistic accomplishments, although noteworthy, did not yet warrant a central place in France's cultural pantheon. Still, they represented the new French cinema gaining traction worldwide.

The reporter described Varda as one of the New Wave's first auteurs, and then gave Resnais disproportionate credit for *La Pointe Courte*. This portrait of the auteur as a young woman was notable for three things. Already at this early stage in her career, Varda was on the phone advising a teenager about how to become a filmmaker. Asked if she and Demy collaborated, she replied with an emphatic "No way!" Finally, a boy-meets-girl sketch of the Demy-Varda relationship: "One evening, at the Tours Festival, she meets a tall, joyful ingenuous boy," Reyer wrote. "We started chatting, Varda said, and we never left each other." Reyer concluded, "It's their whole story. A story without a story. Very new wave."

In April 1965, Demy and Legrand flew to Los Angeles for the Academy Awards, where *Umbrellas* was a best foreign language film nominee. Taking advantage of the trip, his agent scheduled a number of meetings with Hollywood executives including Gerald Ayres, then executive assistant to the vice president of production at Columbia Pictures. Ayres, Francophile and Francophone, would be instrumental in convincing Columbia to hire the French director.

Demy returned to Los Angeles a few weeks later. When he and Ayres met for lunch, Demy confided his dream to visit Bodega Bay in Northern California, where his idol, Alfred Hitchcock, had made *The Birds*. Within the week, Ayres arranged to take the director on what was, before Interstate 5 was completed, an eight-hour drive up the coast. It would be a two-day jaunt. According to Ayres, to their mutual surprise, they became lovers. When Ayres wanted to prolong the relationship, Demy demurred, reminding him, "Oh, Gerry, we are both married men."

Whether Varda, at the beginning of making three films about married couples, knew about the affair is unknown. Ayres, who would soon become a producer and screenwriter, remained a lifelong friend and supporter of both filmmakers.

Varda and Demy had never formally collaborated on a film, but that spring the possibility of doing so was floated by Louis Aragon, the esteemed poet, and his wife, Elsa Triolet. The first volumes of their collected works had been published the prior year. Aragon proposed that Demy and Varda make a documentary portrait of them, or, better yet, two interconnected portraits.

Varda was game. But Demy, working with Legrand on the words

and music for *The Young Girls of Rochefort*, decided that it made more sense to put his creative energies into a feature film than a short. Varda proceeded without him.

She met the literary giants at La Coupole, the legendary Montparnasse brasserie where the couple had first clapped eyes on each other in 1928. Instantly, an image of Elsa entering through the restaurant's swinging door as Aragon beheld her came to Varda. She hired actor Michel Piccoli to recite Aragon's effusive poems about Elsa, "like a priest rushing through Mass," pairing the recitations with film footage of Elsa's inscrutable face.

Varda draws the difference between Aragon's idealized Elsa, his muse, and the real woman. Aragon's poems have the effect of eclipsing her and enlarging himself. When Varda asks Triolet, "Do [the poems] make you feel loved?" she tersely replies, "Not the poetry." Her matter-of-factness punctures the hot-air balloon of Aragon's verse in the abrupt way that *Le Bonheur* deflates romantic love.

The disparity between Aragon's dramatic lines and Triolet's succinctness makes for a fascinating dynamic, one that may have informed Varda's next film, the long-aborning *The Creatures*, featuring Piccoli as an unusually emotive husband and Catherine Deneuve as his mute wife.

A CAREFREE husband and wife are speeding along the road in a Ford Zephyr, the breeze softly blowing their hair, headed for an island retreat. With a playful smile and a caress of his forehead, she asks, "Humor me and slow down." No less playfully he responds, "Humor me and let me drive," explaining, "When I race, my thoughts race too!" The camera pans to a picturesque coastline dominated by a fortress-like structure. We hear the wife, insistent now, demand, "Slow down." Next, the wail of a skid and the moan of crumpling steel. Cut to the carcass of a totaled car.

The opening sequence of *The Creatures* is fast and engrossing. Few would make that claim for the remainder of the movie. The film, conceived at Noirmoutier as well as filmed there, is dedicated "To Jacques."

The husband, Edgar, survives the crash with a vertical suture on his forehead. His wife, Mylène, also survives, though the accident has rendered her mute, perhaps from shock. Like the husband and wife in *Le Bonheur*, Edgar and Mylène are an amorous traditional couple. He is a novelist exploring the external world for inspiration; she is a lovely homebody, communicating with her husband via a slate. Soon, she is an expectant mother.

The film begins with a scene of ordinary spousal friction, proceeds to contrast a creative husband with his procreative wife, and without warning becomes a science fiction yarn about a writer's desperate search for a plot. Compounding Edgar's literary desperation is an archvillain who via remote control renders his human targets irrational. Piccoli mugs through the film, Deneuve is the picture of serenity, and the penultimate chess game between good and evil plays like a parody of Ingmar Bergman's religious allegory *The Seventh Seal*.

The Creatures opened in Paris in September 1966, and was generally greeted by the sound of audiences scratching their heads. A *New York Times* correspondent who saw it at the Venice Film Festival wrote an item headlined "Varda Film Bewilders Festival Audience." Varda was able to joke in interviews that her sci-fi experiment had two stars yet didn't succeed. But it was not a failure. Henri Langlois, supremo of the Cinémathèque française, admired it, writing Varda a warm letter after reading the Paris reviews that variously called it silly, bad, and lacking poetry. "Your film is as silly as Jean Renoir, as bad as Rossellini, as unpoetic as Méliès," comparing the movie to those made by his directorial holy trinity. Mike Nichols, the rookie director of *Who's Afraid of Virginia Woolf?*, a Varda fan and friend since *Cléo*, was her date to a preview screening in New York.

PROFESSIONALLY, VARDA had much to be proud of. She had made three features, two of which firmly established her as an auteur.

But financing was increasingly challenging to find, and an unsuccessful movie made it even more so. She wrote a script titled *Christmas Carole*, about a female student and two young men toughing it out over the holidays without money. To attract financing, she shot a six-minute sequence that included what would have been the screen debut of Gérard Depardieu. She abandoned the project for lack of investor interest. Until he found regular acting work, Depardieu supported himself by babysitting for Rosalie.

Other New Wave filmmakers, including Godard and Truffaut, also struggled to find financing. It would be a decade before Varda received another CNC advance. Yet her cultural reach at home and abroad was burgeoning. In New York, Mike Nichols was openly besotted with all three of her 1960s features. In Rome, Federico Fellini adored *Cléo*, pronouncing the movie "marvelous." In Warsaw, Agnieszka Holland, then a fourteen-year-old high school student and film buff and today the Oscar-nominated filmmaker of *Angry Harvest, Europa Europa*, and *In Darkness*, saw *Cléo* in 1962: "It made a lasting impression." Two years later, she said, "I watched *Le Bonheur*, and then rewatched it many times. It was so revolutionary. It was an enormous influence. Those two movies made Agnès my hero."

While Varda made largely female-focused stories with unconventional editing, she was also helping to change the face of the French film industry by hiring women for key production and creative roles. She employed or encouraged two generations of female assistant directors, cinematographers, and editors who continued to work in cinema in various capacities. Some, like Lynne Littman and Patricia Mazuy, would themselves become award-winning directors.

Renowned filmmaker Chantal Akerman never worked for Varda, but, like Holland, she was inspired by Varda's professional and personal example. In a 2011 interview, Akerman contrasted Marguerite Duras and Varda, filmmakers of the older generation. "Marguerite built up airs around herself that she would promote and with Agnès, we were sometimes competitive. But Agnès is capable of moments of great generosity toward women, where Marguerite was only capable of generosity to men."

For Holland, "Agnès was a mother figure to many women film-makers." She recalled, "When I picked up a camera for the first time as an adult, I felt that it gave me permission to look and the power to tell the subject what to do. That's part of the joy of being a filmmaker, having the license to do both." This, reflected Holland, is what she "absorbed" from Varda's example.

Varda may not have been conscious of it, but even at this early stage of her film career, she already was turning the ground and seeding it for future filmmakers, male and female. While frequently cited as proof that gender was no impediment to becoming a director, her struggle to make the movies she wanted is just as often invoked as proof of the contrary.

8

Rosalie recalled that "each time the phone would ring [at rue Daguerre], Jacques would say, 'It's Hollywood!' Of course, it wasn't Hollywood. But then, one day, it was."

In 1966, not long after the location shoot of Demy's *The Young Girls of Rochefort*, the call came. Gerry Ayres, Demy's friend at Columbia Pictures, had scored financing for the filmmaker to direct a film for the studio in Los Angeles.

At the time, Columbia was the studio most actively involved in producing youth-oriented movies (e.g., *To Sir, with Love*; *Head*; *Easy Rider*), and thought Demy's idea for a film about a young Angeleno drafted for Vietnam service fit the bill. Demy was over the moon and asked Varda to join him on the California adventure.

Late that year, they flew to Los Angeles and stayed with the Legrands while looking for a rental of their own. Varda marveled at the city "where people of all colors dressed in all colors." She was wowed by the streets in Beverly Hills, where a cream-and-brown Tudor stood between a pink château and a yellow Italian villa. Scorners of pretense, Demy and Varda were amused that the Legrands' housekeeper drove a long white Cadillac. Soon the newcomers would lease his-and-hers white convertibles of less pricey models.

Within three days, they found what Varda described as a "cliché house" and Ayres "a modest cottage" on North Alpine Drive, in the flats of Beverly Hills. Landscaped with palm trees that swayed in the breeze, it had shag rugs, a color TV (not yet available in France), and the obligatory kidney-shaped swimming pool. When Demy mentioned to Gene Kelly that he was thinking of buying the cottage, the actor "snorted in contempt," recalled Ayres. Kelly thought that the $40,000 price was too high. "Jacques took his advice and later resented it," said Ayres.

After signing the lease, Demy and Varda invited everyone they knew in Los Angeles to a housewarming. Ayres came with his wife, Anne, and an underemployed young actor under contract to Columbia named Harrison Ford. Ayres had recently introduced him to Demy, who in turn thought "Harry," then moonlighting as a carpenter, was perfect for the script he was writing. Varda enthusiastically agreed, volunteering her services to shoot his screen test.

At first, the house on North Alpine was a canteen for French actors and directors in Hollywood. Around the pool it wasn't unusual to see sleepy-eyed Simone Signoret nursing a Scotch or the electric Michel Piccoli—then making *Topaz* with Alfred Hitchcock—bringing Hitch's gift to him, a case of Château Lafite Rothschild, to drink it with his countrymen. Varda scrubbed vegetables and greens for crudités and guests brought offerings for the buffet table. With its warmth and informality, the house on North Alpine soon became a salon of many nations.

Demy and Varda welcomed Ingrid Bergman (in LA filming a TV adaptation of *The Human Voice*), Michelangelo Antonioni (preparing *Zabriskie Point*), and their good friend Bernardo Bertolucci. Among the regulars was former UCLA film student Jim Morrison, an aspiring movie director fronting the rock group the Doors. Alain Ronay, a French-born classmate of Morrison, made the introduction.

In Paris, Demy and Legrand had taken English lessons. Varda claimed that she'd learned English "by watching the dubbed version of *Cléo from 5 to 7* shown on TV." While it's unlikely that *Cléo* was responsible for Varda's graceful English, she was a quick study. Her sister-in-law Hélène Demy recalls that the disciplined Varda took daily lessons from a tutor in Los Angeles.

The sojourn in Los Angeles from late 1966 to mid-1969 was a happy one. Demy worked on his screenplay for *Model Shop*, Varda on two screenplays in English. Before she could complete them, she had to see to a prior commitment in Paris. In 1966, Demy and Varda each agreed to make an episode of the collective documentary *Far from Vietnam*, protesting the U.S. war in Indochina. Godard, Joris Ivens, William Klein, Claude Lelouch, Chris Marker, and Alain Resnais were the other members of the collective. When Demy's colleagues disparaged his proposed sketch, which involved an American soldier and a Vietnamese prostitute, he chose not to participate.

Varda's segment was about a Frenchwoman who in her delirium confuses demolition in her Paris neighborhood with the American bombardment of Hanoi. She shot her segment, but Marker did not include it in the finished film. Instead, he used her footage to flesh out other episodes. It was another disappointment, but not a setback. The news reached her at a time when *The Young Girls of Rochefort* was doing well in Paris, and she observed diplomatically, "Strong and intelligent personalities gathered in a group are not . . . the most effective in signaling the urgency of awareness." She looked ahead, investing her anti-war views and countercultural sympathies in the scripts she wrote in California.

"Some people get eaten up by resentment; Varda kept busy," observed the film historian Sandy Flitterman-Lewis. She wasn't the type of filmmaker who suffered, as the old school Hollywood action directors joked, of "paralysis from analysis."

Albert Johnson invited Demy and Varda to the San Francisco Film Festival in October 1967, asking them to present a program using clips from their work to discuss film style. As *The Creatures* was to screen at the festival a few days before their joint program, Varda flew up before Demy. Greeting her at the airport was Tom Luddy, Johnson's assistant and a recent graduate of UC Berkeley. It was serendipity. Both Varda and Luddy seemed to know everybody and introduced their acquaintances to like-minded friends who could help them with their other projects.

On the drive into the city, Luddy wondered aloud whether Varda was related to Yanco Varda, a painter he knew who lived on a houseboat in Sausalito, across the Golden Gate Bridge in Marin County. She asked to know more about Yanco. Luddy described him as a Greek artist who'd been in the Bay Area for years and was in Henry Miller's circle of friends in Big Sur. Indeed, it was Yanco who had introduced Miller to the town and people of Big Sur, and one of his collages, "Women Reconstructing the World," was the cover of a book by Anaïs Nin, a lover of both men. Would Varda like to meet him? Yes, she would. She wondered if he was a long-lost uncle. He was around seventy and had been born in Izmir, according to Luddy. This Varda whom she had never heard of had been born at about the same time and in the same place as her own father, Eugène.

Luddy drove Varda to the festival office, where he asked a friend of Yanco's to deliver an important message to the houseboat. There was someone special the artist needed to meet. He would bring said person to Yanco's houseboat the next day. And so it was that Luddy drove Varda to the SS *Vallejo*, described by film scholar Homay King as a "patchwork quilt of a houseboat built from the shell of a passenger ferry."

When Luddy introduced the two Vardas, the filmmaker was overwhelmed. She hugged the titanium-haired hipster with a Fu Manchu moustache, who was wearing pink pants. He told her that Eugène Jean Varda was his first cousin. "He instantly became the image of the artist/father I had always dreamed of," she later said. After years of estrangement from her father, here was a new connection to him, one who was bohemian and demonstrative like her. She felt compelled to preserve the moment when they both realized that they were kindred spirits as well as kin. She enlisted Luddy to find a 35mm movie camera, a cameraman (David Meyers), and a Nagra (a portable audio recorder). Three days later, with Luddy, Meyers, and nine-year-old Rosalie, she embarked on the two-day shoot of *Uncle Yanco* (1967), reenacting her meeting with her "uncle."

If a producer is one who makes it possible for a director to make a movie, then this was Luddy's first producing gig. Not only did he help Varda find her first cousin once removed; he also suggested the subject for her second film made in California. In 1974 he cofounded the Telluride Film Festival and would produce several films for Francis Ford Coppola's American Zoetrope, including Paul Schrader's *Mishima*, Norman Mailer's *Tough Guys Don't Dance*, and Agnieszka Holland's *The Secret Garden*. Luddy and Varda would be lifelong friends.

As their first year in California wound down, Varda assisted in Demy's effort to prove to Columbia that Harrison Ford possessed the star quality for the male lead in *Model Shop*. In crafting his screen test, she used her considerable talents to show that his mischievous, laid-back personality in life as well as on-screen had the effect of making others lean forward. She took Super 8 footage of him facing the camera and in profile. She shot sequences of him smiling his crooked smile, which seemed to make the scar on his chin smile too.

Demy and Ayres took Varda's reel to Bob Weitman, the interim studio head, to persuade him to cast Ford in *Model Shop*. Weitman did not recognize that the late 1960s were unconventional times and, when he looked at Varda's reel, he predicted that Ford, who had had a forgettable walk-on part as a bellhop in the 1966 film *Dead Heat on a Merry-Go-Round*, had no future in Hollywood. Weitman insisted on casting Gary Lockwood, the conventionally handsome TV actor who had played Dr. Frank Poole in *2001: A Space Odyssey*. Lockwood's appearance in the Demy movie was one of his last leading roles on the big screen. It might have been Ford's first.

IN THE 1960s, female directors rarely worked for major studios. They made low-budget indies like Susan Sontag's *Duet for Cannibals*

(1969) and Barbara Loden's *Wanda* (1970); exploitation films with a feminist twist like Stephanie Rothman's *It's a Bikini World* (1965) and *Student Nurses* (1971); or underground films like Shirley Clarke's *The Connection* (1961) and *Portrait of Jason* (1971). Ida Lupino made her last studio film, *The Trouble with Angels*, in 1966; Elaine May made her first, *A New Leaf*, in 1971.

Given this context, when Columbia Pictures executive Gerry Ayres read Varda's screenplay *Peace and Love* in 1967 and persuaded the studio to let her direct, it was extraordinary news. The film fit into the studio's artistic and economic mandates to produce movies about contemporary youth that could be made for peanuts. Varda described it as a tale of a young American, a star of television ads, who impulsively abandons her career when she falls in love with a French lawyer about whom she knows very little. Varda hoped to cast Sharon Tate, a model and actress just then emerging on the scene. Ayres remembered that the lawyer character was based on Régis Debray, a French journalist who had fought alongside Che Guevara in Colombia and was imprisoned at the time Varda wrote the screenplay.

When Ayres brought Varda to Weitman's office, they chatted pleasantly. Then the interim head of Columbia mentioned that the only thing the studio required was final cut. "Agnès balked," Ayres remembered. In America, final cut was a standard studio demand. In France, a filmmaker could negotiate with the producer for the prerogative. The atmosphere of the room grew charged. Ayres defused it with, "Let the lawyers work out the fine points of the deal," restoring peace, if not love. Then, "Bob walked us to the door where he smiled at Agnès and pinched her cheek. Agnès slapped his arm away. End of deal."

That slap communicated swiftly to Weitman that pinching her was not acceptable. It was unprofessional. It was condescending. It was also sexist, a word not yet commonplace in 1967. For both, the situation was unprecedented. Swatting Weitman's arm was a defense of Varda's professional and personal dignity and an affront to Weitman's authority. For the remainder of her California sojourn, and with few exceptions for the remainder of her working life, Varda worked outside film production hierarchies.

WHILE IN the U.S., Varda and Demy socialized with both counter-culture and establishment figures. Varda marched in anti-war demonstrations. She and Demy attended "be-ins" and "love-ins," alfresco happenings celebrating peace and love that were scented with the earthy perfumes of patchouli and marijuana. They went to rock concerts where the Doors or the Grateful Dead performed, delighting in the music, the dancing, and the illusion of figure and ground merging so that revelers' flower-patterned garb appeared to intertwine with the bougainvillea and jasmine around them.

They likewise enjoyed dining with figures such as director George Cukor and his favorite actress, Katharine Hepburn, who stayed in his guesthouse when she was in California. Varda found her "brilliant, funny, and incredibly mean." Demy wrote a script for Hepburn and Jim Morrison about a fading actress who wants out of Hollywood and hires a limo driver to take her to Las Vegas. Danny Selznick, the producer son of legendary producer David O. Selznick, invited the Demys to lunch with Mae West, then seventy-five, whom Varda described as "a monument of platinum curls" draped in white satin. West flirted with Demy while reprising her most suggestive movie lines. He didn't know whether to laugh or cry, because what was groundbreaking about the sex-positive actress in 1933 sounded quaint in 1967. At another soirée, Varda thought that Demy *would* cry when he realized that the tall, slim redhead standing motionless and looking lost was Rita Hayworth, whom he idolized, in the early stages of dementia not yet diagnosed.

Varda preferred to hang out with anti-establishment types like Yanco's pals Henry Miller and Anaïs Nin. "Mischievous as the devil," wrote Varda of the *Tropic of Cancer* author. Of diarist Nin, who lived in a grand LA home designed by Eric Lloyd Wright, grandson of the famous architect, Varda recalled, she "received me in an Oriental dress slit to the thigh . . . 65 years old [and] talking with the liveliness of a seductive suffragist." Varda was happy to see two of Yanco's paintings in the house, one hanging in Nin's living room and another above her bed.

In May 1968, a month after the assassination of Martin Luther King and a month before that of Bobby Kennedy, Varda and Demy listened to reports of the violent student demonstrations in Paris, the shuttering of the Cannes Film Festival, and the general strikes across France. At the time, Demy was in preproduction for *Model Shop*, which he would shoot in June and July. Varda was immersed in the books of English-language feminists—among them Shulamith Firestone, Germaine Greer, and Kate Millett—when Tom Luddy phoned to tell her that he could get her an interview with Huey Newton. The cofounder of the Black Panthers was in an Oakland prison, charged with manslaughter of a policeman. Luddy thought that Varda should document the group's efforts to free Newton. Varda concurred.

As with *Uncle Yanco*, Varda recruited Luddy's help in procuring equipment and crew for *Black Panthers*. He is credited as one who assisted in its "realization." Whenever he spoke about Varda, he would invariably say, "You can't say no to Agnès. She will pester you until she gets what she wants."

Before Demy began production on *Model Shop* and Varda on *Black Panthers*, Rosalie celebrated her tenth birthday. She invited ten girls from her class—and Jim Morrison. The charismatic musician sat at the foot of the long table, nursing a bottle of cognac. The girls smiled at him; he smiled back. When the alcohol hit his bloodstream, he face-planted into his dessert plate. Varda recalled that "the girls continued their joyful racket as if nothing had happened."

While Demy shot *Model Shop*, Varda flew to Oakland on three consecutive weekends to conduct the filmed interviews for her documentary short. Every Sunday, those defending Newton's innocence gathered in the gardens of the Alameda County courthouse. Presenting herself as a representative of French television, she moved freely among the crowd. Varda had Pascal Thomas' interview with Newton and access to Bobby Seale, activists Eldridge and Kathleen Cleaver, and H. Rap Brown, chairman of the Student Nonviolent Coordinating Committee. The movie opens with happy children dancing on the green as their families watch, smiling. The twenty-eight-minute short is neither objective nor propagandistic. It is exploratory. Its interviewees are modulated and calm. Varda listens to an unidentified group member enumerate the Panthers' ten-point platform, which advocates for full employment, better education, decent healthcare, livable housing, and an end to police brutality. She allows her subjects to speak conversationally, without framing them as armed militias or separatist radicals, as much of the media did at the time. She understands that a quiet listener elicits more information than an adversarial interlocutor.

Likewise in 1968, Varda met Lynne Littman, a budding director whose 1977 documentary short *Number Our Days* would win an Oscar and who later directed the well-received 1983 feature *Testament*. Littman assisted Varda in the editing of *Black Panthers* and during the conception and execution of her subsequent film, *Lions Love*. During the edit of *Black Panthers*, Varda and Littman planned to document a Panthers demonstration one evening. Before they went, they joined Demy and Rosalie for a family dinner at North Alpine. Littman wrote about it in a diary entry dated September 20, 1968:

> Jacques Demy is as gentle as Agnès is ferocious. Little Rosalie parodies a love scene with papa who mimes himself a victim to her charms and we all struggle with the frozen purple Jell-O and green grape dessert prepared by Monique, the Moroccan housekeeper with deep cleavage.... Next we're running through the streets of Hollywood, me carrying lenses and Agnès darting through Black Panthers and demonstrators wearing her new red shoes and a red shawl. Strange camera, strange people, strange cops—but she's making a film.

Varda self-financed the modest documentary with the understanding that the Office de radiodiffusion-télévision française (ORTF), the national broadcasting service, would be interested in showing it. "But the agency had a tense exchange with her over editing the narration. She said they thought it was 'perhaps just a little violent' " and asked if it could be removed. She agreed to do so if the interviewees were not edited. The evening it was scheduled for broadcast, it did not air, and ORTF offered no explanation. Since then, Varda's footage has been used in documentary accounts of the Panthers. Other radical movements have used extracts from the film.

Littman, who had worked in public television prior to meeting Varda, had never seen anything remotely like the Frenchwoman's directing method. "They say that filmmaking is a collaborative medium. Not for her," observed Littman. "Agnès, cigarette dangling from her mouth, was an expert at everything, a solo act. The film happened on her energy. She knew what she wanted and got it. She directed and edited like a painter. She had freedom of direction and then editing control of the [footage] she had freedom over. And still, her films feel like they happen by accident."

VARDA AND Demy's time in California coincided with the movie industry's seismic shift from Old Hollywood to New, and they witnessed the rise of American counterculture in its birthplaces of San Francisco and neighboring Berkeley. Varda wrote with considerable wit about her impressions. But rather than collect them in a book, she spun them into the kaleidoscopic *Lions Love . . . and Lies*. The feature reflected those she met, the movies and plays she saw, emerging social arrangements, and the omnipresence of television in American life. She shot it just as Demy's *Model Shop* was released without fanfare and received without enthusiasm.

The prior year, Varda had met aspiring producer Max Raab, a longtime admirer of her movies. After World War II, the ready-to-wear manufacturer invented the shirtdress, the foundation of his fortune and his Villager brand, a clothing line marketed to "collegiennes." The Philadelphia-based Raab also owned a repertory theater where he programmed Varda's films. When they made a date to meet in a Los Angeles café, she pitched *Lions Love*. He liked her idea of three outsiders, "too old to be hippies and too young to be adults," circling Hollywood, waiting to be discovered. She liked his idea that making movies and manufacturing clothes were similar processes, in that both were produced in pieces and put together in unique ways. "I gave her money because I loved *Le Bonheur*," Raab said in 2005. When he met Varda, Raab, who was widely read, had options on the novels *Walkabout* and *A Clockwork Orange* for adaptation to screen and has executive producer credit on both of these 1971 films.

Through Michel Legrand's agent, Varda and Demy had met Gerome Ragni and James Rado, pied pipers of the counterculture. The pair wrote and starred in *Hair*, the wildly popular "tribal rock musical" then drawing standing-room-only audiences on Broadway and in Los Angeles. Varda had hoped to cast Jim Morrison in *Lions Love*, but he had a concert tour with the Doors. Rado and Ragni were the next best choices for the movie, a kind of hippie *Jules and Jim* about Hollywood hopefuls. They said yes. For the last member of the threesome, she wanted Viva, the sylphlike "superstar" of Andy Warhol's 1968 underground movie *Lonesome Cowboys*.

At his invitation, Varda had met Warhol in 1967. The following year she was in New York and visited the Factory, the artist's hybrid studio and salon, to ask if he would persuade Viva to work with her. Varda's escort was Carlos Clarens, a convivial film historian who was living at North Alpine while writing a book. They rode up the creaky industrial elevator, which opened onto a vast space, a onetime piano factory. Under a cloud of cigarette and marijuana smoke, the place was crowded with models, art collectors, scene makers, and those who aspired to be. Varda was pleased that "[Warhol] was there, royal and a little removed from all those who film, smoke, and argue. We chat, he's funny and smart." In his high-pitched voice, the platinum prince of Pop Art introduced her to Viva, telling his superstar that *Cléo* was a "divine" film. Varda returned the compliment, telling Warhol that he was a "daring" artist.

Viva agreed to join Varda's cast. A photo of the actress and the French filmmaker on set would grace the cover of the inaugural edition of Warhol's *Interview* magazine in 1969.

Lions Love is a metafiction about an underground filmmaker (real-life filmmaker Shirley Clarke as Varda's stand-in) in Hollywood to negotiate a deal for a movie "using movie stars as real people." While in Los Angeles, she stays with "Jim" (Rado), "Viva," and "Gerry" (Ragni). In this largely improvised film, the principals play versions of themselves, enabling Varda to blur the boundary between fact and fiction, between acting a part and behaving naturally. Set during eventful weeks in May and June 1968 but filmed in February and April 1969, the film also enables Varda to blur the boundary between documentary and reenactment. Like so much of her filmography, the result is unclassifiable, an episodic film that snakes through the twisty streets of the Hollywood Hills as it meditates upon stardom of both the screen and political kinds. It inventories the hippie bona fides of natural hair, au naturel swimming, and pot smoking— this last all the better to enjoy the stoner lassitude that results. As the trio watch *Lost Horizon*, the 1937 film about a plane that crashes in Shangri-La, they are amused they are in a real-life Shangri-LA, watching a film about another utopia.

Many of the sequences are larky, such as one in which the three eternal Peter Pans test their readiness for adulthood by tending children. When the studio suits tell Clarke that she cannot have final cut, she returns to the communal house where she is supposed to act out a suicide attempt by overdosing on pills. Clarke balked, telling the off-camera Varda that she can't, because it's "not my style." Miffed that her colleague has broken her promise to play Varda's surrogate, Varda performs the scene in Clarke's stead.

For most of the playful film, Varda distills the atmosphere, style, and soul of a city and its most famous industry. Slowly, LA's verdant foliage begins to look discolored under the toxic yellow shroud of smog. And the flummoxed moguls always looking for the new thing stick with the old because it's familiar.

As May gives way to June in the film's chronology, a political storm cloud eclipses the sun, and even the smog. Concurrent with Clarke's fictional suicide attempt is the real-life assassination of political hopeful Robert Kennedy in Los Angeles and the news that Warhol has been shot at the Factory by Valerie Solanas, a thwarted playwright who believed Warhol had stolen her work, compounding the grief and angst.

The introduction of these life-and-death events abruptly weighs down the film's lighthearted tone, which led *New York Times* critic Vincent Canby to gripe, "There is so much so pleasant about *Lions Love* that I wish Miss Varda hadn't tried to give it a larger significance." Yet the political and cultural assassinations are what give the movie resonance. While viewing TV replays of the scene at the Ambassador Hotel, where Kennedy was fatally shot, Viva pronounces, "Televised death is the national pastime." That insight is a takeaway from Varda's first California sojourn—and an entire era.

SIX MONTHS after *Lions Love* wrapped, it had its premiere at the New York Film Festival, along with Susan Sontag's feature debut, *Duet for Cannibals*, Marguerite Duras' second feature, *Destroy, She Said*, and Paul Mazursky's *Bob and Carol and Ted and Alice*. Implicitly or explicitly, all touched on nonmonogamous social arrangements.

Varda and Sontag sat for an interview with *Newsweek* editor Jack Kroll on an episode of *Camera 3*, a Sunday morning culture review produced by WCBS television in New York. When Kroll condescendingly described both of their films as "touching on the grotesque," Varda visibly bristled. "Neither Susan's movie nor mine are grotesque," she said firmly, reminding him of the world of difference between grotesques and hippies. Sontag praised *Lions Love* for capturing how real people talk and speak over one another. Varda in turn praised *Duet for Cannibals* as "a brave story about vice." Bonding, they reframed and broadened Kroll's narrow definition of their films.

Canby found it "ironic that Miss Varda, whose husband, Jacques Demy, the gifted French director, tried unsuccessfully to capture the banal beauty of Los Angeles in his *Model Shop*, does just that in *Lions Love* without trying very hard." Varda succeeded in distilling the zeitgeist; her film was accessible and madcap without malaise.

9

WHEN DEMY AND VARDA returned to Paris and resettled in the 14th arrondissement in the summer of 1969, they reconnected with old friends, and Los Angeles friends like Jim Morrison and Gerry Ayres would drop in at rue Daguerre as they once did at North Alpine. Wherever they lived or traveled, Demy and Varda were the hub of an ever-widening circle. As Ayres noted, something that impressed him about both filmmakers was that "they were like Bedouins, they took their universe with them . . . pitching tent wherever they stopped and continued writing, their treatments, their scripts, and finally, their films."

Now seventeen, Hélène Demy enjoyed the time she spent with her brother, who, she said, "introduced her to painting and cinema," and her sister-in-law, who "opened her up to literature and feminism." Jacques was the same as before, remembered Hélène. "Agnès was larger than life." In Los Angeles, Hélène had enjoyed meeting Ayres, and was happy when the producer joined her and her brother at the windmill in Noirmoutier. The three were together when they learned of the murders of Sharon Tate and her friends by the Manson Family. Demy, his sister, and Ayres had all met the actress, who made *The Wrecking Crew* at Columbia while Demy was directing *Model Shop*, and were shaken by the news.

Earlier that summer, Hélène remembered, fresh off the release of *Mississippi Mermaid*, François Truffaut had come to Noirmoutier with his leading lady, Catherine Deneuve. "Truffaut and Agnès would talk about the production side of the business," she said. "Jacques wasn't interested in business chat." For fun, Hélène recalled with a grin, "Agnès made a home-movie parody of *Lions Love* with Jacques and me. She dressed me up as Viva." Hélène had never encountered anyone like her sister-in-law. "The way she talked, how she dressed, how she ate olives and tomatoes for breakfast in the summer. I admired her, even though I was intimidated."

After their summer respite, Demy and Varda didn't waste a minute in resuming projects that had been in limbo during their California stay. Although Demy's project was the more commercially successful, Varda's was a daring and imaginative experiment as well as an object lesson in how excellence does not necessarily correlate with box office returns. His film was the rainbow-colored, fairy-tale musical fantasy *Donkey Skin* (1970), which was immediately embraced by the public. Hers was a hybrid documentary/fictional narrative about the 1967 Greek junta and the resulting exodus of Greek nationals to France, *Nausicaa*.

Varda had proposed the film to ORTF in 1967. After her return to Paris in 1969, the public broadcaster belatedly expressed interest. In the film's surviving cut, Varda plaits three parallel stories in as many narrative forms: a fictional coming-of-age narrative in which an art history student connects with those displaced by the coup, documentary testimony of Greek refugees, and a personal essay on Varda family history. *Nausicaa* thus provides three ways of looking at a junta. Aside from the starling description of her father's death at the casino in *Jane B. by Agnès V*, it is the only one of Varda's films that considers her father's experience as an ethnic Greek immigrant.

Varda created this hybrid of narrative feature with documentary testimony a decade before Warren Beatty did the same in *Reds*. But its impact cannot be measured, since authorities deemed it too controversial to broadcast on television. Varda said in an interview that the likely reason *Nausicaa* was never broadcast was that "France sold a lot of Mirage planes to the Greek colonels"—the junta controlling Greece at the time.

Despite her recent spate of unrealized proposals and scripts, Varda was undeterred. She took solace in the memory of having once gone with Demy to meet Jacques Prévert, the beloved poet and screenwriter of the film classics *Daybreak* and *Children of Paradise*. The young filmmakers had been taken aback when Prévert showed them his many unrealized screenplays. Varda recalled that, rather than grieve the unrealized projects, he celebrated the ones that were made. She calculated that only one in three of her completed screenplays got made. Prévert's example encouraged her to look forward, not back.

The French film industry had changed markedly since she and Demy decamped to California. The New Wave was no longer new and the movement had lost its momentum. "Many had come to think of the New Wave as a moment that had come and gone," reflected historian Richard Neupert.

By 1970, three of the New Wave's most commercially successful auteurs had developed relationships with a single producer, an all-around troubleshooter who managed financing and distribution. Claude Chabrol had André Génovès; Éric Rohmer had Pierre Cottrell, and François Truffaut had Marcel Berbert. Often these directors based their films on preexisting material, such as novels and short stories. Not Varda. While she admired experimental literary forms, as a rule she believed that a literary work created to be read was almost inevitably diminished in the process of adaptation to the screen. Cinema involved words, yes, but it wasn't strictly literary.

There were exceptions. Jeannine Aeply's novel *The Music Box* interested Varda—not the entire book, but a sequence around which she wanted to build a movie, *Viveca, the Wise*. In it, a furious husband awaits a wife who seems to have abandoned him and their infant son. As he waits, he rehearses the many ways he will reproach her on her return. Varda wanted to explore the possibility that Viveca does not return. She wrote the script in French and in English. Actress Anna Karina was interested. Alas, Varda failed to find a producer who was.

In 1970, two of Varda's California films opened in Europe. In April, *Black Panthers*, which never aired on French television, won the top prize at the Oberhausen Festival of Short Films in Germany. In December, it screened on a double bill with *Lions Love* at the Studio Parnasse in Paris, where it was politely ignored. The following week, Demy's *Donkey Skin* opened and swiftly became one of his most commercially successful films. Over time, it gained a reputation as a film that families would watch together annually, similar to *It's a Wonderful Life* in the United States.

WHILE DEMY and Varda were in California to witness firsthand the 1967 Summer of Love, that mass migration of anti-war, back-to-nature, music-loving, pot-smoking youth to San Francisco and its environs, they had missed the 1968 demonstrations that rocked France. For seven weeks, student protesters demanding social change were joined by striking laborers demanding fair wages, united against a government that feared insurrection. Ranging across the political and class spectrum, the demonstrators sowed the seeds of social and sexual liberation. De Gaulle would resign the presidency in 1969.

The events of 1968 helped transform a culturally conservative, majority-Catholic nation into one where advocates of sexual freedom, women's liberation, and gay rights challenged the status quo. May 1968 marked a dividing line between before and after, old guard and new. Demy and Varda's return to Paris in 1969 was to a politically charged, and fundamentally changed, city and nation.

In California, Varda had female friends who didn't like how they were regarded in the anti-war movement and split from the New Left. She was seeing similar exasperation among her female friends in France. She recognized that where suffrage had been the chief objective of first wave feminism, legal birth control and abortion were primary goals of what would be known as the second wave. Varda had advocated for reproductive rights since the early 1950s, when she was among the women lobbying the wife of the leader of France's Communist Party to challenge its opposition to legal contraception. In 1970, the Mouvement de libération des femmes (Women's Liberation Movement, or MLF) took root. The following year, the collective called on Simone de Beauvoir, author of *The Second Sex* (1949), that indispensable work of twentieth-century feminism, to help achieve their aim.

The result was the "Manifesto of the 343." "One million women in France have abortions every year," began the document drafted by de Beauvoir. "Condemned to secrecy, they do so in dangerous conditions; under medical supervision, this is one of the simplest procedures. Society is silencing these millions of women. I declare that I am one of them. I declare that I have had an abortion. Just as we demand free access to contraception, we demand the freedom to have an abortion."

It was signed by 343 notable Frenchwomen, including Varda, and published in *Le nouvel observateur*, a leftist magazine, in April 1971. Each signatory understood that the public admission of having had an illegal procedure made her vulnerable to prosecution.

Like Varda, most of the signers were leading figures in French arts and letters. Joining de Beauvoir were writers Marguerite Duras, Françoise Sagan, and Monique Wittig. Along with actresses Catherine Deneuve and Jeanne Moreau there were Stéphane Audran, Françoise Fabian, Bulle Ogier, and Delphine Seyrig. Signer Gisèle Halimi, a prominent attorney, and de Beauvoir cofounded the abortion advocacy group Choisir (To Choose) to defend those who might be prosecuted for signing the document.

The manifesto was less a petition than it was a provocation. Within days, this opening salvo in the fight for legalization of abortion and greater access to contraception was dubbed "The Manifesto of the

Sluts." The front page of *Charlie Hebdo*, the satirical weekly spawned in the wake of May '68, printed a cartoon ridiculing a male politician who asks, "Who got the 343 sluts from the abortion manifesto pregnant?" But despite the derision in the politcian's question, and thanks to four more years of concerted effort and organized protests, in January 1975 the Veil Law, named for Minister of Health Simone Veil, was enacted, making abortion legal.

Participating in the women's movement prompted Varda to think critically about female representation on-screen. "I realize something has to be changed because the image of women in film has been strongly built up by men, and accepted by them, but also accepted by women—because as women we have accepted that women should be beautiful, well-dressed, loving and involved only in questions of love, etc.," she said in 1974. "In films the only thing we are able to accept in a woman is her relationship with love. . . . But you never see a woman relating to her job; you cannot accept that the subject of a film would be a woman doctor and her difficulties with an operation, her patients, etc. . . . [This] should be changed. I really think we should prepare ourselves as women and as an audience."

Varda didn't need a relief map to see how she and her sister activists were reconfiguring the social landscape. She set out to capture that evolving feminist consciousness on film. In 1972, she wrote the screenplay for a musical, *My Body Is Mine*, hoping that either her MLF compatriot Françoise Fabian or Vanessa Redgrave would play a doctor who performed abortions. Though unproduced, many of its themes would be reprised in her 1977 musical *One Sings, the Other Doesn't*. In 1975, she made *Women Reply*, an eight-minute short for a series aired on France's Channel 2 in which respondents answer the question, "What does it mean to be a woman?"

While these projects percolated, Varda fulfilled a pledge to Bernardo Bertolucci, who had solicited her help in translating his script for *Last Tango in Paris* into French. According to her agreement with Bertolucci, in June and July 1971 she would improve the translation and work with him on a "new construction" of the script. At the time, Demy was in Germany shooting *The Pied Piper*, a film fairy tale starring the Scottish-born troubadour Donovan.

Earlier that year, the Doors had recorded the band's final album, *L.A. Woman*. By March, Jim Morrison was in Paris. He hoped that he could live anonymously, that in the country of Apollinaire and Baudelaire he would find his muse as a poet. In his suitcase was a print of *HWY* (1969), a *cinéma vérité* film in which he'd starred. He sought the advice of Demy and Varda about getting it shown in Paris, and would often pop by rue Daguerre when in the neighborhood.

According to one of his biographers, "Jim had developed a real fondness for Agnès." The singer and the filmmaker recognized in each other an artist and anti-authoritarian. It is also likely that Morrison, accustomed to bending others to his whims, appreciated Varda's spine and the candor delivered in her husky, cigarette-cured voice. He visited rue Daguerre frequently that spring and early summer, often accompanied by their mutual friend Alain Ronay.

On July 2, 1971, Ronay spent the afternoon strolling with Morrison through the Marais district of Paris, where the musician and Pamela Courson, his longtime partner, had rented an apartment. Ronay had dinner plans with Varda that evening and was shaken when he arrived at rue Daguerre. When he had left Morrison at a bar, the singer wasn't himself. Ronay confided to Varda that the musician's face had looked different—like a death mask. After dinner at a nearby Vietnamese restaurant, Ronay and Varda returned to rue Daguerre. She went upstairs to sleep while Ronay spent a restless night downstairs. At 6 am he was awakened by the sound of a ringing phone, or so he thought. It turned out to be an audio hallucination.

Around 8 am the phone rang, this time for real. Even though Ronay was a houseguest, he sprang up to answer it. As he feared, it was Courson. "Jim is unconscious and bleeding! Call an ambulance!" she pleaded. Ronay roused Varda, who phoned the fire department to report a medical emergency in the Marais before slipping a madras dress over her nightgown and rushing by car to Morrison's rented apartment.

When Varda and Ronay arrived, firefighters crowded the second-floor landing, where Courson told them that Morrison was dead. Ronay did not want to see his friend's corpse in the bathtub. After consoling Courson and brewing a pot of chamomile tea to calm her, Varda entered the bathroom. "I saw him dead," she later told a *Paris Match* reporter. "Jim's head was on the left, leaning over the white enamel rim, and the dark water [red with blood] covered his body like a cloth. . . . I did not approach."

Because Ronay didn't want the authorities to know that the dead man was a celebrity, he identified the singer as American poet Douglas James Morrison, inverting his first and middle names. Ronay and Varda's tacit objective was to get their friend buried before the news of his passing became public and his funeral a circus. Courson informed the medical examiner that "Douglas" had asthma and a chronic cough, emphasizing that he was an alcoholic and not a druggie.

While the medical examiner surveyed the corpse, two unfamiliar figures came to the apartment. Ronay correctly suspected that one of them was Jean de Breteuil, aristocrat, junkie, and candyman to the stars. He supplied heroin to Courson and Marianne Faithfull, and was widely rumored to be the one who had furnished singer Janis Joplin and Rolling Stones guitarist Brian Jones with fatal doses of the drug. Varda immediately pegged the visitors as dealers and left the apartment. As there were neither needle marks on Morrison's body nor signs of foul play, an autopsy was not required. On the official certificate, cause of death was given as heart failure. For twenty years, neither Ronay nor Varda spoke publicly about the singer's final hours.

They broke their silence on the twentieth anniversary of Morrison's death in 1991, acknowledging that when they arrived at rue Beautreillis, Courson told them that she and Morrison had snorted heroin the previous evening. It may have been the singer's first time, as his preferred self-medications were whiskey and beer, though others have reported that heroin was what caused his collapse at the Rock'n'Roll Circus, a Paris disco, that night. A third possible scenario was that

Courson and Morrison had gone to see the noir western *Pursued*, directed by Raoul Walsh, and returned to the apartment, where the mixture of heroin and alcohol killed him.

Ronay credited Varda's connections in the media—most likely Bodard and Lazareff—for keeping a lid on the singer's death for four days. "I did something I knew Jim would have wanted," Varda said in the French documentary *Les derniers jours de Jim Morrison*, posted on YouTube after her death. "In the spirit of his life in Paris, I hid the news of his passing."

On July 7, Morrison was interred at Père Lachaise, the cemetery where his beloved Apollinaire—not to mention Balzac, Marcel Proust, and Gertrude Stein—is buried. Courson recited the last stanza of Morrison's "Celebration of the Lizard." There were five mourners and the funeral lasted eight minutes, making it shorter than the Doors song "The End." Did Varda, as Morrison biographer Stephen Davis suggests, memorialize her parting glance of the singer in the *Last Tango* screenplay? In the film, the wife of Paul (Marlon Brando) has committed suicide in a bathtub. Later, when she is laid out on a bier of pink hydrangeas, Paul rages over her corpse: "You, who the hell were you?"

Varda almost surely told Bertolucci about seeing Morrison in the bathtub. While she did not write the *Last Tango* screenplay, she contributed to its language and shape. But the nature and extent of her contribution remain a mystery. In a contract signed in October 1971, Marianne Films promised Varda $5,000 for her work. Later that year, Marianne bowed out and a French and an Italian company stepped in to coproduce. Varda ended up receiving the credit "dialogues by Agnès Varda." Although she later retained high-profile attorney Georges Kiejman to file suit against the Italian coproducer, it is not known whether there was a settlement, and *Last Tango* is absent from her official filmography. Perhaps she did not want a personal association with Bertolucci's *succès de scandale*.

10

BETWEEN 1966 AND 1971, Varda wrote scripts for six features and one short that failed to find backers. And though during the same period she made *Uncle Yanco*, *Black Panthers*, *Lions Love*, and *Nausicaa*, the first three failed to find significant distribution and the last, politically censored, never aired on French television. Over the same years, Demy directed four films that were produced and widely distributed: two hits, *The Young Girls of Rochefort* and *Donkey Skin*, and two misses, *Model Shop* and *The Pied Piper*. She was "discouraged," Varda told interviewer Mireille Amiel in 1975. "I was also feeling the contradictions of my feminine condition." Ruefully she admitted, "I didn't accomplish much between 1966 and 1975." While she may not have accomplished what she'd hoped to as filmmaker, she had thought a lot about those contradictions.

Varda defined the contradiction to Amiel: "There are two problems," she observed, "the problem of the promotion of women in all professions in equal number to men and the problem of society: How can women who still want to have children be sure to be able to have them when they want, with whom they want, and how are we going to help them raise the children? . . . These problems of the place of women within society are very important. In the meantime, there is only one solution and that is to be a kind of 'superwoman' and lead several lives at once and to not give in and to not abandon any of them—to not give up children, to not give up cinema, to not give up men if one likes men."

In 1972, the most obvious contradiction in Varda's life was struggling to legalize abortion while herself pregnant. She learned that she was expecting in February. Varda enthusiastically threw herself into the research for *My Body Is Mine*, a group portrait of women fighting to legalize abortion. Her script failed to win a CNC advance.

Demy was in Los Angeles, where he may have been working with Legrand on *Anouchka*, their proposed musical based on *Anna Karenina*, when Varda called with the news. Demy himself was feeling his own contradiction. According to Ayres, by then divorced and living with a male partner, Demy had recently confided that he and David Bombyk, a twenty-six-year-old story editor at Warner Brothers, had leased a small cottage in Venice early in 1972. Ayres knew that Demy loved Varda deeply and that the director "dreaded being thought he was gay." Possibly Demy wanted both a spouse and a lover, and, as Ayres believed, "wanted to pull it off without France knowing much about it." Soon after Demy told Ayres about Bombyk, the filmmaker called the executive from a pay phone at LAX. Demy was headed back to Paris. Agnès was pregnant, he said, telling Ayres how proud he was to become a father.

"What about David?" asked Ayres.

"He will have to understand," Demy replied.

In many ways, Demy was a man of his time, born and raised Catholic in a country that criminalized homosexuality until 1968 and considered it a pathology until 1992. According to Varda, Demy did not want others to know of his bisexuality. And Varda, who had lived with both Valentine Schlegel and André Bourseiller, did not speak publicly of her own.

What Demy shared about Bombyk with Varda, if anything, is unknown. But his return to Paris after receiving her news suggests that at the time, his marriage was a primary concern.

In October, Varda was eight and a half months pregnant when she and actress Delphine Seyrig, her friend in feminism, drove to Bobigny, a suburb northeast of Paris. Along with hundreds of other women, they protested the trial of Marie-Claire Chevalier, who had been raped by an older classmate. The teenager had sought an illegal abortion because she did not want to raise the child of a "thug" and because her single mother was cash-strapped from raising three children. Defending the teenager, attorney Gisèle Halimi called upon Seyrig, one of the notorious 343, to testify that although she, too, had had an illegal abortion, she was never prosecuted. Why, Seyrig asked provocatively, was anti-abortion legislation applied so inconsistently? Why was the rape victim on trial and not her rapist?

Of the Bobigny demonstration, Varda recalled with amusement, "There were hundreds of women. There were barricades. We were screaming. I was huge." Seyrig joked to Varda that an excellent way to get positive attention for the cause would be for Varda to deliver her baby on the spot. "Give birth!" she ordered Varda. "We'll make the front page!" The protest was serious, but Seyrig's levity provoked Varda to convulsive laughter as the two got jostled against the barricades by the police. Within the week, Mathieu Demy was born. Varda was forty-four.

She was both thrilled to have a child with Demy and ambivalent about the ramifications. "Despite my joy, I couldn't help resenting the brakes put on my work and my travels. I was unhappy that I couldn't do 'my' films," she said.

CATHERINE DENEUVE was expecting at the same time as Varda, ' they were often together. The actress and her partner, actor Mastroianni, visited Noirmoutier and told Demy that they were interested in making a comedy together. Did the director have any ideas?

Demy did.

His 1973 farce *A Slightly Pregnant Man* "began as a joke," he said. "My wife was pregnant, and she was always talking about what was going on inside.... It became the sole topic of conversation, and it started to get out of proportion; so jokingly, I said I thought that if I was pregnant, I wouldn't talk about it so much. And as I said it, I realized that I had a subject."

His film, the first in a cycle of male maternity movies that would include Joan Rivers's *Rabbit Test* (1978) and Ivan Reitman's *Junior* (1994), was not a success. Yet a half century after its release, its anecdotes of the corporate exploitation of expectant parents, Mastroianni's quiet befuddlement, and Deneuve's relief that this time her husband can deal with the morning sickness and sleep deprivation, remain amusing.

In the period after Mathieu's birth in 1972, both Demy and Varda wanted to be as near to the newborn as possible. While Demy filmed *A Slightly Pregnant Man* in the 14th arrondissement, Varda made *Daguerréotypes*, a documentary portrait of married couples who worked together as shopkeepers in her neighborhood.

Though she expected that she wouldn't be able to travel because of Mathieu, in June 1973 she accepted an invitation to Toronto for the Women in Film Festival, a ten-day immersion into the past and present of movies made by women. She introduced screenings of *Le Bonheur* and *Lions Love*, took part in lively conversations with audiences and other directors, and for the first time saw films by pioneers such as Dorothy Arzner, Alice Guy-Blaché, and Olga Preobrajenskaya as well as new films from American directors such as Barbara Loden (*Wanda*), Elaine May (*A New Leaf*), and Stephanie Rothman (*Terminal Island*).

In "Notes on Toronto," an article about her experience there, Varda did not touch on questions of whether men and women had different ways of seeing. After all, as painter Barnett Newman said, "Aesthetics is for artists like ornithology is for the birds." She was too close to the subject to codify it. For her, "the heart of the problem was the images of women in cinema." After listing the binary prototypes of women she sees on-screen—mother/whore, wife/mistress, saint/sinner—she notes, "Women, the female audience, are beginning to become aware of the false image of women in cinema." Where, she asked, were the courageous women who didn't make a fetish of their courage? The intelligent women who weren't also prudes? The professionals struggling with the fascinating difficulty of their professions?

Varda's tone alternates between species recognition (there were other women like her!) and awe. Never had she encountered so many women who did what she did, nor seen so many movies that, like her own, focused on female lives and experiences.

"I had lots of surprises," she wrote. "First, I didn't realize that there were so many films by women." Here was a movement she was already part of. She was wowed by Anne Severson's short *Near the Big Chakra* (1972), which featured extreme close-ups of thirty-eight vulvas. "A new approach to our femininity," she observed approvingly.

The kind of movies she wanted to see, Varda wrote, were those "that tell the story of people's relationship with events." This was, pretty much, a definition of every film she had made up to this point and many of those she would make in the future. Her report from Toronto ends on a high note of sisterhood and optimism. "Above all, I expect the reactions of the female public to intensify to the point of making a tidal wave of tidal waves, to the point of creating a demand, of demanding another cinema, parallel, if necessary, but resolutely made to please women who are finally awake."

If Varda had come to Toronto in a postpartum slump, she would leave reinvigorated. And, as she customarily did when encountering new ideas, she set out on a self-assigned curriculum of study.

Hélène Demy remembered that in the period between 1974 and 1976, summers at Noirmoutier were different. Varda would invite Hélène, who turned twenty-two in 1974, to come with her to the nearby home of the Ringarts, whose daughter, Nadja, a feminist sociologist and filmmaker, visited each summer. Varda and Ringart discussed issues in the movement while Hélène listened.

"I learned a lot, thanks to Agnès," recalled her sister-in-law. "This is when I started reading Germaine Greer and Betty Friedan and articles on the subject... Agnès certainly opened up the doors of feminism to me. Although I was never an activist, I strongly supported the cause."

EXCEPT FOR Truffaut and Resnais, who enjoyed successes in 1974 with *Day for Night* and *Stavisky*, respectively, it was not the best of times for New Wave filmmakers in France or internationally. Varda nevertheless pressed on, determined to make her own films in her own way. Soon after returning from Toronto, she revisited the CNC-unloved screenplay *My Body Is Mine*. She resolutely believed that there was a movie to be made about the women's movement in France. Once again, she rethought the story and rewrote it, making it more accessible. While reshaping the script, she received carte blanche from German television company ZDF for a project of her own choosing. After four years of financing limbo, the good news was both an affirmation and a relief. Could she leverage ZDF money by becoming her own producer?

She could. Since *La Pointe Courte*, when she founded a collective in which each of the collaborators had a share in the outcome, Varda had been open to alternative funding models. Her flexibility would prove to be the key to her long career. At the suggestion of Resnais, she had accepted commissions to prove that she could make films within industry norms. She had self-funded her experimental shorts, such as *L'opéra-mouffe*, under the banner of her company Tamaris. She had found producers for *Cléo*, *Le Bonheur*, *The Creatures*, and *Lions Love*.

"Tamaris went dormant as a producing enterprise until the mid-1970s, when Varda resuscitated it and renamed it Ciné-Tamaris," noted the film historian Kelley Conway. The restructuring of Ciné-Tamaris enabled Varda to leverage the ZDF grant to coproduce the documentary *Daguerréotypes* (1975) as well as a narrative film about the women's movement ultimately titled *One Sings, the Other Doesn't* (1977), which would go on to become one of her most polarizing films.

Prior to making the two films, Varda observed in an interview, "Little by little the feminist movement built up and a lot of women began to think of their position in society. And in the last five years it has become not only something very strong and very good, but very fashionable as well—which is the worst part of it, because it is 'in' to speak about women. Ten years ago, it wasn't 'in,' and maybe in ten years, even though the movement will still be growing, maybe society will have another topic to think about. Right now, we are in the middle of it."

As for herself, she "felt a bit stuck and suffocated by home and motherhood," she confided in a 1975 interview. In the spirit of turning lemons into lemonade, she wondered if something sweet could come out of the "limitations" of keeping close to her toddler, Mathieu. Since many women with young children are tethered to the home, she would make *Daguerréotypes* while physically and symbolically tethered to hers. The figurative umbilical cord for the film would be a 90-yard cable attached to the electric circuit panel at rue Daguerre, limiting the range within which she was able to move with camera and sound equipment.

Unstated to her subjects on rue Daguerre was the goal of better understanding the so-called silent majority, the political conservatives who neither protest nor otherwise express their political opinions, such as the voters who elected Richard Nixon in the U.S. in 1968 and Valéry Giscard d'Estaing in France in 1974. Before the shoot began, she brought the shopkeepers together with a performance by Mystag the Magician.

Varda and her crew set up as unobtrusively as possible inside the nearby bakery, butchery, clockmaker's, and so on, and it's clear that her subjects are even more tethered to their shops than the filmmaker is to her home. Varda seems most taken with the Debrossians, proprietors of Blue Thistle, vending homemade eau de cologne, hosiery, underwear, and buttons. The director describes the goods as "an inventory suspended in time." The couple is representative of the street's mom-and-pop stores, in which the husband is usually the artisan and the wife the cashier. Because Mme. Debrossian exhibits signs of dementia (including getting agitated at sundown), her spouse handles both sides of the business while keeping a loving eye on her.

Like the shopkeepers but without their customers, Varda lived with her spouse in a workplace. For the filmmakers, there was no division of labor, but rather a marriage of mutually supportive artisans. In that sense, their marriage was more like that of the husband-and-wife tailors cutting fabric at adjacent tables, and the married coiffeur and coiffeuse cutting hair at different stations. From this angle, the film is kin with Varda's other explorations of marriage, in *La Pointe Courte* and *Elsa la rose*.

Also like *La Pointe Courte*, *Daguerréotypes* both reports on a community and seeks to bring that community together. The magic performance that opens the film is intercut with the realist vignettes of butcher, baker, tailor, and filmmaker, effectively introducing the neighborhood stalwarts to their customers and one another. For those who wonder what the magician is doing in this distinctly realist context, it may be that Varda is contrasting two strains of early French film: the documentary tradition begun by the Lumière brothers and the fantasy element pioneered by Georges Méliès.

Among Varda's many gifts was her genuine interest in the lives of others. Throughout the film, her curiosity and warmth are mirrored in the animated and engaged responses of her subjects. Years later, *New Yorker* critic Richard Brody would credit Varda as the progenitor of "affectionate anthropology" in film. This might have surprised her. Despite the fact that *Daguerréotypes* attracted viewers and won prizes, Varda was disappointed that the closer she got to her neighbors, the more their politics made them seem less approachable.

A month after its June 1975 premiere on ZDF, Varda arranged

an open-air screening on rue Daguerre, a block party where film-maker, subjects, and their customers drank rosé and talked. In terms of meaningful political discussion, it wasn't what Varda had hoped. Still, in taking interest in what their workday was like and showing the shopkeepers what her own workday was like, Varda created a portrait of a community and a work of human connection that rises above political and social differences.

SERENDIPITOUSLY, AS Varda was preparing to shoot *Daguer-réotypes*, word came that her rewrite of *One Sings* had been awarded a CNC advance. While seeking a producer for *One Sings*, Varda received another television commission, this time for the news mag-azine *F... comme femme* (W for Woman). The show polled female lawyers, sociologists, and filmmakers to answer the question, "What does it mean to be a woman?" Varda responded, "I want to talk about the woman's body, about our bodies."

She told the producers that she wanted to frame her eight-minute contribution "as an affirmation and not an exhibition," a pithy description of the difference between presenting the human form and objectifying it. Varda had matter-of-factly shown nudity since *L'opéra-mouffe*. She negotiated with the producers to include a close-up of female genitals, but that sequence was cut before the program aired. Afterward, the producers allowed her to restore the shot and commercially distribute her short. She called it *Réponse de femmes* (*Women Reply*).

She shot the eight-minute film over one day in February 1975 with women of all ages, shapes, and sizes. Like many of her best works, it wrestles with contradictions, specifically those inherent to being female. Some of its assertions, such as "To be a woman means being born with female genitals," would today be viewed as quaint or essen-tialist. It is very much a movie of its time, but while it may define imperfectly what it means to be a woman, it keenly captures the new spirit of the women's movement, one that wants to do the defining rather than being defined. The women talk about what it feels like to be reduced to a pair of breasts and a vagina, to be a body detached from a mind. They talk about feeling diminished by ads using nude women to sell cars and office furniture, as though women were appliances. They chuckle at the very mixed messages of "Cover your body, be discreet" and "Show your body, it sells stuff." When a prescriptive male voice off-screen pronounces, "A woman who has not known motherhood isn't a real woman," one of the women challenges his statement with, "Is a man who is not a father any less than a man?"

The short aired on French television in 1975 and the following year was nominated for best documentary short at the Césars, France's equivalent of the Oscars.

BETWEEN THE making and the broadcast of the short, Demy and Varda traveled to Morocco over Easter. The Club Med in Marrakech offered the couple accommodations in exchange for screening and discussing their films. Rosalie, then studying for her baccalaureate, was with them. Laura Truffaut, daughter of the filmmaker, was there with her mother and sister. She remembered that "Demy and Varda were always together, happy in each other's company." While the younger woman's encounters with Varda typically were brief, she recalled her as "warm, open, and curious."

Despite the positive reception of *Women Reply* and the advance in hand for *One Sings*, Varda was unable to attract a prospective producer. She saw only two paths forward: cast movie stars, which would be expensive but attract other production money, or produce it herself. She chose the latter, devoting her efforts to creating a production system that did not strand her work in the eddies, but would enable her to attract mainstream distribution. Never mind that producing and directing a movie was twice the amount of work, comparable to a fashion designer raising the sheep, shearing it, carding and spinning the wool, then weaving her own fabric before designing and making a dress. Varda wanted to make a popular movie about how the women's movement mainstreamed the fight for abortion rights. It would not be didactic like *Women Reply*. It would be a musical with a happy ending.

Just as Varda was regaining her professional momentum, Demy hit his own bumps in the road. He and Legrand had conceived *Anouchka*, a sung-through movie musical of *Anna Karenina*, and in late 1973 met with a Soviet production company about support. Shortly thereafter, he traveled to Los Angeles to write a screenplay based on Wagner's *Tristan and Isolde*. As Varda planned her utopian feminist musical, both Demy scripts about doomed love went unproduced. When a third script, *A Room in Town*, a tragic musical to star Catherine Deneuve, was about to go into production in early 1976, Deneuve insisted that her voice not be dubbed. Production shut down. In 1983, Demy would make the film with Dominique Sanda.

Before Demy shut down *A Room in Town*, Varda went to New York for the U.S. premiere of *Daguerréotypes*, which was showing in a program of new French cinema at the Museum of Modern Art. "It was a venue beloved by French and Italian directors because it acknowledged that films *were* art," said Laurence Kardish, then associate curator of film. "[Varda] struck me as very personable and very focused on what she wanted," he recalled of this first encounter. "She was there to engage the audience." Engaged they were, with the documentary, its maker's unassuming humor, and her interest in what they thought.

From March to June 1976, Varda finally shot *One Sings, the Other Doesn't*. Locations included Paris, Bobigny, Hyères, Amsterdam, and Tehran.

FOR THE first time since the silent era, in the 1970s female filmmakers made their mark on international cinema. Buoyed by second wave feminism, they came from Berlin, Hollywood, New York, Paris, Prague, Rome, and Sydney. Among them were Chantal Akerman, Gillian Armstrong, Jane Campion, Věra Chytilová,

Martha Coolidge, Elaine May, Jeanne Moreau, Joan Micklin Silver, Margarethe von Trotta, Claudia Weill, Lina Wertmüller, and, of course, Varda.

Their protagonists weren't looking for marriage (Armstrong's *My Brilliant Career*, Chytilová's *The Apple Game*). More often than not, their films looked at men through gimlet eyes (May's *Mikey and Nicky*, Silver's *Hester Street*). They were inclined to emphasize sex work rather than sex (Akerman's *Jeanne Dielman, 23 quai du Commerce, 1080 Bruxelles*). They celebrated female friendship (Moreau's *Lumière*, von Trotta's *The Second Awakening of Christina Klages*, Weill's *Girlfriends*, Varda's *One Sings, the Other Doesn't*).

Varda's musical chronicle of the formative years of France's feminist movement showed how an unplanned pregnancy could prevent a woman from pursuing her career path and from being able to support her other children. It likewise illustrated how the women's movement enabled women to build a bridge across the class divide, raise consciousness about reproductive rights, and create alternative families of the like-minded. The film captures women from different walks of life emerging from the modern dark ages into the light of liberation.

It begins in 1962, as the teenage Pauline (Valérie Mairesse) enters a photo gallery lined with images of melancholy women that, like the film's cinematography, might be inspired by Picasso's Blue Period. She recognizes one of the women as Suzanne (Thérèse Liotard), her former neighbor. Suzanne is twenty-two, a mother of two, pregnant again with a child she cannot support and a married partner whose wife will not give him a divorce. Middle-class Pauline asks her father for money and quietly gives it to Suzanne for an illegal abortion. For the first time, Suzanne has control over her body and life and inspires both women to work for reproductive rights.

The story jumps to the Bobigny protests in 1972, to the barricades where Varda and Seyrig had marched and laughed. There, Suzanne, now running a family planning center, sees Pauline, now known as Pomme (Apple), a folk singer advocating for political and reproductive equality. During the film's second act, the women regularly exchange postcards about their lives. Pomme falls in love with an Iranian man and has a baby in Tehran. Suzanne is drawn to a married doctor yet tries to keep her distance.

In its final act, Varda's most conventionally structured feature resolves happily for the women of France, its leading characters, their partners, and their children. Abortion is legalized. The two friends find men who elevate rather than suppress them. The women have consequential work and meaningful relationships with their children. As with *Daguerréotypes*, Varda narrates the film in the tender, maternal voice of one telling a bedtime story. Aptly, both Mathieu Demy and Rosalie Varda are in the film, Mathieu as the impish son of one of Pomme's partners and Rosalie as Suzanne's teenage daughter, the glowing embodiment of feminism's future. It is Varda's only (intentionally) feel-good movie, opening with the icy blues of Picasso and closing with the rosy pinks and celadon greens of a Matisse idyll. The film offers the comforting assurance that while romantic partners come and go, female friendship is forever. "In a woman's life, in the long run, men are not *that* important," Varda told American journalist Ruth McCormick.

One Sings opened in Paris in March 1977. It was well received on the festival circuit, winning Varda the Silver Medallion at Telluride, opening the New York Film Festival, and taking the grand prize at Taormina. While it played for twenty-seven weeks in Paris, the U.S. box office was disappointing and the reviews were all over the place. Molly Haskell wrote that the film "does for the spirit of sorority what the films of Renoir and Truffaut do for the spirit of fraternity." For Vincent Canby, "At key moments [*One Sings*] is as phony—and as relentlessly schematic and upbeat—as Soviet neorealist art. It's of less interest as a movie than as a statement of position." Still, it was seen by 350,000 people in France. In Varda's reckoning, that was 345,000 more than would have seen it had she made a political film.

McCormick told Varda that many viewers resisted *One Sings* because the director made women's lives and problems seem simpler than they are. How, asked the reporter, could an oppressed woman like Suzanne become an independent feminist organizer? Gently, Varda reminded her interviewer, "Look, for once you have a film where women are without guilt, without shame, without dependency, without stupidity, fighting against laws and institutions, getting value and putting value into women's ventures. Don't you think you are already getting quite a lot?"

For many filmmakers, meeting fellow directors and talking about movies is the greatest dividend of the film festival experience. At Telluride in 1977, Varda met Martin Scorsese. He was thirty-five and had just made *New York, New York*. She was forty-nine. "Agnès was one of the Gods," he recalled in 2019. "We became friends. And we stayed friends. . . . She was a wonder to me, reinventing constantly." Scorsese said that he always depended on her to tell the truth. Their friendship was affectionate and collegial. Varda was thrilled when Scorsese's Film Foundation helped restore Demy's and her own films.

His respect for her film work meant a lot during this period, as she was feeling regularly condescended to by "feminist men"— mostly journalists and directors—who held a "not bad for a woman" attitude toward her work. During the publicity blitz for *One Sings*, Varda pushed back against this paternalism. She said, "We, blacks and women, have only recently been decolonized, and we must find our own way. . . . We should not be ready to go along with the anxiety of so many male artists who [project their issues on women], like Modigliani, Giacometti, or especially, Ingmar Bergman."

"A man is entitled to bring his fear, his guilt, his suffering to his art," Varda said. "But as a woman artist, I wouldn't want to project my anxiety onto men." In this, Varda was in accord with feminist film critics like Molly Haskell, who observed that Bergman, at the time America's favorite foreign filmmaker, criticized his women for attributes he himself had given them.

Respect from American filmmakers and critics was welcome validation for Varda. Still, in 1976 she was stung when *Paroles . . . Elles tournent*, a book by France's Musidora Collective about women in film, made no mention of Varda or her work. It happened again in

1980, when she read two special issues of *Cahiers du cinéma* devoted to French film and neither she nor her films were cited. "That really hurt," she said. "If *Cahiers du cinéma* . . . was excluding me, it really felt like an exile."

EARLY IN 1978, Demy received a phone call from London. Despite his many supporters, he had not made a film since *A Slightly Pregnant Man* in 1973. Would he meet some Japanese producers for lunch?

The producers were planning a movie adaptation of *The Rose of Versailles*, a manga series that had become a phenomenon in Japan, and considered him the right director for a history-based fable about the end of France's *ancien régime*. In this version, Marie Antoinette has a bit of a crush on her bodyguard, Lady Oscar, who was raised by her father as a boy because males were more likely to advance professionally and socially in the monarchy.

Demy found the producers amiable and liked that they "seemed to have unlimited means at their disposal." Indeed, Shiseido cosmetics, the Japanese counterpart of Estée Lauder, was a major backer of the film. It would be a musical, meaning a reunion for Demy and Legrand. All the director needed was a screenwriter who would help him telescope an episodic ten-volume manga into a smooth narrative in English. Varda would receive an executive producer credit for hiring the crew and keeping the film on time and on budget.

Patricia Knop, the American screenwriter of *The Passover Plot*, "somehow got on Demy's radar," recalled Gillian Lefkowitz, the younger of Knop's two daughters. Varda and Knop, who was likewise an artist in multiple media (painting and sculpture as well as screenwriting), took to each other immediately. Lefkowitz remembers Varda being hard on her mother about her painting. "Agnès was no-bullshit, and they had a loving, deep relationship. Agnès and Jacques were a *huge* part of our lives." And vice versa.

Knop's elder daughter, Chloe King, now a screenwriter, remembers Mathieu, always dressed as Batman or Superman, and especially

Varda, whom she thought of as a godmother. "She scared the shit out of me sometimes," King said. "For sure she didn't suffer fools, and she was very judgmental. But that judgment forced you to explain, go deeper, do better. She had the most beautiful core."

Production on *Lady Oscar* commenced in July 1978. Varda had just celebrated her fiftieth birthday and Demy his forty-seventh; they had been together for nearly twenty years. The producers persuaded Demy not to spend money on name actors, feeling that the story was the star and arranging for the film to be shot partly at Versailles. The result was a Fragonard painting come to life, in macaron colors and with a lively score, occasionally clever lyrics, and the plot U-turns common to melodrama and manga. The British actors were good-looking and politely stiff, perhaps more plausible as English butlers and head housekeepers than as French royals and proletarians.

Lady Oscar was at least five years ahead of its time, anticipating *Tootsie, Victor/Victoria*, and *Yentl*, the principal movies of the early 1980s gender-bender genre in the U.S. Demy's film found distribution only in Japan, failing to attract interest from distributors in France or elsewhere. Demy scholar Darren Waldron observed that, like the director's *A Slightly Pregnant Man*, "the target of the film's critique is not gender roles, but institutionalized sexism." The film set in eighteenth-century France openly admires contemporaneous American social freedoms. Oscar's closest friend tells him that "equality exists in America . . . a man can love whomever he wants."

IN 1979, with Mathieu in tow, Demy and Varda went to Los Angeles for their second California sojourn. Both had films in the works. For Varda, it was *Maria and the Naked Man*, based on a real-life murder in the Echo Park neighborhood. For Demy, it was *Skaterella*, a contemporary *Cinderella*, in which the title character loses her roller skate during a midnight escape from a rink. The two directors leased an apartment in Venice and, with the help of Patricia Knop and her husband, Zalman King, combed side streets, dumpsters, and second-hand stores to furnish it.

What drew Varda to *Maria and the Naked Man*, the true story of a policeman who killed an unarmed man who was walking outside stark naked, was the contrast between a nonviolent hippie, an engineer and neighborhood guru, and the cop who saw him walk out of his home and shot him fatally from his cruiser. The policeman pleaded self-defense and was acquitted. Maria H, who is pregnant with the child of the deceased, wants to find out what made the cop shoot. She finds an eyewitness, Betty (a role coveted by Simone Signoret).

Varda had a "step deal"—where screenwriters are paid in installments for completed work—with the film subsidiary of the British music corporation EMI. EMI liked the script, which, rather than following the conventions of a whodunit, instead asked *why*. They insisted that Varda, who often said that she was intimidated by stars, cast an American star in the lead, but all the established and rising stars passed on it. In 1979, Jill Clayburgh had signed to make *Starting Over*, Sally Field was cast in *Norma Rae*, Jane Fonda was attached to *9 to 5*, and Sissy Spacek to *Coal Miner's Daughter*. Without a star, EMI would not proceed.

Skaterella, on the other hand, seemed like a sure thing. Roller rinks were the new discos. Francis Ford Coppola had approached Demy to write and direct this updated version of *Cinderella*. Instead of a glass slipper, there would be a leather roller skate. Nastassja Kinski, fresh from her breakthrough in *Tess*, was to play the lead. Yet it, too, was scuttled. At the time, the gossip was that despite being taught how to roller skate, Kinski found it a challenge to act and skate at the same time. What is certain is that Demy's pal Gene Kelly was slated to direct *Xanadu*, a kindred musical fantasy on skates with Olivia Newton-John as Terpsichore, the muse of dance. Whether due to Kinski's lack of confidence or because two roller skating musicals were thought to be too much for the market—or both—*Skaterella* was canceled.

The cratering of both projects occurred at a particularly difficult juncture for the filmmakers, further straining an already stressed relationship. Five years earlier, Demy had rushed home to be with Varda during her pregnancy. Now forty-eight, after twenty-one years of living together, he wanted to live with David Bombyk.

Only their closest friends knew of their separation. For a time, they continued to entertain as a couple in Los Angeles. Demy moved in with Bombyk not far from the apartment where Varda and Mathieu remained. In Paris, Demy purchased an apartment on rue Daguerre across the street from Varda. These arrangements enabled them to co-parent Mathieu.

Understandably, Varda was shaken, said Lynne Littman, her assistant at the time, who remembered the filmmaker coming to her house to tell her of the breakup. "Agnès spent her time doing, not talking," said Littman. From the evidence of Varda's semi-autobiographical 1981 film *Documenteur*, shell shock better describes her mindset. "At this moment in our lives, Jacques and I are in a silent rage against each other," she would recall later in *Varda par Agnès*.

Almost immediately, Demy was asked to make a telefilm in France based on Colette's autobiographical novel *Break of Day*, which she wrote in her early fifties following the breakup of her second marriage. It was a subject he could relate to. He wrote the screenplay and shot it in June 1980 at La Treille Muscate, Colette's former home near St. Tropez. It's a handsome biopic, played with nuance by Danièle Delorme. Rosalie, who had interned as a costumer on *Lady Oscar*, received her first solo credit as costume designer on the film. To Tom Luddy, Demy confided, "Colette reminds me so much of Agnès."

Varda found solace with Littman, Patricia Knop, and others. She mothered Mathieu, made the films *Mur Murs* and *Documenteur* in Los Angeles, and mourned the end of the relationship.

She didn't know at the time that it wasn't the end.

11

"I HAD A CAR and spoke French," said Lisa Blok-Linson of her qualifications when Varda hired her as Mathieu's caregiver in 1979. An undergraduate at UCLA film school, Blok-Linson had seen *One Sings, the Other Doesn't*, which she liked. She also liked Mathieu, age seven, "a bright, precocious kid who captured my heart."

When Varda began the research for *Mur Murs* (1981), a documentary about mural artists in Venice and other parts of Los Angeles, Blok-Linson was promoted. Her first film job was as the documentary's "production assistant and whatever-needed-to-be-done girl." Over the next thirty years Blok-Linson worked variously as a production manager and line producer on several of Varda's films, and she also produced Mathieu Demy's directorial debut, *Americano* (2011). Her work with Varda segued into a career as a location manager for blockbusters like *The Rock*, *Mercury Rising*, and *Blade*, as well as production manager for low-budget documentaries and features.

When Blok-Linson met Varda, Venice was a transitional seaside community with a colorful backstory and an uncertain future. Developed by a tobacco millionaire in 1905 as a beach resort with rental bungalows, canals, and gondolas, it was abandoned during Prohibition when bars were shuttered, only to become an industrial area when oil was discovered. From the 1950s through the 1970s it was a run-down neighborhood, home to artists and surfers, beloved for its low rents, high ideals, and amiable resistance to development. Resident artists painted murals on its crumbling walls, and Venice began to resemble an open-air gallery. The art and the artists were more diverse than in traditional art spaces.

The murals were variously photorealistic, Pop, surrealistic, and trompe l'oeil; others were in the styles of naïve, folk, political, and graffiti art. Some of the painters were art school graduates, like Terry Schoonhoven and Victor Henderson, cofounders of the LA Art Squad, and Judy Baca, administrator of the Citywide Mural Program. Others were self-taught. Venice was a derelict neighborhood unified into a community by the muralists. Here was a documentary camera-ready for Varda, who filmed from majority-Hispanic East Los Angeles to the city's western beachfront.

With backing from France's Ministry of Culture and its state-owned television channel, Varda made *Mur Murs*. Its title is a bilingual pun. In French, it means "wall walls." In English, whispers. "The pun is a mistake," joked Mireille Amiel in her 1982 review. "These walls don't whisper, they howl!" And how.

Like Varda's commissioned documentaries of the 1950s, *Mur Murs* takes an inventory approach to the LA murals. She worked organically, first looking at the artworks, then meeting and interviewing their makers. "Agnès ended up on my doorstep one day," recalled Baca, lead artist for the mural *History of Venice* (1971) and general of the army of artists young and old who created *The Great Wall of Los Angeles* (1974–84), a history of the city from prehistoric times through the 1960s.

"Initially, she was looking at murals by white males," recalled Baca, one of three female muralists interviewed in the film. Baca and other artists encouraged her to visit Watts and East Los Angeles, where many Black and Latino muralists lived and worked. "Varda didn't come with preconceived ideas," said Baca. "I remember thinking that she worked more like an artist than like a filmmaker." The muralist appreciated that Varda felt her way through the material rather than illustrating a preexisting thesis. "She brought her own enthusiasm to it."

When it came to asking questions, "[Varda] had no hesitation getting into your face." She was just as interested in the makers as she was in what they made. "I've taken thousands of people to see the murals," Baca said. "Usually, they wait for me to give them a read on what they're seeing. Not Varda. She needed to discover rather than to be shown."

She discovered that walls don't listen, they speak. They speak of the city and its people. They speak of artists disgruntled with the gallery system. They speak of their wish to communicate with passersby. She likewise discovered that walls are not always barriers, but often mirrors that reflect the community. Other times, they are backdrops for the urban drama and for performance artists. Walls celebrate both the living and the dead. They comment upon what a city is and what it could be. They express personal visions and collective daydreams.

Rather than provide captions identifying each artist, Varda hired someone—a wall whisperer?—to murmur the name of the painter or painters of the image on-screen. In this way, the murals introduce themselves. "Murals mean, 'I exist' and 'I sign what's mine,'" says an unidentified voice. Suzanne Jackson, a Black artist working in the Mid-City neighborhood, explains that the Black Panthers asked her to paint guns and clenched fists and other symbols of resistance. She resisted, instead transforming the concrete walls of St. Elmo's Village into a sanctuary of birds, trees, and whales. A Latino artist in East LA looks at the faces on the walls and explains with pride that his forebears are Aztec, Maya, and Toltec, and that the local murals celebrate these notable ancestors. Kent Twitchell, a white muralist, talks about how his 20-foot portraits of locals painted on the exterior wall of an unemployment office heroize these workers while giving viewers the childlike experience of being among giants.

At a time when exclusion was commonplace and marginalized artists were not part of the conversation, Varda ensured that those on the fringes of the art world were central to the discussion. At this joyless juncture in her personal life, she made a contemplative and joyful survey of public art.

The Isle of California, Terry Schoonhoven's imagining of Los Angeles after a magnitude 9.0 earthquake, is the final image of *Mur Murs* and the first of *Documenteur*. It depicts a crumbling segment of ramp broken off from a freeway after a seismic event has separated Los Angeles from the mainland. Did Varda see herself in the image of the sundered isle? It mirrors the rupture in her marriage and the ensuing physical separation from Demy.

In English, *Documenteur* translates as "documenter." In French, it's an oxymoron meaning "docu-liar." The film telescopes Varda's post-Demy stint in Los Angeles. Its documentary aspect comes from its powerful depiction of Varda's melancholy. The Varda surrogate character, Émilie, has been left not by her husband but by her boyfriend and father of her son.

Just over an hour long, the film recycles some of the narration and footage from *Mur Murs*. The film opens with a car that stops in front of *The Isle of California*. Émilie and her son, Martin, played by Mathieu Demy, get out of the car and play catch. This moment is a literal illustration of a woman finding her feet after an emotional earthquake, and its tone has the foreboding of a film noir. Varda called *Documenteur* "a shadow of *Mur Murs*, Los Angeles without sun and wonders." To best capture the darker side of LA, Varda shot *Documenteur* only on overcast days, said Blok-Linson. "If it was sunny, we went indoors."

In the voiceover narration by Delphine Seyrig, Émilie confesses that she is lost. Lost in a sea of faces, submerged in a tsunami of words. She looks in the mirror and doesn't recognize her face. She asks, does being separated from a man mean being in exile from all men? Only one face has a name: Martin. Only one word has meaning: pain.

As Varda remembered, while she and her film editor, Sabine Mamou, worked shoulder to shoulder on *Mur Murs*, Varda would rehearse a line or describe an image she thought of for *Documen-*

teur. "Sabine listened. . . . Later, at Christmas, she gave me a school notebook. She had transcribed by hand . . . what I had said out loud speaking out of the blue."

Mamou was not an actress, but, as she recalled, Varda "said to me, 'I saw you play with my son Mathieu yesterday and thought you could act in the film.'" Varda "wanted to do a home movie," Mamou remembered. "The characters were her son, and friends of hers or mine. What I lived through with this film was being very close to the process of creating."

"Our core crew on *Documenteur* were women," said Blok-Linson. The director of photography was Nurith Aviv. "Sabine Mamou as actress and editor, me, and of course Agnès at the center of everything." They shot all morning and then broke for lunch, "where we would all pitch in and cook, then eat and chat about anything but the film. It was very egalitarian. Of course, this is not how mainstream Hollywood works! What I learned was how collaborative an art filmmaking is and should be."

In the movie, Mamou and Mathieu have such a natural rapport that it is easy to believe they are mother and son. She is a parent who sets boundaries for her child while trying not to burden him with her sadness. He is a child who tests Mom's authority while trying not to make her sadder. That they don't always succeed makes this quasi-documentary feel like a real one.

The narration is as minimalist as a *nouveau roman*. Varda thought this was the result of her reading Nathalie Sarraute's *The Use of Speech* while she was writing it.

Near the film's conclusion, mother and son play on the beach, pretending to be crabs. Martin tells the giggling Émilie that he loves it when she laughs. Both are surprised by joy. So is their audience, as this portrait of melancholy somehow morphs into an antidote for it.

Documenteur, wrote Rosalie, "is the only time Agnes opened the door to show what she usually would hold back."

"Agnès processed her life through her films," observed Blok-Linson. "Even though her separation from Jacques was a painful time in her life, she created this circle that became a family of sorts. Agnès never felt sorry for herself . . . and didn't want anyone to feel sorry for her."

In 1981, *Mur Murs* debuted at Cannes. It went on to win prizes at the Florence and Mannheim film festivals.

To hear Varda tell it, "Solitude in California made me make some progress. Following *Mur Murs* and *Documenteur*, and back in France, my work refocused."

In January 1982, a double bill of the documentary and the semi-autobiography opened in Paris. Later in the year, Valentin Vignet, the eldest of Rosalie's three sons, was born, making Varda, fifty-three, a grandmother, and Mathieu, nine, an uncle.

AFTER MAKING *Salut les cubains* in 1963, Varda disengaged from photography to the extent that when she returned to Paris from California in 1969, she had replaced the darkroom at rue Daguerre with an office. Upon her return from California in 1981, she would later tell an interviewer, the odds against finding money for feature films were so high that she nearly gave up trying to make another.

Happily, in 1982, Antoine Cordesse and Lucien Clergue, organizers of "Encounters with Photography" workshops and exhibitions in Arles, invited her to present an event at the Théâtre Antique, a Roman amphitheater dating from the first century AD. Creating the work was a formative experience as she mixed photography, film, and recorded commentary, prefiguring her twenty-first-century installation art.

It was an opportune moment for her to reconsider the photograph. Since the publication of *On Photography*, a 1977 essay collection by her friend Susan Sontag, serious examinations of the form were multiplying faster than Polaroids. Roland Barthes' *Camera Lucida* (1981) and Jean Mohr's *Another Way of Telling* (1982) were among them. Varda's contribution to these investigations would contrast moving and still images.

She dove into the ocean of her own photographic work and, to her surprise, rediscovered an abundance of images. After organizing this trove of visual material, she called upon the amazing technicians of the Centre Pompidou to put together an antecedent of a Power-Point, a system that could toggle between projecting still images and projecting film clips on videotape as her audio track delivered commentary throughout.

"The evening conceived by Agnès Varda . . . was a success, a real 'audiovisual' show," wrote novelist and photography critic Hervé Guibert in *Le Monde*. He was delighted by the breadth of the spectacle projected on the screen of the Théâtre Antique, documenting Varda's work at the TNP and her trips to China and Cuba, "where she saw with generous eyes." He was moved by this "family album of a mother who became a grandmother."

He noted, "There was something particularly mysterious, which made itself understood, in a lively way, and better than a theoretical dissertation: [we saw] the boundary between the still image of photography and the movie image blurred."

Reconsidering her photographic work inspired Varda to look more closely at photography in general and one image in particular, a photo taken near St. Aubin in 1954, before she made *La Pointe Courte*. On her summer break, she reexamined it. She thought a deep dive into one photograph might help her to better understand the strengths and limitations of the medium. The trouble was, she found that the deeper she went, the more elusive the image became.

In the DVD introduction to *Ulysse*, the twenty-two-minute color short she made in the autumn of 1982, Varda says, "The Man was naked, the goat was dead, the boy was named after the hero of the *Odyssey*." The man stands in the deep background, naked, gazing toward the English Channel. The boy, also naked, is in the middle distance, wearing sandals, sitting knees to chest on the rocky beach looking at the goat. The goat is in the foreground, lifeless, eyes open. An observer familiar with Homer who knew that the photograph's title was *Ulysse* might think it a photographic reen-

Between screenings of *Cléo from 5 to 7* at the Cannes Film Festival in 1962, Varda plays pinball as husband Jacques Demy watches.
Reporters Associes / Gamma-Rapho via Getty Images

Flanked by first-nighters, Varda and Demy share a moment at the 1965 premiere of *Le Bonheur* (Happiness) in Paris. *Reporters Associes/ Gamma-Rapho via Getty Images*

During the 1966 New York Film Festival, Varda takes a field trip to Stony Point, New York, to see experimental filmmaker Stan VanDerBeek's *Movie-Drome*. *Robert R. McElroy / Getty Images*

Varda and Demy at the 1966 Cannes Film Festival. *François Pages* / Paris Match *via Getty Images*

On the set of *Nausicaa* in 1970, Varda finds the best angle for a scene. *INA via Getty Images*

Varda with cinematographer Nurith Aviv framing a shot on the set of *One Sings, the Other Doesn't*, 1976. *Roger-Viollet via Getty Images*

Varda and the star of *Vagabond*, Sandrine Bonnaire, get respite from the winter cold on set in 1985. *Micheline Pelletier / Gamma-Rapho via Getty Images*

Varda with son Mathieu, circa 1995, in the courtyard of rue Daguerre. *Jacques Lange / Paris Match via Getty Images*

Varda in a potato costume created for the 2003 Venice Biennale installation *Patatutopia*. The installation was reprised for the 2011 exhibition *There Is No Sea* in Sète. *Pascal Guyot / AFP via Getty Images*

Varda at her 2007 installation *Les Justes* at the Paris Panthéon. Her multimedia exhibition celebrated the French citizens who sheltered Jews during the German occupation of France in World War II. *MAXPPP / Alamy Stock Photo*

Varda with her two children, daughter-in-law, and four of her five
grandchildren on the set of *The Beaches of Agnès*, circa 2008.
Ciné-Tamaris / France 2 / Album / Alamy Stock Photo

Varda with her son, Mathieu Demy, and daughter, Rosalie Varda, at the 2013
Cinémathèque française retrospective, *Tales of Love: The Enchanted World of
Jacques Demy. Miguel Medina / AFP via Getty Images*

Varda at the Paris Grand Palais in 2014 in front of a retrospective of her photographs. The first image from left is *Potato Heart*, from 1953, and the second is *Alexander Calder and His Family* from 1954. *Photograph Matthieu Alexandre / AFP via Getty Images*

Varda in her birthplace, Ixelles, Belgium, for her 2016 exhibition at the Ixelles Museum, *Patates et compagnie. Luc Castel / Getty Images*

Varda receives an honorary Oscar in 2017, presented by Angelina Jolie.
Kevin Winter / Getty Images

Varda helping to lead the Women's March at Cannes in 2018. *Loic Venance /
AFP via Getty Images*

Varda with director Martin Scorsese at the Marrakech International Film Festival, 2018. *Abaca Press / Alamy Stock Photo*

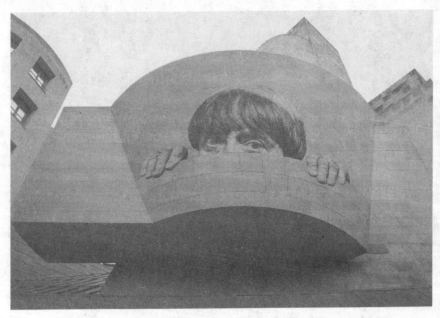

A mural of Varda created by the artist JR for the Agnès Varda retrospective *Viva Varda!* at the Cinémathèque in Paris, 2023. *Abaca Press / Alamy Stock Photo*

actment of Homer's hero on the island of goats, turning his back on a bad omen.

For the film essay, Varda interviews its human subjects twenty-eight years later. Fouli Elia, the adult, is an editor at French *Elle*. Ulysse Lorca, the young boy, now an adult, owns a bookstore on the rue de Rivoli. Their memories are fuzzy. "Didn't you carry the boy to the beach?" asks Elia.

She did. Ulysse is the son of Bienvenida Lorca, Varda's rue Daguerre neighbor and onetime lab assistant. We learn that the young Ulysse suffered from hipbone trauma and doctors predicted he would have a lifelong limp. Varda remembers that she traveled with the Lorcas to Normandy seeking a cure. Ulysse remembers nothing at all, even when Varda presents him with a painting that he made while looking at the photo. "Everyone has his own story," he says, brusquely dismissing the filmmaker. Yet in a larger sense, they are in accord. "Rather than fix a meaning, Varda is content to let her film reveal the photograph's . . . subtly subjective appeal," observed scholar Ari Blatt.

Varda then interviews schoolchildren, each of whom offers a different read. She correlates the date the photo was taken with history: May 9, 1954, was the day that the Vietnamese defeated the French at Dien Bien Phu. Then she correlates it with her own personal history: it was one of the last photos she made before shooting *La Pointe Courte*.

Making *Ulysse* reconnected Varda with the artist she was before motherhood and marriage. For her, the process communicated what an image could and couldn't say. The subjects and viewers of the photograph all have different recollections, as in *Rashomon* (1951), the film by Akira Kurosawa in which the characters have contradictory recollections of the same event. Varda's short debuted at Cannes in 1983. The following year it won a César for best documentary short subject.

In the wake of *Ulysse*, Varda hatched an idea that had both pedagogical and entertainment value and took it to Robert Delpire, publisher, gallerist, and head of the Centre national de photographie. She asked what he thought of a series in which every day at the same time a photograph would be shown on television. She proposed to show the photo for ten or fifteen seconds without saying anything about its subject, location, or meaning. Afterward, an unidentified person— maybe a street sweeper, a housewife, a movie star, or a taxi driver— would comment on it. Each episode would have a running time of roughly ninety seconds, beginning with the unidentified image and ending with the name of the photographer and a way to understand it. The narrative frame borrowed the structure of a police procedural one might see on television.

Delpire loved the idea. He and Varda approached Fr3, channel 3, a public-television station, which immediately signed on. The engaging result was *Une minute pour une image* (One Minute for One Image). In 1983, between January and June, *Une minute* aired every night at 11 pm. The next day *Libération*, the leftist daily, published the photograph discussed the prior evening, with excerpts from the commentary. Varda involved photographers including Robert Doisneau and Henri Cartier-Bresson, cultural figures such as Marguerite Duras and Delphine Seyrig, and members of the public such as her baker friend from rue Daguerre.

Had the late André Malraux been alive to watch *Une minute*, one imagines the minister of culture and architect of the CNC advance would have loved it. It applied his concept of the "museum without walls"—the distribution of culture outside traditional channels—to the widest possible audience. The key difference, observed essayist Joseph Pomp, between what figures like Malraux hypothesized and what Varda achieved was that her compendium of images "is both educational and supremely fun." The so-called grandmother of the New Wave was becoming a TV personality known for her arts commentary.

The month after *Une minute* debuted, Demy's ambitious *A Room in Town* (1982), a kaleidoscopic musical melodrama about a real-life dockworkers' strike in Nantes in the 1950s and the interconnected figures participating in or observing it, was nominated for nine César awards. A mélange of impassioned politics, startling violence, impotence, and sexual cruising, the film, starring Dominique Sanda and Danielle Darrieux, was Demy's most operatic. It was to be his last masterpiece.

VARDA'S NEXT film, her least-known masterpiece, was a short commissioned by French television, *The So-Called Caryatids* (1984). Created as an episode in a series devoted to the nude in art, Varda's film suggests that the male gaze is as unheeded a factor of urban life as it is in film. With a running time of thirteen minutes, Varda's contribution to the series was emblematic of her style: poetic commentary combined with equally poetic images of a subject that, however common, largely goes undiscussed.

In classical Greek architecture, a caryatid is a draped female figure that functions structurally as a column, supporting the roof or entablature above. Vitruvius, the Roman architect, dubbed them caryatids after the Peloponnesian city of Karyes, where women in ancient times hefted weighty items on their heads. When the Romans won a war against Karyes, they killed the men, enslaved the women, and designed caryatids to perform the architectural support.

Varda's film inventories the late nineteenth-century carayatids of Paris, where the load they carry is considerably lighter than in ancient times. In Paris, they are undraped, voluptuous paragons of beauty, typically decorating a building's façade. "In the street," she observes puckishly, "the nude is more often bronze or stone than flesh." In Varda's informal census, the caryatids greatly outnumber their male counterparts, called atlases. They carry their burdens lightly, in contrast to the atlases, who exhibit muscular power and the obvious strain of their labor. Varda doesn't question why this is so: she doesn't need to. The gendered architecture makes clear to the presumed male observer that female nudes are here for our sexual pleasure and men for the heavy lifting. She scores her polemical points with visual and verbal wit, humor rather than harangue. *Caryatids* was invited to the Venice Film Festival and later won the prize for best documentary at the Festival of Architecture and Urbanism in Lausanne.

When Varda made the film in 1984, only a fraction of New Wave directors remained active. That year, Truffaut died of a brain tumor at fifty-two. Still working were Chabrol, Demy, Godard, Marker, Resnais, Rivette, Rohmer, and Varda. While she hadn't made a feature film since *Documenteur*, she was having great fun making lively shorts.

Her second short of 1984 was *7p. cuis. s. de b., . . . à saisir* (7 Rooms, Kitchen, Bath . . . [Will Go Fast!]), her entry in "The Living and the Artificial" exhibition at the Avignon Festival. Like *Caryatids*, it was inspired by architecture. In this case, the subject was a former rest home in Avignon where the works of other invited artists were also on view. *7p.* documents the exhibition while at the same time creating a new narrative work. Staged and shot over a week in August, its conceit is that an unseen real estate agent is showing the property, once a hospice for the elderly, to a young lawyer, also unseen. The "living" aspect of the film is the property; the "artificial" is the story Varda spins about original residents, former tenants, and the tableaux of other artists.

In Varda's surreal short, the original residents have been relocated and a geriatrician and his family move into the building, where he opens a consulting room connected to a living space. Sometimes the doctor and his wife are wax mannequins. Sometimes they are played by actors. We see ashen patients in the waiting room and ghostly plaster busts that resemble death masks. We see the doctor in the bedroom with his wife. We see his family of eight around the breakfast table laid with model food including a plastic fish and silicon replicas of sunny-side-up eggs. Fortunately, the parents spend mealtimes enforcing table manners and don't force their children to eat the artificial food.

Doctor and wife are credited with transforming a once spartan industrial kitchen into an avian dreamscape where counters are carpeted with grass, a wild turkey roams free, and live chickens socialize.

As they age, the doctor grows increasingly pedantic, his wife increasingly pudgy, and their daughter, Louise, a young woman with a bowl haircut, increasingly oppositional. Often, the hospice's original residents return as ghosts to haunt the place, lending the short a soupçon of *The Shining*.

7p. is at once the story of a building and the life cycles of its inhabitants, and a farcical look at a nuclear family, punctuated by startling encounters with the work of other artists. As Varda recalled, "This film came out of me with great jubilation, this totally free film born of a stream of associations and impressions."

"The experience of improvising this experimental short provoked in Varda an 'irresistible' desire to shoot again right away," noted Kelley Conway. "I felt it worked for me not to wait, not to prepare so much," said the filmmaker. It was important to replicate the freedom she'd felt on *7p.*, making decisions in the moment, without a shot list and with the most minimal of scripts. Since that experimental film was confined to interior spaces, she looked forward to the greater freedom of shooting outdoors. Despite the financial hurdles, she was hopeful that after the success of several shorts, she would be able to make another feature.

Varda, who tracked the box office in France and the United States, was optimistic. It appeared to her that a new generation of female filmmakers was rising. In 1984, for the first time in seventy years, one needed two hands to count the films made by women. There was France's *Entre Nous* by Diane Kurys, which was nominated for best foreign language film at the Academy Awards. There was *Mrs. Soffel*, a Hollywood studio film by Australia's Gillian Armstrong. There was Argentina's *Camila*, by María Luisa Bemberg, which received a best foreign language film nomination in 1985. America's Martha Coolidge and Marisa Silver had breakthroughs with *Valley Girl* and *Old Enough*. Besides Kurys in France, there were Catherine Breillat's *36 Fillette* and Coline Serreau's *Trois hommes et un couffin*. Serreau's film, remade in the U.S. as *Three Men and a Baby*, would vie with Varda's next feature at the 1986 César Awards.

IN 1984, Varda enlisted the help of Patricia Mazuy on a prospective feature about plane tree plague. They had first met in 1980, when Mazuy, then a business student from Dijon, France, was hired as an au pair in Los Angeles. She was twenty, had little money, and spent the pittance she did have on making a short film. She used a song by the Doors on the soundtrack, not knowing that she needed to acquire the rights to do so. A friend mentioned that there was another French filmmaker working in LA. Maybe Mazuy should ask her advice?

Varda, who was then editing *Mur Murs*, recognized Mazuy's talent when she saw the short, and suggested that Mazuy use Sabine Mamou's editing equipment for free at night. Two years later, Mamou hired Mazuy as her assistant on Demy's *A Room in Town*. Mazuy would go on to become a successful writer and director in France.

Still in the planning stages of the plane tree feature, Varda asked Mazuy to co-edit it. On one of her many scouting trips to Nîmes, where she hoped to shoot, she picked up a female hitchhiker, Setina Arhab, who told her tales of being a single woman on the road alone. Varda was fascinated by the enigmatic drifter and thought of changing the film's focus.

During Varda's scout in Nîmes and its environs, she photographed and interviewed people who would inspire characters in the movie that became *Vagabond*. One was a policeman who told her about the frozen body of a young man he'd found under an apple tree in winter. In this region, a mere ninety-minute drive from Sète, Varda encountered shepherds, vineyard workers, and garage mechanics, many of whom would be cast to play versions of themselves.

"To a degree, Agnès was her own archivist and historian," said film scholar Richard Neupert. "Sometime her stories change. She was a marvelous force of nature." With *Vagabond*, Varda decided to make the original story about plane tree plague subsidiary to that of the human plague of poverty.

As Varda told it, the idea for *Vagabond* was inspired by a news story. It wasn't an item trumpeting the triumph of France's productivity, which in 1980 surpassed that of all other European nations and ranked third globally behind Japan and the United States. It was a stinging look at France's *Nouveaux Pauvres*— the "New Poor" for whom hunger and cold were a daily reality.

An early alarm was sounded in *Le Monde* in 1982: "The New Poor are growing more and more numerous." A spokesman from Catholic Charities reported, "We have seen an increasing number of young people aged nineteen and twenty arrive; they often come from the provinces to look for a job in Paris and then, of course, they can't find one, they don't have a penny left, and they are in a very high-risk situation." Varda would discover that the social problem was not limited to the capital. All across France, rootless young adults encountered risk.

Varda went on many more excursions south, usually solo, in the fall of 1984. Driving through the region enabled her to pick up hitchhikers and talk to them about their solitary journeys. Scouting locations led to meeting locals and listening to their stories about the drifters they encountered.

"Characters began to exist... inspired by those I had met," recalled Varda, "including a mechanic who speaks malevolently of girls on the road. Because they slept [around], he called them all sluts!" Varda took photos and made a list of the kind of people a wanderer could meet outside. "Road-menders, pruners, shepherds, masons, gas-station attendants, etc." She wrote some dialogue and made a shot list. She met a philosopher, a post-1968 dropout now living on the land and herding sheep. She would cast him as a version of himself.

During the research period, Varda's film about the New Poor had a male protagonist and chronicled his interactions with those he encountered on the road. It then morphed into a story about two male dropouts who meet a female counterpart, initially following all three of them and eventually following only her. In Varda's version of *Vagabond*'s evolution, soon after she settled on a structure, she picked up Setina Arhab and reaped the character of a woman willfully indifferent to the opinions of others. This social outsider lives outside by choice. She doesn't want anything or anybody telling her what to do.

Arhab's brassy defiance became central to Varda's vision of the movie. "She was such an extraordinary character that I began to realize how much more interesting it is to see a girl hitchhiker than a guy," said Varda. "That's when I decided that my main character would be a girl. It presupposes more physical courage, more endurance, more guts, [and] a greater capacity to say, 'up yours!' to people." Here was someone who could share her experiences of being a woman on the road and the constant movement that characterized her life.

By the Christmas holidays in 1984, Varda knew she had a film. She had decided on the principal locations. Her nonprofessional actors were at the ready, Arhab included. For a time during preproduction, Arhab stayed with Varda in Paris.

Without a script—like her protagonist, Varda wanted freedom—she was able nonetheless to secure some professional actors. The main character, called Mona Bergeron in the film, there was played by Sandrine Bonnaire, seventeen, whose film debut at fifteen in Maurice Pialat's *À nos amours* had both a bedrock believability and fiery volatility. For the tree doctor Madame Landier, who admires Mona's moxie, there was Macha Méril, a gifted actress in cinema and theater. If Varda thought these excellent actresses would be draws for potential investors, she was unfortunately mistaken.

Funding, always a challenge, was this time even more so. The CNC passed. Varda cast her net wider, to French and European television. Only France's Channel 2 expressed interest. In exchange for broadcast rights, it would put up 10 percent of the film's $722,000 budget. She didn't know where the rest of the budget would come from.

She empathized with the cultural arbiters who turned down the project, observing wryly, "It must be said that when you talk about a dirty and rebellious girl who says nothing, or rather [says] 'shit,' and ends up freezing to death in a ditch, you don't awaken the desires of the deciders." This is not a spoiler: Mona's end is known at the film's beginning.

Mazuy and Varda were at rue Daguerre when Varda received a letter from the Légion d'honneur, a national award bestowed on military, political, and cultural figures. She was invited to become a *chevalier*, the first of five ranks in the national order of merit. "Varda took a red pen to the invitation," recalled Mazuy, and wrote back, "I want to trade the Légion d'honneur for money for my new film."

Soon after, Varda learned that she had received a $1.4 million grant from Jack Lang, minister of culture in the administration of François Mittérrand, the Fifth Republic's first socialist president. Mazuy postulated that perhaps it was through the good offices of Danielle Mittérrand, the president's wife, that Lang had learned of Varda's informal funding request.

Happily for Varda, Lang believed that cinema was an art as well as an industry. He had discretionary funds for filmmakers, domestic and foreign, whose work he deemed significant. While it may be incongruous for a socialist minister of culture to be a committee of one giving direct grants to moviemakers, the films Lang supported proved to be noteworthy. They also included Andrzej Wajda's *Danton*, Robert Bresson's *L'argent*, and Claude Lanzmann's *Shoah*.

Like *Citizen Kane*, *Vagabond* begins with the discovery of a dead person, then proceeds to interview those who encountered the deceased before his or her end. Varda likened this approach to a jigsaw puzzle with missing pieces. The intentional gaps in the puzzle oblige the viewer to fill them in. In interviews, she cited the influence of Nathalie Sarraute.

Varda had spoken of how Sarraute's *The Use of Speech* had helped her shape the terse dialogue of *Documenteur*. She also claimed a more direct connection between Sarraute's influence and her own approach to *Vagabond*. Sarraute dispenses with character, plot, and time in order to magnify the texture of an emotion rather than tell a story. When interviewer Fabian Gastellier asked why Varda so admired Sarraute, the filmmaker said, "Because she talks about what we don't want to say, just like that, between two words. Because she's a woman of impulses. Because she's a literary rebel. Like Mona, Nathalie Sarraute walks alone."

The interviewees who encountered Mona try to grasp her, but

default to their own value judgments. To a garage mechanic, she is a slut. To a teenage girl, she is the embodiment of freedom. To a one-time philosophy professor who is now a shepherd, Mona is not wandering but "withering." To the female agronomist, she is a woman wielding her own power and living the life she wants. To a Tunisian vineyard worker, she is a helpmeet and lover. To a male vagabond who wants to pimp her, Mona is a "good fuck." The viewer considering these verdicts will note that men largely see Mona in sexual terms and women in terms of her independence and strength.

Those who encounter this human Rorschach blot on the road or in the movie theater project onto her their different interpretations, which makes Mona even more enigmatic. We don't learn many facts about her. Mostly, we learn the contradictory emotions she provokes in others. Varda's withholding of Mona's biography and of showing her in close-up has the effect of making viewers lean into her movie.

When the ten-week shoot of *Vagabond* began in March 1985, Varda lacked a conventional script. She had twenty-five pages in hand, a collage of locations and shots annotated with fragments of dialogue that she had written, or overheard, during preproduction. To achieve the immediacy she had enjoyed while making *7p.*, Varda rose every morning to write the day's dialogue, read it aloud to her assistant, edit if necessary, and photocopy it for the actors. That way, the professionals could not over-rehearse their lines and the nonactors would not feel expected to memorize them too far beforehand. Varda's idea of a script differed radically from the Hollywood definition. Her screenplay for *Vagabond* united notes on story, dialogue, sound, music, points of view, and edits. In other words, it was a broad-stroke map of the narrative, with a minimum of dialogue. More often than not, she found the story's fine grain in the moment or in the edit. While Varda had spoken of *cinécriture* (film writing) for years, *Vagabond* is the first of her films to carry the credit *"Cinécrit et réalisé par Agnès Varda."* While she often worked to engage the heart, the mind, and all five senses, in this respect *Vagabond* is the summit of her achievement as a filmmaker.

Five weeks into the shoot, she and Mazuy assembled a preliminary cut. Varda was happy with the acting and cinematography, but the footage lacked the feel of the road. Where was the thud of Mona's boots on the frozen ground? Where was the endlessly unspooling panorama Mona trudged through? To heighten *Vagabond*'s rhythms, texture, and visuals, Varda filmed Bonnaire walking, walking, walking in different geographical contexts, with the camera mounted on dolly track and moving laterally from right to left. This implied, as Kelley Conway put it, "that walking is the central, defining fact of Mona's life, more fundamental than her interactions with people." The camera movement is counter to the way most languages are read, subliminally suggesting that Mona moves against the prevailing tide. The dissonant strings of the score by Joanna Bruzdowicz underline Mona's abrasiveness and refusal of social norms, such as regular bathing. While many in the audience are unaware of the ways in which the film's form conveys its content, they are nonetheless unsettled while watching Mona's journey.

Bonnaire remembered that when Varda asked her to play Mona, she explained, "[Mona] smells, she's contemptuous, and she never says thank you." The seventeen-year-old had everything she needed to know about her enigmatic character. While the story revolves around Mona, initially the camera keeps its distance. It is as if Varda wants to suggest that Mona is a rare species that may be observed but not disturbed.

During the shoot, Arhab bunked with the cast and crew in a dormitory donated to the production by the city of Nîmes. Varda offered her a paid job, answering the phone and taking messages, but the arrangement soon fell apart when the director discovered her dozing in a sleeping bag in the production office. Varda suspected that the drifter, conditioned to constant movement on the road, found the repetitive rhythm of filmmaking like being stuck in time, and wasn't surprised that her muse decamped for the Pyrenees before production's end. But not before she had a chance to appear in a cameo in the film, with her nimbus of curls and large, probing eyes, talking to an elderly man on a train station bench.

Production wrapped on May 8, the same day that the Cannes Film Festival began. Varda hoped to edit the film quickly and show it to Unifrance, which was deliberating on which French films to suggest to the Venice festival for its September slate. The organization tasked with raising the profile of French film internationally did not include *Vagabond* on its nomination list. Was there no end to the roadblocks for Varda's road movie?

Varda sidestepped protocol and directly asked the Venice organizers to consider her film. It was accepted for official competition. But on the eve of Venice, it was still without a distributor. Swallowing her pride, Varda phoned Marin Karmitz, who twenty-three years earlier had worked as her assistant director on *Cléo*. Now he was the principal of MK2, a thriving production company and theater chain. She didn't make a blunt appeal that he distribute *Vagabond*, instead telling him, "You should probably take [*Vagabond*] before I give a press conference and say that no one in France wanted it."

In the end, the astonishing success of *Vagabond* made up for all the setbacks. The production brought to Venice 1,000 bottles of wine from the Gard (the French region where *Vagabond* was filmed) to share with the audience after its first screening. Cast and crew mingled with festivalgoers, drinking à la Mona, out on the street. As Varda raised a glass to toast Bonnaire and Méril, standing nearby were Danielle Mittérrand and Jack Lang. A young man sitting astride his Vespa scooted over to Varda and asked her in Italian, "Did you really make this film? I thought [the director] was young." Varda was fifty-seven. This would not be the first time her later films appealed to those a fraction of her age.

Vagabond won first prize, the Golden Lion, at Venice. As Varda accepted the award, the moment was made even sweeter by the sight of her friend Federico Fellini cheering her on from the audience. He wasn't alone. According to the *New York Times*, "The choice for the top prize was popular among film critics here and won thunderous applause when it was announced this afternoon. The critics were nearly unanimous in their praise of the Belgian-born director's success in offering a sympathetic view of an outcast without romanticizing her lot."

After *Vagabond*'s warm reception at Venice, MK2 formalized a distribution agreement. Varda had a hand in creating the poster. At its center was an image of the unsmiling and scruffy hitchhiker walking purposefully down the middle of a country road. In handwritten script: "She's cute, she stinks, and she doesn't say thank you. Would you offer her a ride in your car?" In France alone, the film had over one million admissions, at the time the strongest domestic box office for a Varda film. For the first time since *Cléo*, she had both a critical and commercial success.

In early 1986, the César Award nominations were announced. *Vagabond* received four: best film, best actress, best supporting actress, and best director. At the February ceremony, Bonnaire won the prize for lead actress. Over the past year, the script of *Vagabond* had been denied a CNC advance and the finished film was rejected by the makers of Unifrance's film festival shortlist, yet still the film won the top award at Venice and a César for Bonnaire. Varda was indefatigable.

Bonnaire, who had made two well-received films before *Vagabond*, graciously credited Varda with making her into an actress. At the Cinémathèque française memorial to Varda after her death, Bonnaire directly addressed the filmmaker. "When I met you, I was a flower, maybe a flower of the season," she said. "And when we made a beautiful film together, I became a tree."

12

THE RESPONSE TO *VAGABOND* was a boost for Varda. Soon after, she received a commission from the Cinémathèque française to make a short film in celebration of its fiftieth anniversary. The three-minute short, *You've Got Beautiful Stairs, You Know*, reminded a younger generation of the action seen, the fun to be had, and the tears shed in the Cinémathèque's auditorium at the Palais de Chaillot, which was accessed by a graceful flight of stairs. With an eye on the steps that countless cinephiles, still in thrall to the film they'd just seen, had descended, Varda compiled a clever montage of memorable stairway scenes, from the criminal mastermind Fantômas blowing up his adversary in *Juve contre Fantômas* (1914), to the handsome jewel thief in *Pépé le Moko* (1937) threading down the human anthill that is the Casbah in Algiers, to the Odessa Steps skirmish in *Battleship Potemkin* (1925), on through clips from *Citizen Kane* (1941), *Cover Girl* (1944), *Contempt* (1963), *Ran* (1983), and more, ending with Isabelle Adjani in *The Story of Adele H* (1975) scaling the Everest of unrequited love as she races up a staircase.

Adjani narrated the short and appears in its final shot as a movie lover waiting for a friend at the bottom of the Cinémathèque stairs. While it may be Varda's least significant (and briefest) work, the clip choices and editing rhythm are irresistible. And there are almost as many actresses depicted as actors.

The film is further evidence that when Varda looked at the world, or through the camera lens, she saw women. As late as 1991, the U.S. Screen Actors Guild reported that two out of every three people on-screen in Hollywood movies were men. This was never the case in Varda's films. The short has added significance as one of the five films Varda would make about film. At its end, the director signs off with a personal endorsement: "Come to the Cinémathèque and you won't be disappointed.... Take it from Agnès Varda." *You've Got Beautiful Stairs* is an early instance of the filmmaker assuming the persona of wise elder. Still only fifty-eight, she had grown more comfortable with narrating and/or appearing in her own movies. Rooted in realism and blessed with a poetic imagination, her on-screen presence had the effect of making her shifts between the imaginary and the documentary more fluid.

WHILE FOR most of the 1980s Varda and Demy lived apart, they occasionally entertained as a couple and traveled together. Lisa Blok-Linson remembers helping them host a Sunday brunch in 1980 at Eastwind in Venice, where Varda and Mathieu lived after the couple separated. In that the invited guests—Greek director Costa-Gavras, B-movie king Roger Corman—were both European and American, it was like their informal salons on North Alpine. They made a formidable pair. Gerry Ayres observed, "Jacques enjoyed his partnership with Agnès, loved the volume they displaced in any room they entered."

In 1986, the couple received an invitation to show their films in Cairo. Mathieu, almost fourteen, accompanied them. After photographing Mathieu astride a camel, the celebrated Egyptian filmmaker Youssef Chahine told the visitors how best to "do" the sights. Which is how the family found themselves in Luxor, "crossing the Nile on these pontoon-ferryboats, with our bikes," Varda recalled. Sometimes they pedaled from tomb to tomb. Then they discovered it was easier to climb the hills between burial sites than to bike the paths in the scorching sun. Varda remembered that she and Demy improvised a turban for Mathieu. Still, so stifling was the heat that there came a point when she didn't know whether they were looking at the tomb of King Tutankhamun or Thutmose II. They retired to a shaded patio, where they drank tea and nibbled at bread and onions. Drunk from the heat, Varda fell asleep on the bench. Recalling the day, she wrote, "A slightly grotesque happiness passed between us."

Vagabond prompted correspondence from friends and filmgoers profoundly moved by the chronicle of Mona. This included a hastily scribbled note, a scrawled fan letter from Jane Birkin, the celebrated singer and actress. Because it was illegible, Varda invited the actress to rue Daguerre to decipher it. Its text didn't matter as much as its subtext: Birkin wanted to work with Varda.

As the two chatted in the kitchen, the conversation turned to their children. Rosalie was twenty-eight and Mathieu fourteen. Birkin also had children by different fathers. Her eldest, Kate, whose father was composer John Barry, was nineteen; Charlotte Gainsbourg, whose father was Serge Gainsbourg, was sixteen; Lou Doillon, whose father was director Jacques Doillon, was four. The mothers made a date to go to Parc de Sceaux. Birkin complained that she was about to turn forty. Varda told her not to be silly. Their budding friendship spawned two companion films released in 1988: *Jane B. by Agnès V.* is a portfolio of Birkin posing as various figures in painting and in history; *Kung Fu Master* is a fiction based on an idea by Birkin, starring her as a fortyish mother erotically fixated on a fifteen-year-old boy.

For the first, Varda proposed to Birkin that they would make the opposite of those tributes to deceased actresses that excerpt scenes from their films and interviews. Instead, they would "show excerpts from films you haven't made, films we've made up, and we'll fabricate some interviews." While the resulting mash-up of an imaginary actress's demo reel and a real artist's varied portraits of her muse are occasionally diverting, it's like watching a random collection of screen tests. A willowy androgyne with a whispery voice, ethereal presence, and legs long as the Seine, Birkin in tableaux arranged by Varda is a lovely woman who embodies Joan of Arc, the Virgin Mary, and Titian's *Venus of Urbino*. But none give Birkin the scope to communicate a feeling, a mood, or an inner life. A few weeks into the production of *Jane B.*, Birkin handed Varda a ten-page treatment that became the basis of their subsequent collaboration, one that gives the actress the opportunity to sustain a performance.

In *Kung Fu Master*, Birkin plays Mary-Jane, single mother of fifteen-year-old Lucy (Charlotte Gainsbourg) and four-year-old Lou (Lou Doillon), the actress's real-life daughters. As Mary-Jane ponders Lucy's blossoming sexuality and how to talk about it with her, she becomes inappropriately attracted to her daughter's friend Julien (fifteen-year-old Mathieu Demy), and he to her. The film takes its title from Julien's favorite video game, in which the goal is to rescue a damsel in distress.

Mary-Jane narrates the story about the boy, whom she first encounters after he has drunk too much pilfered vodka at Lucy's party. She holds Julien's head over the toilet and in thanks, Julien returns the next day to give her a bouquet of daffodils, kissing her hand like a suitor in a nineteenth-century French novel. Given that the age of consent in France at the time was fifteen, Mary-Jane's affair with Julien would not have been prosecuted as a crime. Yet, barely legal or not, it's difficult to overlook how wildly inappropriate the film seems to contemporary eyes. However, it focuses on the mutual romantic longing between Mary-Jane and Julien rather than sex. Moreover, there are other dramas unfolding on-screen and off. The characters worry about AIDS and encounter activists on the street. Behind the scenes, it is a film about two mothers of teenagers creating a psychodramatic structure that might prompt conversations with their children. The conversation between Birkin and Gainsbourg takes place on-screen; that between Varda and Mathieu happens off-screen, in the creation of Julien, charming and chivalrous with females and macho with his male friends.

Mathieu Demy and Charlotte Gainsbourg are both genuinely affecting in the film. And both found the experience invasive. Demy later recalled, "At the time, I was like, 'I'm in a story with a girl who could be my grandmother. But, if it can make my mother happy . . .'" When he was younger, acting was a game. In this film, he was surprised by the "violence of communicating personal emotions." For a time, he cooled on acting and didn't open scripts sent to him by interested filmmakers.

For Gainsbourg, the experience was invasive in the literal as well as the emotional sense. "[Varda] sort of camped in our living room and there was a whole cinema crew that lived with us for a year . . . Being a teenager, I wanted to shut myself off in my room." Gainsbourg was quick to add how much she loved Varda, "but I didn't have that awareness of what I was doing."

Both of Varda's Birkin films opened in Paris to disappointing box office. Despite a sympathetic review from Roger Ebert in the *Chicago Sun-Times, Kung Fu Master* failed to win wide distribution in the United States.

TWO MONTHS after the release of *Kung Fu Master*, Demy began production on what would be his final film, *Three Seats for the 26th.* The musical melodrama with a score by Michel Legrand is a quasi-documentary of its star, Yves Montand. Its making was a blended-family effort: Rosalie designed the costumes, Mathieu and his cousin Katy Varda have roles, as does Antoine Bourseiller, Rosalie's biological father. Montand described the film as an "Oedipal wink." Its release, too, was a disappointment.

The box office results coincided with crushing personal news: Demy had AIDS. As did David Bombyk, who would die in January 1989, one of the nearly 22,000 HIV-related deaths in the U.S. that year, according to the Centers for Disease Control. In France, the figure was 2,064, according to Santé Publique France, the CDC's French counterpart. During this first decade of AIDS awareness, to be HIV-positive was in most cases a death sentence. It would be some time before doctors spoke of "living with AIDS." Demy returned to rue Daguerre to live with Varda. "For the next two years, his life would be a long autumn," wrote Legrand.

At first, Demy self-medicated with work, polishing his script of *Kobi the Bumper-Car*, a story set in the world of amusement parks. Though the screenplay received a CNC advance, Demy declined to direct it due to illness. He would paint, and he would write his memoirs. He lunched frequently with Legrand. "He's sick, but I didn't know it," remembered the composer. "When I found out, I desperately refused to admit the seriousness of his condition."

In March 1989, Demy, Varda, and Mathieu won a trifecta of sorts. All three were invited to speak at the Hong Kong Film Festival: Demy would introduce *Three Seats for the 26th*; Varda would introduce *Kung Fu Master*; and Mathieu, who was in both, would speak about them. "We all went together, and my son was so excited," Varda told a reporter for the *South China Morning Post*. She had not been in Hong Kong since her 1957 trip to China.

While the filmmakers were not gamblers, they were casino enthusiasts. Demy had filmed *Bay of Angels* at Monte Carlo, and Varda had filmed a scene for *Jane B.* at the Knokke casino in Belgium. Varda liked to recount the story of their first visit to Las Vegas with "a shady producer and his girlfriend," unexpectedly winning "kilos of coins" at a wonky slot machine. So they were excited, Mathieu especially, to visit the storied casino in Macau, across the Pearl River from Hong Kong. Alas, even with his parents as chaperones, the sixteen-year-old was not permitted to enter. Nonetheless, the trio enjoyed the Macau adventure and the return to Hong Kong's Kowloon district to show and discuss their films.

When they came back home, Varda recalled, "Jacques was tired, and he began talking more than usual about his childhood." And once he started writing about it, "it was like a pump being primed; the more he wrote, the more he [remembered]."

During his last two years, Demy often went to the hospital for tests or observation. When home, he wrote. Before dinner, he showed Varda the day's writing, which they discussed over dinner. Sharing the pages became their preprandial ritual. Reading his imagistic recollections, Varda told him it was a screenplay awaiting a director. When she proposed that he film, rather than write, a memoir, Demy told her that he wasn't up to the task. "You should make it," he said. "I know, I know," she replied. But how? It seemed to take all the energy that she and Demy possessed to deal with his health. Yet, as *La Pointe Courte* had enabled her to process the decline and death of her friend Pierre Fournier while distracting him during its making, *Jacquot de Nantes* was a means of doing the same for Demy.

A caregiver to someone terminally ill knows the cognitive dissonance of feigning cheer while facing loss, of wielding hope against fears of the worst, and the unbearable weight of physical and mental fatigue. Nonetheless, during Demy's final year, Varda poured everything from her heart and his memory into *Jacquot de Nantes*. She made it, this first of three films celebrating his artistic legacy, to keep both hope, and him, alive.

When Varda commenced production in April 1990, *Jacquot's* working title was "Evocations of a Vocation." It told the story of a movie-mad kid from the provinces, son of a hairdresser and a car mechanic, who live in an apartment above the father's garage before and during World War II. This boy decides he wants to be an artist and teaches himself how to make animated films. Despite his father's insistence that the boy train as a mechanic, a professional filmmaker recommends that the young animator go to film school in Paris and arranges for a scholarship. When Varda's shoot began, Demy was still writing his memoirs.

While rereading Demy's pages, Varda envisioned it as a 1940s period film. She wanted to shoot in black-and-white—but with a twist. Should Jacquot experience a moment that prefigured a scene from a Demy movie, she would intercut a passage from that film, often in color, underscoring the connection between his life and his art. Thus, a black-and-white scene of young Jacques leaving his father's garage is intercut with a color sequence of Guy (Nino Castelnuovo) in *The Umbrellas of Cherbourg* leaving his employer's garage. A scene of young Jacques watching his hairdresser mother style a client's hair is intercut with one of Irene (Catherine Deneuve) doing the same in *A Slightly Pregnant Man*. One need not be familiar with Demy's filmography to recognize how an artist mines his life for his work. Varda described the insertion of movie clips as "little flashes, like premonitions, as if [Demy] had found, in his childhood, hints of the most beautiful . . . scenes he would later make as a filmmaker." Neither biopic nor hagiography, *Jacquot de Nantes* is an affectionate portrait of the artist as a young man, showing how humble entertainments, like puppet shows, inspire a youth to create his own storytelling forms. It also provided Varda a way of expressing her love for, and saying goodbye to, Demy.

From financing to hiring of actors and crew, Demy left the production of the film to Varda. His involvement was to supply the narrative details; hers was to write the dialogue and direct. He insisted that it was *her* film. She began and ended it with footage of Demy off the shore of their beloved Noirmoutier.

"The making of this film became their last shared act," observed Kelley Conway. "In fact, one of their only artistic collaborations, as if Demy and Varda had instinctively understood the incompatibility of their styles and missions for all those years while retaining the greatest esteem for what the other achieved."

Funding for the film came from multiple sources, including the CNC, the Ministry of Culture, and various municipal, regional, and departmental councils. The shoot took fifteen weeks spread over three separate time frames, between April and October 1990. Varda was able to shoot scenes in the Demys' former apartment and garage in Nantes while its new owners were on vacation.

During a break in production, Varda wrote, "Jacques hasn't been to the cinema for months. But we went to see Godard's *New Wave*. [We are] happy. During the film and after. We talk about it a lot afterward . . . about Jean-Luc, his cinema, the path he takes to tell the alliance (somewhat painful) between a man and a woman." Godard's film, something of a metaphor for the Old Wave and the New, was the last one Demy saw.

Varda was a professed agnostic about psychology and psychotherapy, but after *Jacquot de Nantes*, she noted the salutary effects of keeping busy at such a fraught time. As did Demy. Occasionally he would come to the set as she shot the story of the movie-mad child becoming father to the man. She would show him a little boy who looked like him, an actress cast as his mother who looked like her, and an actor playing his father who resembled him. Photos of Demy on the set show him smiling, with a faraway look in his eyes.

Before Demy left Nantes for Paris, he was able to watch Varda's footage at the editing table alongside film editor Marie-Josée Audiard. Audiard reported back to Varda that frequently he smiled in remembrance and recognition. He was, however, critical of one scene: when eight-year-old Jacquot visited his grandfather's grave, the boy did not doff his beret in deference to the dead. Varda acknowledged the gaffe. But given the state of Demy's health and the crowded shooting schedule, she wasn't sure if there was time to reshoot it.

One August weekend, Demy and Varda went to Noirmoutier. On Sunday, Varda proposed to Demy that they go to the shore, just the two of them and the movie camera. She wanted footage of Demy on his beach towel, looking out at the Atlantic as it splashed on the sand. When her camera came in for a close-up of his face, she trembled. Although he smiled weakly and was physically there, he was on his way to a place where she could not follow.

On October 15, Mathieu's eighteenth birthday, Varda was still in

Nantes when she received news that her good friend Delphine Seyrig had died of cancer. Production wrapped the following day, and Varda returned to Demy at rue Daguerre.

As Michel Legrand told it, on the evening of October 27, he was at a play. At intermission, a publicist approached him and quietly asked if he had heard that Demy had died. Legrand raced to rue Daguerre. When he rang the doorbell, Varda greeted him and they fell into each other's arms. Legrand was inconsolable, likening his sorrow to the end of *The Umbrellas of Cherbourg*, when the lovers go their separate ways.

On the day of Demy's funeral, *Le Monde* and other Paris newspapers reported that the fifty-nine-year-old had died of *congestion cérébrale*—a stroke. The *New York Times* attributed the cause of death to a brain hemorrhage due to leukemia. Varda suppressed the truth, she would admit twenty-eight years later, because that's what Demy wanted. "He thought he could hide it. And it took a lot of energy to hide it." Not only for Demy, but for his family and friends.

He was buried at Montparnasse cemetery on October 30, 1990, his plot within view of an old mill that reminded close friends of the family retreat in Noirmoutier. As mementos of the director's life and work, Varda thoughtfully gave to the attendees, who included Anouk Aimée, Catherine Deneuve, and Michel Piccoli, cards onto which were stapled 35mm frames from *The Umbrellas of Cherbourg*.

In late November, Varda had completed an essay about Demy's final months for *Cahiers du cinéma* when her mother, who had dementia, passed away. In six weeks she had lost a close friend, a husband, and a mother. Yet she pressed on through the release of *Jacquot*.

Reid Rosefelt, an American publicist, worked with Varda on the film's U.S. run. "We had the same idea about how to distribute it," he said. Namely, "If you don't keep talking about the departed, they really die."

In January 1991, before the release of *Jacquot*, Varda returned to Nantes to reshoot the graveyard scene Demy had criticized. This time, when young Jacques approaches his grandfather's grave, his mother puts a beret on his head and smiles at him.

THE TRIBUTES and memorials to Demy lasted for years, as did Varda's grief.

On June 5, 1992—which would have been Demy's sixty-first birthday—Mag Bodard, Hélène Demy, Catherine Deneuve, Michel Legrand, and Varda flew to Rochefort for the twenty-fifth anniversary of *The Young Girls of Rochefort*. The musical starring Deneuve, her late sister Françoise Dorléac, Danielle Darrieux, Gene Kelly, and Michel Piccoli was a milestone in the city's history. On that day, Cherbourg dedicated a thoroughfare to Jacques Demy.

During the film's production in 1966, Varda had shot behind-the-scenes footage. While attending the anniversary celebration, she shot more. For the documentary *The Young Girls Turn 25* (1993), she intercut her 1966 footage with extracts from the film itself, adding new sequences shot in 1992. Among them was a speech by Legrand, after Hélène Demy had rechristened the street for her elder brother. "Jacques was like a brother to me," Legrand said. "Long ago, I dedicated much more than a street to him: it was a main artery, the artery leading to my heart."

The Young Girls Turn 25 premiered at Cannes in 1993. Five days later, it was broadcast on French television. While not as accomplished a film as *Jacquot*, it stokes the appetite to see the original film. In the documentary, Varda has the last word, expressing a sentiment about the original film and about Demy himself: "The memory of happiness is also happiness."

Unsurprisingly, the process of preserving Demy's legacy made Varda start to think about her own. Unlike out-of-print books or rare albums, which are sometimes available at a library or in a book or record store, out-of-circulation films, and their makers, often get forgotten. The work of cinema's female pioneers Alice Guy-Blaché and Lois Weber went missing after 1920. Few recognized that film had residual value. Guy-Blaché's early films with sound, color, and multiracial casts, and Weber's socially conscious movies about class inequality and reproductive rights, so radical in their day, were neglected for decades.

"When Alice Guy-Blaché died in 1968, she thought three of her films were extant but couldn't locate any. In the early 1990s, some 40 were known," says Joan Simon, curator of the 2009 retrospective of Guy-Blaché's fims at the Whitney Museum of American Art in New York. "By the time of the retrospective, 130 of her movies were extant—we screened 90 over a three-month period." Today, of the estimated 1,000 films credited to Guy-Blaché, 150—just 15 percent of her work—have been identified.

While assembling *Jacquot de Nantes*, Varda found that many Demy films from which she sought extracts were in dismal condition. The fiery reds of *The Umbrellas of Cherbourg* had faded to Pepto-Bismol pink. Prints of *Lola* had disfiguring scratches. Not only were the films themselves in less than optimal condition, Demy's papers and other archival materials were in disarray.

When Demy died, said Bernard Bastide, Varda's archivist from 1991 to 1999, Varda was "compelled to put things in order," as he delicately put it, "before leaving" herself. In making certain that Demy was properly memorialized, she had to locate negatives of his films, check for fading and decomposition, and, if necessary, supervise their restoration.

During this time, Varda was approached by producer-director Claude Berri, flush with profits from *Jean de Florette* (1986), who asked her to write an adaptation of Balzac's *Père Goriot*. She repeated her mantra: she didn't believe in adapting novels. Besides, there were too many more pressing items on her to-do list.

She negotiated for the rights to Demy's and her own films, preserved them, and said yes to almost everything else that came her way. She bought the bicycle store across the street from her building, converting it into a storefront editing room. Passersby stopped to watch her edit as they would look in at other artisans on the block at their ovens and sewing machines. Soon she would stock Ciné-Tamaris videotapes, and later DVDs, there.

She signed on to write her memoirs and to make two documentaries, *The World of Jacques Demy* and another about cinema's hundredth birthday. She committed to a book about the making of *Vagabond*. In dedicating herself to these simultaneous ventures, she validated Margaret Mead's claim that "there is no greater power in the world than the zest of a postmenopausal woman."

While the *Vagabond* volume did not materialize, the memoir, *Varda par Agnès*, was published in 1994. In 1995, both *The World of Jacques Demy* and *A Hundred and One Nights*, a fantasy about a century of film, were released. That year, she also completed the preservation of *The Umbrellas of Cherbourg* and *The Young Girls of Rochefort*.

By the time *Varda par Agnès*, more of a self-portrait than an autobiography, was published, she had been making movies for four decades. An unsigned review in *Le Monde* hailed it as "seriously joking and joyfully precise." Its collage form combined diary, scrapbook, and photo album without concession to chronology except for the list of her films. The book mapped Varda's first sixty-six years, divulging the absolute minimum of personal information most entertainingly. *Le Monde* credited her with having "opened most of the paths of modern cinema" by making *La Pointe Courte* "with no other qualification or professional authorization than an imperial nerve and a talent ready to leap."

The publication of *Varda par Agnès* was timed to coincide with Varda's first complete film retrospective at the Cinémathèque française in March 1995.

Enthusiasm greeted *The World of Jacques Demy* when it opened in France that September. It combines television interviews with its subject and testimonials from actors and fans. The love for Demy and his work is palpable, evoking the panorama of his career while distilling the prismatic color and jazzy rhythms of the "Demy-monde." For lay viewers, it is a graceful introduction to the Demy filmography. To those for whom he is a film god, it is a holy artifact.

Alas, what Varda intended as a buoyant tribute to film's first century, *A Hundred and One Nights*, landed with a thud. The conceit of her star-studded story is that at the age of one hundred, Simon Cinéma (Michel Piccoli), the human embodiment of movies, is losing his memory. So he hires a comely film student (Julie Gayet) as a Scheherazade to tell him stories of his celebrated life and times, which are illustrated by film clips, gossipy digressions, and a constellation of film stars paying their respects. They include Jean-Paul Belmondo, Sandrine Bonnaire, Catherine Deneuve, Alain Delon, Robert De Niro, Gérard Depardieu, Jeanne Moreau, Marcello Mastroianni, and Hanna Schygulla. The cluttered and clumsy film, set in what resembles an upscale movie nostalgia store, is one hundred minutes of nonstop verbal and visual double-entendres interrupted by celebrity cameos. It is occasionally funny, but the cumulative effect is one of exhaustion, with Varda as the pilot of a breakneck comedy on the order of *Airplane!* but without as many laughs.

Ordinarily sympathetic to Varda's work, *Le Monde* critic Jean-Michel Frodon took the film to task. "The evocations of great moments in film history," he wrote, become "a laborious game of Trivial Pursuit." More to the point, he despairs, "Here, she seeks a 'Fellinian' phantasmagoria that is not her style and that soon turns into dreamy, commemorative bric-a-brac." Even so, there are moments to treasure in the misfire. One is a my-death-was-bloodier-than-yours game between Piccoli and Depardieu, to determine who suffered the most horrific end in movies. It plays like a diabolical critique of movie violence. Another is a scene in which Bonnaire, clad as grubby Mona from *Vagabond*, tramps up to Monsieur Cinéma's villa where she morphs, magically, into the Beauty of Jean Cocteau's *Beauty and the Beast*. The film received a few positive reviews, but none persuasive enough to have an impact at the box office.

Cinema's centenary was taken seriously in France, and Frodon, among others, felt provoked, reacting as if *A Hundred and One Nights* was a crime against the Republic. Some (incorrectly) assumed that *A Hundred and One Nights* had been made with public money and were up in arms. It was, in fact, a commission from the First Century Association, though the budget was supplemented by the CNC with a loan that Varda had to repay.

Apart from *A Hundred and One Nights*, Varda's films of the 1990s were well received. She was gratified, she said to me in 1998, that "there never have been so many women making films." In 1993, Jane Campion, the New Zealand–born director of *The Piano*, was the first woman to win the Palme d'or at Cannes (she shared the prize with Chen Kaige and *Farewell My Concubine*) and the second to be nominated for best director at the Academy Awards. In 1995, the Dutch filmmaker Marleen Gorris was the first female director of a best foreign language film winner, *Antonia's Line*. In France, Claire Denis, Anne Fontaine, Agnès Jaoui, and Patricia Mazuy (who had worked as an editor on *Vagabond*) were among the next generation's female directors. In the United States, there were Kathryn Bigelow, Sofia Coppola, Julie Dash, Nora Ephron, Nancy Meyers, and Gina Prince-Bythewood, among others. In 1998, when Varda turned seventy, women directed 9 percent of the top 250 films at the U.S. box office—a substantial rise from 1954, when Varda made her first film and women made less than half of one percent of films released internationally.

13

AFTER SIX YEARS AND three films memorializing Demy and one commemorating film history, Varda may have been tired of looking backward. She may have been tired, period.

Possibly still working through the grief that had fueled her since Demy's diagnosis and death, perhaps dispirited by the reception of *A Hundred and One Nights*, she needed a change of scene. Noirmoutier would remind her of Demy.

In 1996, she announced that she would take a break from film-making, joking that she was moving to the south of France to take care of trees. For a woman possessed of a work ethic so extreme that it was more properly a work imperative, she was likely doing more than just tending the three-hundred-year-old cedar at the inn she received in a transaction with her son-in-law, Dominique Vignet.

The hostelry was in Provence, near Bonnieux, famed for its lavender, sunflowers, stone villages, and stunning red rock formations. Now, along with the onetime windmill in Noirmoutier and the former framing shop on rue Daguerre, she had a new property to repurpose as she considered a new direction for herself. Varda christened it La Maison de L'Aiguebrun, after the stream responsible for the lush greenery that surrounded it. During this break from directing, Varda enjoyed a new creative challenge: she planned the design of each guest room to evoke the décor of a different film. In 1998, she also hired a professional manager and continued to attend to Demy's legacy, which proved to be forward-thinking.

Prior to Demy's death in 1990, Bruce Goldstein, programmer of repertory films at Film Forum in New York, visited rue Daguerre to ask Demy if he knew of a 35mm print of *The Umbrellas of Cherbourg* that had not faded. He did not. He also recognized that the film needed restoration. In 1988, he and Varda, realizing that they had neither prints nor ancillary items from their films (e.g., scripts, photos, press kits) had scoured flea markets and film labs, without much luck. Nonetheless, Goldstein was horrified to learn that Demy and Varda didn't know where the negative was.

After Demy died, Varda found the negative and supervised its restoration. When the restored *Umbrellas* played at Film Forum in 1996, attendance was strong, at 90 percent capacity, reported Henri Béhar in *Le Monde*. He also noted that the median age of the crowd was between twenty-eight and thirty-five—roughly the same age as the thirty-two-year-old film. It costs a lot to restore a film, and the revival of *Umbrellas* was proof that classic films could make money in rerelease.

While Demy's films of the 1960s—and even the 1980s—were known in the United States, Varda's movies were mostly seen at North American film festivals. Laurence Kardish, then the curator of film and coordinator of film exhibitions at New York's Museum of Modern Art, sought to rectify that, inviting Varda to participate in a career retrospective.

"Agnès came to New York, sat for many interviews, and was applauded by full houses at our large theater," he remembered. At the retrospective's end, Kardish asked her if she would consider showing her future films at MoMA, and let the museum acquire them. "She replied that she was sixty-nine, and while she intended to remain very active, she could no longer afford to use film either physically or financially."

Not only was the MoMA retrospective an indication of Varda's growing profile in the United States, it may very well have boosted interest in her films licensed for video in North America. Now a producer, Marie Therese Guirgis was in 1999 a cinephile just out of college working at Fox Lorber, a U.S. DVD distributor, when she was introduced to Varda by phone. Because some of her colleagues found dealing with the filmmaker exhausting, Guirgis, who spoke French, became the company's designated "Varda whisperer."

"Initially, it was intimidating," recalled Guirgis. "But I was impressed that she was so on top of the financial life and business of her films as well as those of Jacques." Most of the French directors the DVD rep had met "were interested in staying at fancy hotels and eating in fancy restaurants," said Guirgis. Not Varda, "In practice, she was opposed to excess and waste."

What most impressed the American was that "Varda knew how to read a royalty report. She would find mistakes and call—and she was almost always right." Varda showed Guirgis how to be an artist *and* a businesswoman. "To this day, I've never met another director— let alone one of her caliber—who understood the financials so well."

IN 1999, four years after the ignominy of *A Hundred and One Nights* and the beginning of Varda's break from filmmaking, Rosalie and Mathieu flew to Japan with their mother for another career retrospective, this one at the Kobe Documentary Film Festival. In a kiosk at Tokyo's Narita Airport, Mathieu marveled at a Sony digital camera new to the market. He urged his mother to buy one. She did. "And practiced with it throughout that summer," recalled Rosalie. "That's how she began to shoot *The Gleaners and I*."

Armed with the new camera, Varda would return to directing at a time of fervent debate among cinephiles about whether film was superior to digital video. In 1840, when French painter Paul Delaroche saw a daguerreotype, precursor of the photograph, he predicted, "From today, painting is dead!" Fortunately, it survived his obituary. Varda was in Cannes in 1998 when *The Celebration*, a film shot on digital video, won the Jury Prize. She would have heard the attendant "Is film dead?" discussions. They proceeded along the lines of prior artistic disputes, such as whether painters should trade their slow-drying oil for quick-drying acrylic paint, whether popular musicians should stay acoustic or go electric, and whether audiophiles should ditch their analog vinyl for digital CDs. Some clung to the old ways; others adapted to the new. Varda was one of the latter.

By 1999, American filmmakers like Martin Scorsese and Steven Spielberg told reporters that film offered superior depth of field (which it did) and greater consistency of light and color (ditto). A *Le Monde* survey in 2001 found French directors divided on the issue. Despite greater subtleties of resolution and color in film, Varda found good reasons to embrace video, and not only because digital cameras were lighter and cheaper. Digital cameras enabled her to get closer to her subjects without intimidating them with an apparatus that obscured her face. For a documentary filmmaker, this was a game changer.

The Arriflex 535-B was a popular film camera in the 1990s. While the body weighed a mere 17 pounds, when fully loaded with film and a lens it could weigh 38 pounds. By contrast, the Sony Mini DV DCR TRV900E, one of the two cameras she used to shoot *The Gleaners and I*, weighed less than 2 pounds—lighter than her first Rolleiflex still camera. Varda was seventy-one when she picked up her first Sony digital camera. Immediately she became an early adopter.

While the new equipment was instrumental in telling her twenty-first-century story about the impact of industrial farming on agriculture—and on food waste—she reminded interviewers that digital cameras were not magic; they were only tools. Still, the animated and engaged woman who appears on camera, narrates the film, and interviews the many subjects of her 2000 movie was nothing like the subdued filmmaker I had lunched with two years earlier at Cannes. When I first saw *Gleaners*, I thought the source of her renewed energy was that, after a decade of looking back, Varda was ready to live in the present.

The idea for *The Gleaners and I* came at her from converging directions, Varda told journalist Melissa Anderson. At her neighborhood outdoor market, Varda noticed modern-day gleaners, those who harvest things, often laboriously, bending to scoop up the discolored fruit and vegetables abandoned by vendors. Soon after, she was captivated by a TV program on the subject. What pushed her to begin and continue the film, she said, "was the discovery of the digital camera."

"This is the camera that would bring me back to the early short films I made in 1957 and 1958," she said, referring to *Ô saisons, ô châteaux* and *L'opéra-mouffe*. "I felt free at that time," she recalled of those days of cinematic experiment coinciding with her first pregnancy. In referencing the period prior to meeting Demy, she was not nostalgic for her youth; she was excited by the prospect of recapturing her youthful creative energy.

The Gleaners and I began as an idea for a four-part television series and emerged as a feature-length documentary. It would become her signature work and redefine her film career. It was the template for her unique essay films, in which she herself is the audience's guide, surveying a phenomenon—social problem, community, or geography—and digressing to include others, adjacent or not. Her outward-looking essay films are about serious subjects, yet with a lightness of touch and open-endedness that accepts contradictions and doesn't offer solutions. She shows the audience her findings and expects them to be more mindful, to arrive at their own conclusions. The movie combines her skill at portraiture, her love for landscape, and her journalistic skills as an interviewer with her talents as an essayist and commentator.

Varda had examined fishermen whose livelihoods were threatened by polluted waters in *La Pointe Courte*, the impoverished and hungry living on the fringes in *L'opéra-mouffe*, Black Panthers protesting police brutality and inequality, and the social dropout Mona of *Vagabond*, who depended on the kindness of strangers. *The Gleaners and I* continued Varda's advocacy for those not protected by a social safety net.

It is at once a documentary about food insecurity in the age of plenty, Old Testament directives about gleaning, sixteenth-century laws protecting the practice, and agriculture in the age of mechanical harvesting. Varda, narrator, guide, and resident art historian, playfully presents herself as an aging woman with liver spots on her hands and graying roots beneath a dye job. In other words, she is the human embodiment of the unconventionally shaped and spotted produce abandoned in the field. "The film suggests that our culture is too quick to reject the slightly bruised apples, misshapen potatoes ... and women who don't conform to certain norms," observed Kelley Conway.

As Varda conducts her reconnaissance of field, orchard, granary, and dumpster—likewise the Bible and law books—she finds gleaners and gleaning of different sorts. Consistent with her feature films, her subjects are not generic role models but flesh-and-blood characters.

There is Alain Fonteneau, an economist and ethicist (and, additionally, French tutor to new immigrants), who lives on "almost 100% salvage." He is appalled by agricultural waste. He disparages expiration dates, using his nose to discern the edible and the potable. He agreed to be interviewed, Fonteneau told Varda's assistant, if he could express his opinion that "waste is related to not knowing what to do with waste." In most cases, as Varda shows, gleaners know precisely what to do with it.

There are the rural hungry from nearby trailer camps, combing potato fields for what the mechanical harvester has left behind. Nearly half the tubers are too big or small to meet supermarket standards for the preferred round or ovoid spud. There are the urban hungry collecting broken eggs and yesterday's bread left at the stalls and in trash receptacles of neighborhood markets. And there is Édouard Loubet, a chef who gleans locally grown herbs for his Michelin-starred restaurant because he disdains the European Union crop of "sprigs picked green in Italy three weeks ago."

And then there are the artists and bricoleurs, including Varda herself. In the trash she finds, and repurposes, a clock without hands, enshrining it at rue Daguerre. "You don't see time passing," Varda remarks of the timepiece that, ironically, is now a found metaphor of timelessness. A Russian-born bricklayer shows Varda a "totem tower," a structure he has built with orphaned dolls. Another artist shows Varda how his work made from salvaged materials gives new life to the unwanted.

The link here is Varda, the filmmaker as gleaner of disparate facts and contexts that imagine ways to address problems of hunger and waste. Her warmth, curiosity, and contagious joy in human connection come shining through. And, while her inventory approach to its subject in *The Gleaners and I* follows the form of so many Varda documentaries, her on-camera presence makes it feel new, foregrounding her empathy, humanism, engagement, and wit.

Like Charlie Chaplin and Buster Keaton, Varda makes her presence felt both behind and in front of the camera lens. Her self-presentation as a small round figure with a slightly wrinkled face and mottled skin visually rhymes with the speckled, heart-shaped potatoes abandoned in the field because they are considered unsuitable for the supermarket. Rather than shame the grower who has wasted so much food without announcing its availability for gleaners, she gleans some potato hearts for personal use and alerts a food agency to their location and availability. The agency reaps more than 1,500 pounds of potatoes and distributes them. She does not scold, she does not virtue-signal; she simply shows how easy it is to mitigate waste and hunger.

These potatoes are the symbolic descendants of *Pomme de terre coeur* (Potato Heart), which Varda photographed in 1953. *The Gleaners* established the potato heart as Varda's vegetable avatar. In the U.S., the film contributed to the "waste not, want not" ethos gaining new traction with a generation unfamiliar with Varda's work. On college campuses, it was shown in both business schools and film schools. In France, wrote British scholar Ruth Cruickshank, the success of *The Gleaners and I* "coincided . . . with a convergence of concerns about the increasing impacts of global consumption."

Judging by its robust box office ($150,000 in the U.S., 120,000 admissions in France), the forty awards it won, and the correspondence Varda received, the response to *The Gleaners* was unprecedented in her directorial career. "I think she may have been surprised by its success," said Emily Russo, co-president of Zeitgeist Films, Varda's U.S. distributor. "To be honest, no one could have predicted it. At the time, foreign-language documentaries were not huge draws."

Richard Peña, then program director of the New York Film Festival, guessed at why *The Gleaners and I* struck a chord in the U.S. and internationally. "It really opened up the personal essay film. It was done so humbly, so simply, so sincerely, skillfully weaving together different things, so offhandedly and conversationally." It was different, he observes, from other documentaries, because it was a dialogue rather than a monologue. "It showed us rather than told us."

"Agnès had the quality of constantly changing and expanding," reflected Peña. "Some filmmakers find that their moment has passed. She never did." As remarkable as it is for a filmmaker who had been working for forty-five years to connect with a younger generation in this way, it's even more extraordinary that as Varda grew older, her audience grew larger.

PART III

DIMENSION

14

SOME MAY HAVE BEEN surprised that, after the successes of her feature *The Gleaners and I* and its postscript, *The Gleaners and I: Two Years Later* (2002), Varda would return to making shorts. But as she once said, "A writer does a poem, an essay, a short story, and then a novel. So why not the same, in its fashion, with film?" In the French film community, short subjects had great prestige. Telluride Film Festival director Tom Luddy believed that "in France, the *court métrage*, or film short, is treated with great respect. But in America no one pays enough attention to Agnès's shorts."

For Varda, the chief advantage of digital filmmaking was its ability "to collapse the time . . . between wanting to film something and actually being able to do it." Between 2002 and 2004, she would make three shorts in succession. They were *Tribute to Zgougou the Cat* (2002), a two-minute celebration of her majestic feline; *Le lion volatil* (The Vanishing Lion, 2003), an eleven-minute magical-realist romance that takes place in and around the Lion of Belfort statue in Montparnasse (in which Zgougou has a memorable cameo); and *Ydessa, the Bears and etc.* (2004), a forty-minute documentary of a photo exhibition in Munich.

Varda was a lifelong cat lover. The Ciné-Tamaris logo is a winking tabby, and from *La Pointe Courte* through *Cléo* and from *Zgougou* through her penultimate film, *Faces Places*, cats played a role in her work. Like them, she was small, saucer-eyed, watchful, and unpredictable; she did not so much seize on new ideas and milieus as pounce upon them. In fact, while it is now well known that Varda was a forebear of New Wave cinema, less heralded is her role as a pioneer of the cat video. The eponymous Zgougou, a gift from Sabine Mamou, editor and lead actress of *Documenteur*, was named after a Tunisian pudding of pine nuts, eggs, and cream. Supremely cinegenic, Zgougou is always ready for her close-up, a dominating presence invariably upstaging Bernard, rue Daguerre's recessive male cat.

"If a camera is running, she stands in front," says Varda with a sigh as Zgougou strides into the frame while the director is shooting something else, necessitating a retake. Likewise, when the tape recorder is turned on for an interview, the cat purrs. When Varda turns on the computer, Zgougou drapes herself on and around it, shedding her luxuriant silver fur on and in its surfaces and apertures, which of course clogs its circuits. In this charming portrait, Zgougou is at once feline subject and love object, acknowledged queen of rue Daguerre. Varda may have shared the sentiments of Colette, who pronounced that "the perfect companion never has fewer than four feet."

A larger species of cat rules *Le lion volatil*, a brief mystery-romance in which Frédéric-Auguste Bartholdi's 1880 bronze of a roaring lion vanishes from its plinth in Montparnasse. (In reality, it was temporarily removed for cleaning.) In the short, a pretty tarot card reader notes that the lion's disappearance coincides with that of a ticket-taker at the nearby Paris catacombs (note cat pun). While the card reader misses both statue and ticket-taker, when she looks at the plinth again, a large house cat (Zgougou, enlarged by special effects) has magically replaced the lion. The card reader is enchanted. So are we.

In December 2003, Varda was in Munich screening her films. She took a break to visit the Haus der Kunst, now a museum of contemporary art, built during the Third Reich expressly to exhibit Nazi-approved art. She was flabbergasted by the depth and breadth of the exhibition "Partners," organized by the curator Ydessa Hendeles, who was born in Germany and raised in Canada. Among its many resonances, it took aim at the original purpose of the building in which it was shown.

The galleries, two stories high, were hung with black-and-white photographs from floor to ceiling. They resemble posed snapshots culled from family albums. Each of the three thousand photos featured humans posing with or being consoled by a teddy bear. Vintage teddy bears in vitrines were scattered throughout the exhibition rooms. Varda felt compelled to document the exhibition and its curator. Hendeles had installed the work cinematically, inviting the museumgoer to take in its enormity as one would a master shot in a film, while breaking up the vast space with individual images and sculptures that are the equivalent of close-ups.

The exhibition was an object lesson, and in *Ydessa, the Bears and etc.* Varda explores its components to interpret this mysterious work of installation art. The teddy bear is the common thread of the historic photographs, but what does it signify? They are variously companions, protectors, child surrogates, mascots, spirit animals, and, frighteningly, targets. The first clue Varda identifies is a caption under a photo triptych from 1948. The subjects are Holocaust survivors Jacob and Dorothy Hendeles with their baby daughter, Ydessa, and her teddy bear. Given that the exhibition's venue is a Nazi-built institution, and that its curator is the daughter of survivors, Varda makes the obvious connection that a Jewish woman has assembled this installation in the house that Hitler built. It's a haunting film, though the exhibition itself was more nuanced, and unnerving, than the abridged version Varda shows her audience.

It clearly had a profound effect on Varda herself. At the time she made the film about Hendeles's masterful work of installation art, Varda herself was evolving into an installation artist.

AT SEVENTY-FIVE, an age when many artists and filmmakers are contemplating retirement or putting together their retrospectives, Varda commenced her third career.

When she'd segued from still photography to film in 1954, Varda had embraced a second dimension, that of movement. Nearly half a century later, when she began making installations, she left the world of two dimensions to embrace three. Typically, an installation occupies, and transforms, a three-dimensional space that the viewer can walk around, or through. By this definition, Michelangelo's frescoes in the Sistine Chapel qualify as an installation. Likewise, Judy Chicago's *The Dinner Party*.

In 2003, organizer Francesco Bonami conceived the 50th Venice Biennale as "an exhibition of exhibitions" rather than a collection of one-person shows. He delegated curatorial duties to seven professionals. Hans Ulrich Obrist, the Swiss-born curator then at the Museum of Modern Art of the City of Paris, assembled the group exhibition "Utopia Station," with colleagues Molly Nesbit and Rirkrit Tiravanija.

Varda was one of sixty artists invited to use the idea of utopia as a rubric. The result, wrote art historian Linda Nochlin, was "a heterogeneous, multiform, sometimes messy but always provocative indoor and outdoor large-scale exhibitions of objects, installations, videos, films and performances." For Nochlin, as significant a champion of feminist art as Varda was of feminist cinema, the filmmaker's *Patatutopia*—a mélange of objects, installation, videos, and performance—was a "highlight" of the exhibition.

Patatutopia, which roughly translates to "Tater Utopia," is a video triptych, a human-scaled altar to the humblest of vegetables. It consists of a soundtrack, three simultaneous video projections—each featuring a close-up of sprouting potato hearts—and a bumper crop (1,500 pounds) of actual potatoes below the three screens. Film is a time-based medium, and at least since her 1953 still photo of a potato heart, Varda had been interested in the effects of time on both objects and people. She filmed the three videos of *Patatutopia*—each three minutes and thirteen seconds—in her cellar over a period of six weeks.

The potato heart in the center of the three video panels seems to contract and expand like a pulsing human heart. The accompanying soundscape replicates rhythmic inhaling and exhaling. The left panel shows sprouting, wrinkly potatoes a little further along in the tuber life cycle than the lone potato in the center. In the right panel is a clutch of decomposing spuds tangled in a network of roots. In addition to its visual and audio elements, at Venice *Patatutopia* also had an olfactory component: the odor of the decaying potatoes, which completes the effect of experiencing the tuber's life cycle. In Venice there was also a performance element, with Varda as a busker dressed as a russet potato walking through the Biennale asking visitors to see her contribution to "Utopia Station."

Annette Messager, a leading French artist, was also invited to show in "Utopia Station." "Before the Biennale opened," she remembered, "we made a poster of the potatoes and I was invited to rue Daguerre to have dinner with other visual artists. Agnès did not like the French word *plasticienne* [visual artist]. Agnès was very intrigued about everybody's likes and dislikes."

"At the time she didn't have visual artists as friends, and she would *really* listen a lot," said Messager. The two women shared a love of cats. They traded stories of how difficult it was for women to be recognized as artists and filmmakers when they were starting out. "Another thing we shared was that we both lived with another artist," added Messager, whose partner was installation artist Christian Boltanski.

"Agnès was a forceful woman, an important role model for me," said Messager. "Everyone would recognize her when we walked down the street. She loved that. She loved people. And she really loved people to like her." Varda confided to Messager that, at a time when it had become increasingly challenging to get a film funded, the art world was a welcome outlet for her creative energies. "The difference between visual artists and cinéastes is that films need money," explained Messager. "Agnès felt that the cinema no longer wanted to produce her films, that film was a road that no longer existed."

After Venice, Varda began to experience eye trouble. "At first, tired eyes, then trouble seeing," recalled Rosalie to a reporter. "Some days, her eyesight was blurry and black dots appeared in her field of vision." The diagnosis was macular degeneration, a progressive retinal deterioration. It was a concerning diagnosis for anyone, but for a filmmaker and visual artist it was potentially career-ending. Yet, according to her daughter, for the remaining sixteen years of her life Varda continued working in much the same way as before the diagnosis. "Her strength of character and commitment to her projects gave her the necessary energy."

During Varda's last years, she relied increasingly on her daughter and assistants to make sure photographs were in focus and other details properly attended to. Rosalie gave up her career as a costumer to become her mother's eyes, her uncredited collaborator, and, on occasion, her credited producer, ensuring that Varda could continue with her work and frequent travel.

The gift Rosalie gave her mother was to not have to worry anymore about raising production money. Rosalie and her brother, Mathieu, made it possible for Varda "just to deal with the urgency to create." Varda's children assumed the task of overseeing the preservation of their parents' films for digital projection, raising funds through KissKissBankBank (the French counterpart of GoFundMe) and from government agencies. On June 5, 2004—which would have been Demy's seventy-fourth birthday—mother and daughter attended the dedication of Place Jacques Demy in the 14th arrondissement. In July, Varda traveled to Taiwan for its Biennial, where she installed *Patatutopia* and screened *Gleaners*.

Early in 2005, Varda returned to Asia, visiting Beijing for the first time since 1958. She was there for a retrospective of French cinema at the China Film Archive, which included many of her films. Serge Toubiana, former editor of *Cahiers du cinéma*, was then director of the Cinémathèque and represented France at the retrospective.

Years later, he would recall that he and Varda "were in the main theater of the . . . Archive getting ready for an evening presentation in
which . . . *Jacquot* was to be screened." As the projectionist conducted
film and sound tests, "Agnès heard the voice of Jacques Demy, who
was on screen, and fainted at the sound of the voice of the man she
loved so dearly." Toubiana helped her regain consciousness. "It was
like she [awakened] from a dream."

IN BETWEEN Varda's globetrotting adventures, she received an
invitation closer to home, just a ten-minute stroll from rue Daguerre.
Hervé Chandès, director of the Cartier Foundation for Contemporary Art, commissioned her to put together an exhibition scheduled
for 2006. It would be her first major museum show. Two of the installations ultimately included at the Cartier, *The Triptych of Noirmoutier* and *The Widows of Noirmoutier*, were first shown at the Galerie
Martine Aboucaya in January 2005.

Noirmoutier is the theme of "L'ÎLE et ELLE," the Cartier show,
which opened in June 2006. The literal translation of the title is
"The Island and Her." In spoken French, however, it sounds like
"He and She."

Like rue Daguerre, the island refuge is a biographical through line
for Varda. Together, she and Demy had restored the windmill where
they wrote, dreamed, and gardened. On its beach, she last had filmed
Demy. There, she had discovered La Bonnotte potatoes, a rare species of spud. After Demy's death, she spent time there with friends,
children, and, later, grandchildren. Noirmoutier had many stories to
share. In sharing those stories, she combined photography, film, and
installation art in surprising and memorable ways.

"L'ÎLE et ELLE" is a suite of installations, ranging through the
emotional spectrum from mournful to merry. *The Widows of Noirmoutier* is the former. In front of a large screen are fourteen chairs
arranged in a rectangle mirroring the shape of the big screen, each
one equipped with headphones. Surrounding the screen are fourteen

smaller video monitors. (The polyptych configuration of screen and monitors may have been a tribute to the Ghent altarpiece that Varda saw as a child in Belgium.) On the center screen is a video of women in black—the eponymous widows, Varda included—making a solemn processional around a bier-like table on the beach. The visitor can hear the ambient sound of crashing waves. Each smaller monitor features an interview with one widow. One can see all the women speaking but hear only one at a time by taking a specific seat and headset. To hear them all, one must keep changing seats. The effect is that of a communal confessional.

The installation is at once a group portrait of grief and a collection of individual experiences of mourning, consciously choreographed, an extraordinary convergence of the collective and the personal. As visitors change seats to hear each woman's experience, they mirror the widows on the large screen proceeding around the rectangular table. The attentive gallerygoer becomes aware that the women in the center screen and those changing seats in the rows in front are configured around what film professor Dominique Bluher described as a void, the empty space where the spouses once were. In the widow interviews conducted by Varda, one woman says that she feels amputated—once she was half of a whole and now she is just a half.

In a positive review in *Le Monde*, Jean-Luc Douin quoted Varda to the effect that the exhibition pushed her to "give shape to an emotion" and "to question my relationship to the image and the relationship to the people to whom it is offered." Douin noted that the exhibition "permitted the cohabitation of the serious and the playful." Illustrating the latter, he cited *The Grave of Zgougou*, a brief video about the resting place of Varda's beloved cat, who died in 2005 at the age of fifteen, in Noirmoutier. Varda wanted the cat's tomb, she said, "to have the funereal exaltation of the Mexicans. Death evoked in a light, charming way." She decorated the grave with starfish and shells, and a scarlet paper flower of the sort that she had made as a child. The last shot of the video rises from the grave to the heavens above Noirmoutier.

Likewise playful: *Ping Pong, Tong, and Camping*, an exuberant, primary-colored inventory of beachwear, sand toys, and inflatables stacked architecturally like polyurethane pillars. And yet another: *My Shack of Failure*, a beach cabana with roof and walls indicated by 35mm filmstrips taken from a print of *The Creatures*, Varda's made-in-Noirmoutier 1966 sci-fi film, her first flop. With *The Gleaners*, Varda learned how to recover, recycle, and transform. In this work, she transformed the material of a failed film into a light-filled cabana.

THE CARTIER FOUNDATION show led to another unexpected commission for Varda to create a very different kind of memorial. In 2007, at the behest of French president Jacques Chirac, Varda, then seventy-eight, made a site-specific work at the Paris Panthéon to accompany a public ceremony.

It was called *Les Justes* (The Just), for the French citizens who risked their lives to protect the children of French Jews. Some hid them. Others forged certificates of baptism so they could live openly. Yet others shared their food ration tickets. The Panthéon, originally a church, served as both a sacred space for Catholics and a secular mausoleum for those figures instrumental in the creation of modern France, from Voltaire to Alexandre Dumas and Marie Curie to Josephine Baker. The ceremony celebrated the adding of Les Justes to the Panthéon's honor roll. Varda's commission was a coproduction, so to speak, between the office of the president, the Ministry of Culture, and Jewish organizations including the Museum of the Shoah.

Varda worked shoulder to shoulder with Rosalie, her grandson Valentin Vignet, and set designer Christophe Vallaux to blend theatrical lighting, *son et lumière* effects, still photos, and moving pictures into an immersive atmosphere. They commemorated three hundred of the known heroes in still photographs, and film vignettes acknowledged the bravery of both the known and unknown figures who intervened to save Jewish children.

On a raised platform in what once was the Panthéon's nave,

Varda arranged framed photographs of the priests, nuns, teachers, and neighbors who acted. Above the platform, there were two
pairs of screens, one pair visible to anyone in the building. On the
screens, vignettes of the interventions played. In one example, a nun
witnessing a Gestapo roundup of a Jewish family casually wraps her
habit around a young passerby wearing the yellow Star of David and
walks him to safety.

On these paired screens, a black-and-white vignette (resembling a
period movie) played on the left while a color version with suspense-
ful close-ups and heightened sound played on the right. It's as if the
black-and-white version is the objective story and the color version
the subjective, remembered one. There were also sounds and images
of migratory birds streaming across the sky, evoking the migration
of Jewish children separated from their families as well as the migration of others, Jewish and Gentile, fleeing the Germans, including
the twelve-year-old Varda and her own family.

Initially scheduled to be open to the public only for one weekend
after the January 18 ceremony, the installation remained open for two
more weeks by popular demand.

NATHALIE OBADIA, a contemporary art dealer with galleries in
Brussels and Paris, certainly knew of Varda. She had seen *Cléo from
5 to 7*. And she had lived for a time in Nantes, where "the couple of
Agnès Varda and Jacques Demy were quite well known." She had
seen Varda's installation at the Venice Biennale. However, she did not
meet Varda until 2007, when they were seated at the same table in
Paris for a dinner at the Fondation Pernod Ricard.

"We were at a table of about sixteen. Before coffee, all the young
people left to smoke. And when they left, the two of us started a conversation that never stopped," Obadia said. "She was curious about
everything. She questioned everything all the time." When Varda
said to the gallerist, "I am an old filmmaker but a young artist," Obadia laughed at her candor.

"She was a jack-of-all-trades," said Obadia. "She did not want to be confined to one thing." Obadia looked at Varda, woman to woman, and liked what she saw. Then she looked at Varda as a gallerist looks at an artist. She admitted that initially she thought that because Varda was not a traditional artist, she would not be an obvious figure for collectors to acquire. Neverthless, Obadia gave the "young artist" a show in Brussels in 2010. Since then, she has represented Varda's photographs, collages, and installations.

"What I liked a lot about her work is that she used materials that didn't require a huge cost of production," said Obadia, likening her to Boltanski and Messager. The gallerist was likewise impressed by Varda's outgoing presence. "When she came to the gallery for her exhibition, she engaged with the people who came. She was always connecting, very present, very confident."

As Varda neared her eightieth birthday in 2008, there were requests from filmmakers to make a documentary about her. She saw the value of such a project, but wasn't ready to entrust it to a stranger. So, she invited Didier Rouget, her assistant director on *Jacquot de Nantes* and *A Hundred and One Nights*, to co-direct what became *The Beaches of Agnès*. After she installed "L'ÎLE et ELLE" at the Cartier Foundation, the production of *Beaches* began in Knokke-le-Zoute, on Belgium's coast.

It opens with a dazzling sequence of mirrors in the sand, artfully setting the stage for Varda's reflections on the panorama of her life. "If you opened me up," she announces, "you'd find beaches inside." Her material, as Bachelard might say, is sand. Sand shifts, and it can be sifted and made into mirrors and lenses. Varda begins this chapter of the film walking backward, indicating that she is going back in time while simultaneously embodying Kierkegaard's insight that life is lived forward and understood backward. She liked working with Rouget, but decided to move forward as the sole director and writer of the film, using the Belgium footage as a sizzle reel to attract funds.

She trusted Rouget to make a biographical film. But she wanted it to be a "film-film," and she wanted to tell her story herself in her own *cinécriture*, incorporating clips from her photographs, films, and installations. By the fall of 2006, she was absorbed with *Les Justes*, which she and her crew installed in January 2007. Afterward, the production of *Beaches* continued in Sète, Paris, Venice, California, and Noirmoutier. She edited as she went along, with a goal of having it completed by August 2008 so it could debut in at least one of the fall troika of film festivals: Venice, Toronto, or New York.

Every year during his tenure, Piers Handling, director and CEO of the Toronto Film Festival from 1996 to 2018, went to Paris to look at new French cinema. To save time, he typically screened the films he was interested in at the Unifrance offices. In 2008, his request list included *Beaches*. "Because the sound mix was not yet completed, Agnès couldn't show the film to us at Unifrance," Handling recalled. "We had to go to her."

He went with a colleague to rue Daguerre. "We all were on couches and chairs. She projected the film on a wall. There was no narration. Agnès had a mic and read over the images. It was the most unique film experience I ever had." *Beaches* premiered at the Venice Film Festival in early September 2008. And, said Handling, "Of course we took it for Toronto. It was one of the most important films by one of the most important directors in film history."

The critics concurred about the ciné-memoir and its maker. In *Le Monde*, Jean-Luc Douin: "Tender, playful, maliciously inventive." In the *Guardian*, Peter Bradshaw: "elegant, eccentric, and distinctly literary meditation on the Proustian themes of memory and self." In *The New Yorker*, Richard Brody: "a rapturous tribute to life itself." In France, *Beaches* won the César for best documentary and the best picture prize from the French Syndicate of Critics. In the U.S., the National Society of Film Critics voted it best documentary. Varda also earned her first nomination from the Directors Guild of America for best documentary.

Varda's kaleidoscopic look at her life brims with her vitality, vivacity, and imagination. To suggest the fragmented nature of memory,

Beaches is intentionally nonlinear. Chronology is not a factor in the ciné-memoir where she, literally, dances across the sands of time and rows a boat, it is implied, from Sète to Paris. People and places are paramount. Varda's focus on friends and family is her way of communicating that we are who—and what—we love. Critic Peter Bradshaw nicely described her autobiography as one that "conceals as much as it reveals." Still, there is at least one revelation here: she surprised many viewers by offhandedly disclosing that Demy's death was AIDS-related.

Together, the acclaim for *Les Justes* and *Beaches* reaffirmed Varda's status as one of France's national treasures. Accordingly, in 2009, the Légion d'honneur elevated her to the status of *commandeur*, its third-highest rank. This led to an awkward encounter. As Claire Denis, the director of *Chocolat* and *Beau travail*, remembered, she and Varda went to a screening where Godard was set to introduce a film by his partner, Anne-Marie Miéville. After the film, all the questions from the audience were directed not to Miéville but to Godard, who said disingenuously, "Ask her, she is a real artist, I am no one." For Denis, "It was like a film in which he was acting." She and Varda left to eat at a nearby café, and soon after Godard and Miéville came into the same café—passing Varda and Denis as though they were invisible. Varda stood and called out, "Jean-Luc!" When he acknowledged her, she asked why he hadn't said hello, and he replied that it was because she had accepted the Légion d'honneur. Varda replied, "Unlike you, I cannot refuse anything."

Even in the best of times, Godard, who had moved back to his native Switzerland in the 1970s, was moody and irascible. Was he angry about the Légion d'honneur? Might he have felt upstaged by Varda when her 2006 show at the Cartier Foundation was acclaimed and his concurrent show at the Centre Pompidou was widely slammed?

When Varda made *Beaches*, which concludes with celebratory footage of her eightieth birthday and the eighty brooms she received as gifts from her guests, she suspected it would be her valediction to filmmaking. As did many others who reviewed it.

Were we ever wrong.

VARDA DID not make fashion statements. She reveled in fashion playfulness.

Her dress was aubergine, her leggings purple, and her slippers cardinal red, like the Pope's. Except for the skullcap of silver-gray at its crown, Varda's hair and dress almost exactly matched. In early February 2009 she was in Vincennes, just outside Paris, to receive the Prix Henri Langlois, an award named for the cofounder of the Cinémathèque française and pioneer of film preservation.

Three weeks later, she donned a silver-and-gray tunic over black trousers for the César Awards. Though her garb was sober, she was no less mischievous. On that evening, she accepted her third César, best documentary, for *The Beaches of Agnès*, and joked before the cameras. With both hands, she hefted the eight-pound bronze statuette above her head, pretending it was a barbell.

The period between 1998, when Varda was on her voluntary leave from filmmaking, and 2009, when she was triumphant at the Césars, was one of significant reputational change. She had evolved from a figure working at the margins of the film industry into one central to the conversation. Whether it was natural or consciously planned, she had assumed the persona of subversive grandma. During the last decade of her life, she was ubiquitous at film festivals, TED talks, symposia, and awards ceremonies around the globe, often using these occasions to express her thanks and, increasingly, her social critiques.

During this time, there was greater visibility not only for Varda but for female filmmakers in general. In the 1990s, only 3 percent of filmmakers invited to show their work at Cannes were women. In the 2000s, the figure was 10 percent. And during the same decade in France, female filmmakers did particularly well, making 16–24 percent of the film output annually. In the U.S. during the 2000s, the number of women directors seesawed between 5 and 11 percent.

"In spite of illness, in spite even of the archenemy sorrow," wrote Edith Wharton, "one can remain alive long past the usual date of disintegration if one is unafraid of change, insatiable in intellectual curiosity, interested in big things, and happy in small ways." While it's unlikely that Varda was aware of Wharton's prescription for longevity, she followed it instinctively. In adapting to new film technology and embracing new art forms, she was unafraid of change. Given the interviews she conducted in *The Gleaners and I*, her curiosity was unslakable. She was interested in big things, like the real-life stories she chronicled in *Les Justes*. Small things like *chouquettes*, sugar-sprinkled cream puffs, made her happy.

Reid Rosefelt, the New York publicist who had worked with Varda on the launch of *Jacquot*, kept in touch with her and continued to see her over the years. He remembers visiting her in the late 1990s and being "surprised by the flurry of young people around her, making cinema." They worked with Varda in editing rooms converted from family rooms. They debated film during dinner in the courtyard. "Agnès curated this bunch of filmmakers," Rosefelt recalled, "and the atmosphere they created was electric." The way Varda kept current, he realized, was "by surrounding herself with this youthful energy."

It wasn't only digital cameras that transformed Varda's filmmaking process and spontaneity. As she prepared *Beaches*, she incorporated other aspects of the digital age. She referred to her filmography as a "database of images." She could access clips from her films and still photographs while editing her ciné-memoir.

"Her standard working method now involved the interspersion of reflection, writing, traveling, shooting, the recording of the voiceover, editing, and shooting of still more material," as the critic Kelley Conway put it. Naturally, adding and subtracting visual elements necessitated modifying the movie's narration and musical cues. Varda's tools kept pace with new technology and her own speed of thought.

While recuperating from the first of two hip replacement surger-
ies, Varda prepared her 2009 exhibition "La Mer . . . Etsetera," at the
Regional Center of Contemporary Art in Sète. For that show she
made the Zenlike *Bord de mer* (Seaside, 2009), the simplest and most
powerful of her installations. The viewer hears the sound of waves
and beholds a large still photo of the ocean projected on a wall; in
front of it, a film loop of crashing waves projected on the floor; in
front of it, real sand. In this triptych there seem to be no boundaries
between the still and the moving, the real and the representational.
It's hypnotic.

She thought of a way of combining her filmmaking and artmak-
ing careers by making an informal, but informed, television series
chronicling her travel to artist studios and art institutions—a museo-
logue, if you will—called *Agnès de ci de là Varda* (Agnes from Here
to There Varda, 2011).

Each episode begins with the same vivid visual metaphor. In Varda's courtyard, a tree is pruned, followed by a time-lapse sequence of
its regeneration. The suggestion is that while Varda is off looking at
art, the tree sprouts new shoots, branches, and leaves, while Varda
experiences a similar sprouting and growth of perception.

While she does not approach the series with a thesis, four themes
emerge. Repeatedly she is drawn to paintings and sculptures of angels.
Likewise, images of skeletons and skulls are ubiquitous, from Frida
Kahlo *calaveras* thumbing their noses at death to a solemn Cézanne
memento mori acknowledging its imminence. There are several art
couples interviewed, including her Paris friends Christian Boltanski
and Annette Messager, Los Angeles chums Zalman King and Patricia Knop, and Portuguese filmmaker Manoel de Oliveira and his
wife, Maria Isabel. The final episode of the series focuses on carnal
pleasure—including that of an eighty-year-old indigenous woman
and her younger lover in *Japon*, by filmmaker Carlos Reygadas, and
admiration of voluptuous female forms in sculptures by Niki de Saint
Phalle and Aristide Maillol.

For an unattached eighty-something artist with health challenges, it is unsurprising that Varda is attracted to artist couples or to art about sexual desire and mortality—as well as angel imagery. As the lifelong student of iconography surely knew, angels represent messengers heralding great change.

The iconography of Varda's international museum crawl is less important than her assumption that looking at art is a communal and conversational activity. Particularly memorable is her rapport with artists and her descriptions of their work, such as when she introduces Pierre Soulages as "a painter who works with black the way others work the soil" or when she observes that "Frida Kahlo is loved *for* and *through* her paintings." This implicitly acknowledges the "Fridolatry" that elevated Kahlo, champion of women and of indigenous peoples, and lover of animals, into a secular saint.

Similarly, at this juncture in Varda's life, she herself was an object of Vardolatry. She was not only beloved for her films and art but likewise regarded as the matron saint of gleaners, cats, and potatoes.

Her ascension was noted as early as 2007, when President Chirac commemorated *Les Justes* during a ceremony televised live from the Panthéon. Film historian Tim Palmer observed that Varda herself had "effectively risen to state-sponsored canonization."

15

VARDA TYPICALLY BEGAN HER day with a chamomile tisane. She did not steep the bag; she introduced it to the hot water for approximately one second before removing it. She sipped, sometimes cupping her hands around the vessel while inhaling the earthy perfume. The fragrance, and no doubt the heat, helped her focus on the task at hand.

More and more, the task was related to an art exhibition. She spoke often of her "three careers" as photographer, filmmaker, and gallery artist. At the Musée Paul Valéry in Sète in December 2011, she mounted the exhibition "There is no sea" ("Il n'y a pas de mer"), where she repurposed and reimagined work made fifty years before. A diptych on view was comprised of Varda's 1956 photo *Terrasse Le Corbusier*, an image of five adults and a baby at the architect's Radiant City in Marseille, next to a 2007 digital film, a reenactment of the still image that gives it a fictional backstory. The dynamic between still and moving picture makes demands on the observer. The story in the photo is something the viewer constructs in her mind; the story in the film about the photo is something Varda constructs to give the impression that visitors are seeing the subjects before and after the photo was shot. Once again, Varda was experimenting with stillness and movement. The observer of a photo can capture a moment lasting 1/25 of a second. For the viewer of a film, each moment is elusive.

In 2012, Ciné-Tamaris produced a box set of Varda's features and shorts, *Tout(e)Varda*. She would sometimes use it as a prop in public appearances. Like a spokesmodel, she would show it to the audience with a flourish of a hand and joke, "Sixty years of creation and not even four pounds!" When the box set was made available, many wondered, once again, whether she had made her last work on film.

In 2013, she was invited into the Academy of Motion Picture Arts and Sciences in a year when the organization invited 267 new members, including Ava DuVernay and Lena Dunham, both admirers of hers, in an effort to diversify the organization's ranks. While the invitation affirmed Varda's status as a star on the stage of world cinema, it seemed like too little, too late. Since her first art exhibition at the Galerie Nathalie Obadia in 2010, it had been understood that she was now primarily a visual artist and that her followers would see her latest work in galleries and museums. Those who loved her films could buy the box set, catch the films at retrospectives, or attend one of her master classes at whichever university, film festival, or cinematheque invited her. Whether speaking about her photos, films, or art, she demonstrated that she was an engaging performance artist as well.

Requests for her to speak came regularly—often with the enticement of an artist-in-residence honorarium. "In the ten years between when Agnès was eighty and ninety, she had maybe thirty exhibitions, four catalogues, and two films," Rosalie told journalist Susan Kouguell. Plus an untold number of master classes given at media centers, museums, and universities worldwide.

In 2014, her ubiquity was such that Peter Debruge of *Variety* proclaimed, "This is shaping up to be the Year of Agnès Varda. This week . . . [Varda] will receive the [Leopard of Honor] at the Locarno Film Festival, which is just the latest in a series of honors, distinctions, appearances, exhibitions, restorations, retrospectives, seances, soirees and other all-around cool happenings that this 86-year-old filmmaker, photographer and artist has been involved in so far this year."

Her first U.S. museum retrospective, "Agnès Varda in Califor-nialand," debuted at the Los Angeles County Museum of Art in November 2013 and ran through June 2014. While it focused pri-marily on her work made in California, it represented all three of her careers, celebrating her movies made in Los Angeles and the Bay Area, photographs taken during her two stays there, and an installation: a cabana of film strips from decommissioned prints of *Lions Love*.

The year of peak Varda continued with a February exhibition of photographic and video triptychs at the Galerie Nathalie Oba-dia, a March–April retrospective of installations at Beijing's CAFA Museum, an August appearance at the Locarno Film Festival to collect her Leopard of Honor for directorial achievement, and, in December, a lifetime achievement award from the European Film Academy at its awards ceremony in Riga, Latvia. When Agnieszka Holland presented Varda with the statuette, the audience jumped to its feet for a standing ovation. The recipient ordered everyone to sit, expressed her joy at receiving the prize, and bluntly declared, "More women should be chosen."

Despite the crowded calendar, Varda made time to write and direct a wryly funny salute to film archivist Henri Langlois to celebrate his 2014 centenary—one of thirteen big-name directors asked to partici-pate. Her contribution was a two-minute memoir about accompany-ing Langlois to an eastern European capital, she couldn't remember which. Neither could she remember whether she'd dreamed it or it had actually happened.

Happily, this would not be her last film. About the time of the Langlois project, Rosalie was thinking about the circumstances under which her mother might direct another. Given Varda's macu-lar degeneration, a co-director might be an option. Yet even if Rosalie could persuade her fiercely independent mother to collaborate with someone else, there was the obstacle—two obstacles, really—of Var-da's age. Physically, it would be too taxing for her to shoot every day for six to eight weeks. Financially, what investor would underwrite a project by a filmmaker closing in on eighty-seven? In most cases, an insurance company could not indemnify such a production. And in the event of a medical emergency, who could complete it? There were many variables to consider.

Contemplating a potential collaborator for her mother, Rosalie thought of JR, the Parisian street artist who shot and printed large-format photographs and pasted them on city walls. His photographic work had much in common with the art and artists Varda had profiled in *Mur Murs*. Rosalie phoned JR and asked if he'd like to meet her mother. He would. Rosalie had suspected that, despite the fifty-five-year age difference, the two might be kindred spirits.

JR and Varda had never met, but they knew each other's work. JR came to rue Daguerre and invited Varda to his studio the following day. "It sounds crazy," he said, "but the next day we started working on something... on a little video. We just wanted to do something together and that's what drove the making of [*Faces Places*]."

"Our aims, on his side and my side, had some common points," agreed Varda. Both were interested in photography. Both were committed to telling stories of people whose voices were rarely heard. And as JR had made the 2010 documentary *Women Are Heroes*, Varda knew he was pro-feminist. She recalled, "We decided [to focus] on people who have no power. People you can meet in villages."

Varda realized that JR was an urban artist, and thus wanted to better acquaint him with rural France. Initially, the plan was to collaborate on an installation work. Then plans changed. The new plan was to make a short film. As Rosalie reframed her pitch to investors, her co-directors came back and told her, "It's not a short film, but a documentary."

Rosalie faced a logistical challenge: how to schedule a collaboration between an overcommitted senior artist with physical limitations and an overcommitted young artist with so many demands on his time? Both were enjoying enviable success, she in the middle of a career renaissance and he in his career prime. Because her mother tired easily, Rosalie proposed that *Faces Places* shoot four days a month over a year rather than an intensive six to eight weeks. This enabled the collaborators to meet prior commitments, allowed Varda to travel in small increments, and meant that Rosalie, who produced the film, could raise the funding as they went along.

BY THIS time, Varda had devised a design for living. Besides her customary playfulness, it involved openness to the new and rethinking past work. For a younger generation, she was becoming a model of aging with grace. Alonso Duralde, film critic for TheWrap.com, described its impact on him: "Many filmmakers have taught me how to look at the world; Agnès Varda also taught me how to age." He continued, "As I get older and new technology rolls in, I wonder if I really need to embrace it. Then I look at Varda immerse herself in new technology, experiences, and people. She's not only preserving her prior work but making new and engaging work with the old." Not to mention using social media platforms, like Instagram.

Varda remained productive by accepting help. Rosalie freed her mother from running Ciné-Tamaris. She also found money for film and art projects and planned the logistics of getting her mother everything everywhere all at once. Mathieu, an in-demand actor and director of film and episodic television, supervised restoration of his parents' films for the digital age. In 2006, Varda hired Julia Fabry as a studio assistant. She would serve as assistant director of *The Beaches of Agnès*, *From Here to There*, and *Faces Places*, and grew into the roles of the filmmaker's fixer, personal curator, and installation assistant.

Audiences at film festivals and master classes were increasingly asking Varda about her future projects. "At my age I don't have a future," or a variation thereof, was her standard answer. "I have many projects and not much time, so I need to go fast." Fabry's experience of Varda was of a woman "moving along with her gut and intuition . . . driven by insatiable curiosity. This could mean waking up at 6 am to get the best light and working until dawn to catch the best light again. She worked very hard until the end, with that same amazing energy."

When Fabry went on the road with Varda and JR in April 2015 for the first four-day shoot of *Faces Places*, she wore many hats, including that of advance woman. Often, Varda dispatched Fabry to gauge if a person of interest would agree to speak with the co-directors. Time after time, said Fabry, "I'd come up to this guy in front of his repair shop who'd say, 'No, sorry, it's the end of my day, I want to go home.' Then [Varda would] catch up with us, and he'd immediately start talking to her!" Fabry recalled that when potential subjects saw "that tiny lady with colorful clothes and funny hair trotting up . . . to ask them weird questions, they were intrigued!"

In Cannes on May 24, six days before Varda's eighty-seventh birthday, the festival awarded her an honorary Palme d'or, the prize given to directors who had not previously won an award in competition. Told that Clint Eastwood and Woody Allen had won the same prize, she paused for a moment and said quizzically, "But *their* films made money." Accompanied by Jane Birkin, Varda went onstage to receive the award, dedicating it to "all the inventive and courageous filmmakers who aren't in the spotlight . . . but who keep going." After the ceremony, for a moment she looked at the prize, which resembles an unusually large gilded sprig of rosemary. She may have remembered the night fifty-one years earlier when Demy won the Palme d'or for *The Umbrellas of Cherbourg*. Then she slipped the award into her black satin evening bag.

On her return to rue Daguerre, the award joined Varda's silver-and gold-plated menagerie—Berlin's Silver Bear for *Le Bonheur*, Venice's Golden Lion for *Vagabond*, the Leopard of Honor from Locarno, plus two Césars—in a glass-fronted cabinet that stood in a corner of her living room. She was also receiving comparable honors from the art world, ones that didn't collect dust. Major museums were acquiring her work for their permanent collections. The Cartier Foundation bought *Noirmoutier Triptych*, which was made in multiples, like a photographic or fine art print, and *The Grave of Zgougou*. New York's Museum of Modern Art likewise acquired a *Noirmoutier Triptych*. The Centre Pompidou owned a collection of her 1962 Cuba photos. The Los Angeles County Museum of Art acquired photographs from California and *My Shack of Cinema*, made from footage of *Lions Love*. Beijing's CAFA Museum acquired a suite of Varda photographs taken on her 1957 tour of China.

When Varda and JR were not on the road, she often scheduled a master class or traveled with exhibitions of her work. In October 2015, she flew to Chicago for CineVardaExpo, a University of Chicago event encompassing a master class, art exhibition, and film program of her work. A few days before she left Paris, filmmaker Chantal Akerman, her friend and colleague, committed suicide. Typically, in lectures and master classes Varda would limit the talk to a discussion of clips from her films and documentation of exhibitions. Untypically, in Chicago she veered from her polished and engaging talking points to make an impromptu speech about Akerman and women filmmakers currently active.

"I have a few words to say about Chantal Akerman [whose movies] deal with time in an interesting way.... We will miss her." She spoke of Claire Denis and Patricia Mazuy, who had helped her edit *Vagabond*. She spoke of Céline Sciamma and American independent Miranda July. She spoke of Kathryn Bigelow, adding, "Some of [these women] even make money. That helps the cause." Where another artist might have mentioned her possible influence on, or discovery of, these women, Varda simply expressed her admiration for the rising generation of filmmakers. Like Varda, each of them fought to make her films her way.

A Varda master class was a crowd-pleaser, and her ad libs during the question-and-answer session were almost always a highlight. In Chicago, there was a query about how she had acquired the nickname "grandmother of the New Wave." She quickly reminded the woman who posed the question that this had been her nickname at thirty. "Now I should be called the dinosaur of the New Wave."

While quick to deliver a good laugh line, she wasn't there to entertain. She was there to see how and if the ideas she communicated in her films and her art were received. The film clips and conversation structure of these lectures delivered in Cambridge (Massachusetts), Chicago, Locarno, London, Philadelphia, Venice (California) and elsewhere would become the template of her final film, the posthumously released *Varda by Agnès* (2020).

While she continued the monthly shoot with JR on *Faces Places*, Varda prepared a 2016 exhibition for the Museum of Ixelles, "Potatoes and Company," in the Brussels neighborhood where she was born and raised. On view from February through May, it included a loving tribute to her mother, screenings of *The Beaches of Agnès*, and, of course, *Patatutopia*.

In April 2017, Varda was elevated to *grand officier* of the Legion d'honneur.

AFTER EIGHTEEN months of shooting and five more in the editing room, *Faces Places* premiered at the Cannes festival in May 2017, ten days before Varda's eighty-ninth birthday. Audiences greeted it with great warmth and the jury awarded it the Golden Eye for best documentary. Neither Varda nor JR was present for the ceremony. Varda returned to Paris, ostensibly to spend her birthday with her family. There were whispers that the maker of *Cléo*, the film about a woman waiting for a breast cancer biopsy, had herself been diagnosed with the malady. Only those in her inner circle knew that she had already undergone surgery and a round of chemotherapy.

Yet she soldiered on. *Faces Places* was invited to the North American fall festivals: Telluride, Toronto, and New York. If this was going to be her last film, she was going to promote the hell out of it. And she did, except that it wasn't her last, but her penultimate film.

In September, Varda went to Toronto, where she did triple duty. While the festival doesn't confer awards, the film won the audience vote for best documentary. Varda also was the highest-profile participant in the festival sidebar Women in Film. The festival further honored her by christening its new VIP lounge after her. Festival CEO

Piers Handling recalled, "Agnès spoke and then said that she wanted to take a nap. She took over a sofa." And so Varda became the first filmmaker to nap in the Agnès Varda Lounge.

Prior to her nap, she said, "As the only woman of the French New Wave, now I feel proud to see these women directors coming from everywhere, expressing their visions from their own perspectives." She was supported by the latest statistics. In France between 2008 and 2017, the proportion of films directed by women rose from 20 to 27 percent. In the U.S. during the same period, the rise was from 8 to 11 percent.

Faces Places was unassuming and charming. Few could resist the sight gag of Varda, eighty-eight, roly-poly and small, and JR, thirty-three, stringbean-slim. The fact that the film features two artists who could be grandmother and grandson gave it universal appeal. Audiences everywhere responded to their explicit mission to give voice to those who are rarely heard: the mailmen, miners, waitresses, and dockworkers the pair memorialize in glorious billboard-scale photographs. In the shared belief that those instrumental in feeding or supporting or otherwise connecting a community should be celebrated, the co-directors committed to literally and figuratively enlarging them.

The collaboration and mutual respect of the co-directors in the film is touching. She is dazzled by JR's "magic van," a Mercedes Sprinter equipped with camera and printer that converts a snapshot into three-by-four-foot posters. He is staggered by Varda's ability to approach strangers and get them to talk about their work and their lives.

When the freewheeling documentary was slated for the New York Film Festival, there were innumerable requests from newspapers and magazines to interview the odd couple. At Lincoln Center after a festival screening, critic Amy Taubin, who knew Varda well, hosted the Q & A. Before the co-directors took the stage, Varda told her "that she could not have made this film alone because she was not strong enough anymore." JR took the lead and Varda, more ret-

icent than usual, slowly came to life. Many in the audience wanted
to know what they had learned from each other. Varda looked at JR
and said, "I learn from you a beautiful thing. You enlarge people."
JR confided to the audience that he had learned the secret of Varda's
interview technique: "She never asks someone, 'What do you do?'
She asks, 'Why do you do it?' "

Their sincerity and mutual respect prompted an audience member
to joke, "Clearly, you're lovers. When can we expect the baby?" JR
laughed and replied, "It was friendship at first sight."

An aspiring filmmaker asked Varda if she had advice for someone starting out. "I never give advice," she replied, then immediately
contradicted herself. "Films should find you. Something happens
that pushes you to do it." Then Varda shared a story that wasn't in
any of her master classes. She recalled that long ago—probably in the
early 1980s—she'd taught a film class at the California Institute of
the Arts. She told her students to set up their movie cameras in an
LA restaurant. "No need to load any film," she said. "Now, stay put
and look." She told them to spend an hour looking at what was in
the frame, and what came in and out of the frame. She told them,
"There is a moment something happens." After an hour passed, she
asked them, was that moment expected? Could they predict it? The
audience hung on to her words as if listening to a suspense story.
The implication was, if you look with concentration, you will know
when something is about to happen.

She neglected to tell the assembled that she had taken thousands
of pictures, still and moving. That she could feel the rhythms inside
the frame and knew instinctively when she should engage the shutter.
"She had a talent for seeing things before they happened," observed
Patricia Mazuy.

The questions circled back to *Faces Places* and the co-directors'
takeaways. JR said that they were still processing. Varda said, "The
feedback is the reward."

If she was dealing with the effects of "chemo brain," she hid it well.
Before she came to New York for the festival, news of a reward of

another kind reached Varda. The Motion Picture Academy in Hollywood called with a save-the-date: on November 11, she would receive a Governors Award, an honorary Oscar. John Bailey, the renowned cinematographer who was then president of the Academy, nominated her, and the Board of Governors approved. Varda was in New York in early October when the news accounts of the sexual predations of Harvey Weinstein, principal of Miramax Films, were on every front page. When *Le Monde*'s Laurent Charpentier interviewed Varda before she left for Los Angeles, most of the questions were about close encounters of the Weinstein kind.

Charpentier opened with, "Is this award a feminist act?" Varda politely answered, "No, it is a matter of cinema, but with a lot of women involved." The director explained that actress Angelina Jolie, who was also a director, would present her with the statuette. A few beats later, Charpentier asked whether Varda had ever been sexually harassed. She answered no. Either she had forgotten about slapping the Columbia exec who pinched her cheek or figured that didn't rise to the level of sexual harassment.

Of the many Weinstein-related questions, Varda observed that it was good the scandal broke, "because it allows women to speak out, and because men are being shaken up." The feminists are right to shout, she said, because "as long as there are angry women, things will change."

Often Varda described her films and installations as jigsaw puzzles with a missing piece. Almost all the parts of her life came together on November 11, 2017, at the Ray Dolby Ballroom of the Loews Hollywood Hotel. In the room were the three other honorees: indie filmmaker Charles Burnett (*To Sleep with Anger, Killer of Sheep*), cinematographer Owen Roizman (*The Exorcist, Network*), and actor Donald Sutherland (*M*A*S*H, Don't Look Now*).

Surrounded by family, the pillars of the French film industry, and close friends, Varda was clad in an ivory and pink silk tunic and coordinating pajama-like trousers. Both her French and American families were there, hearts swelling. There were Rosalie and Mathieu and two of her five grandchildren: Valentin Vignet, a cinematographer, and Constantin Demy, a high school student. There were Thierry Frémaux of the Cannes Film Festival, Serge Toubiana of Unifrance, and Frédérique Bredin of the CNC. There were JR, former assistant Lynne Littman (previously an Oscar winner for documentary), Lisa Blok-Linson (now a noted location manager), and her close friends Tom Luddy, with Telluride comrade Julie Huntsinger, and Patricia Knop King.

There was a lot of love for her in the room, as five Academy members successively introduced, thanked, reintroduced, and presented her with the award. Steven Spielberg opened the evening with, "We are here for Agnès Varda," reminding the assembled that after more than sixty years, "She's still going strong with her newest film, *Faces Places*." Kimberly Peirce, director of *Boys Don't Cry* and governor of the directors' branch of the Academy, spoke of *Vagabond* as life-changing, and how Mona "is the kind of woman I had never seen before . . . one who does not make herself into an object."

Kate Amend, governor of the documentary branch, quoted Littman on working for Varda. "The reason no one complained about the low pay and long hours is that Agnès worked longer and harder than all of us put together." Then Jessica Chastain, later an Oscar winner for *The Eyes of Tammy Faye*, noted, "Like the proverbial distinction between tragedy and comedy, the difference between an iconoclast and an icon is time." She continued, "Moviemaking has a way of turning yesterday's rebels into today's establishment." Still, after sixty-plus years, Chastain argued that Varda retained her rebel bona fides. "In [Varda's] words, 'rebelliousness is part of being a woman.'"

At last, Angelina Jolie came up to present Varda with her Oscar. "To be an artist is to be suspicious of labels," she began. "Varda was called 'the grandmother of the New Wave' when she was thirty. 'Female director' is another label she might resist.'" Jolie went on,

"Those women that took the first step showed the way for all of us." Then she addressed the honoree directly. "Once you told me that you 'don't catch people's attention through normalcy.' On behalf of all of us, thank you for being anything but normal."

An overcome Varda hid her face in her hands. Many rose to their feet for a standing ovation. When Varda reached the podium, she thanked "all the bright, beautiful, intelligent women who spoke." Then she demanded, "I want to know, are there no intelligent men who love me in California?" Her question compelled half the men in the audience to their feet, wanting to show their love. Varda introduced many in her entourage. Surely, every piece of the Varda puzzle was there. Then she placed the missing one. "Dear Jacques was here in 1965, nominated for *The Umbrellas of Cherbourg*," which won best foreign language film. She stated that her lifelong goal was "to get the essence of cinema." Balancing seriousness with levity, she deadpanned, "Because I became older and older without losing the desire to create, I started to get lifetime achievement awards."

She thanked "Angelina and Jessica, my feminist guardian angels." A few nights before, Varda said, she had woken up in the middle of the night, anxious about her speech. "I got nervous, started to move my legs and arms in bed. I forgot the weight of my body on the mattress. Tonight, I have the same feeling.

"It's a big event, serious, full of meaning and weight," she said, now balancing gravity with a smile of undisguised joie de vivre. "But I feel, that between weight and lightness, I choose lightness. I feel that I'm dancing," she concluded, "dancing the dance of cinema." To applause, Varda left the podium, raising her pink chiffon scarf above her head and looking as though she would levitate. Much to the audience's delight, Jolie joined Varda in an impromptu dance of cinema.

After the ceremony, Varda and company repaired to Jolie's historic home in Los Feliz. Built in 1913, it had once been the estate of multiple Oscar winner Cecil B. DeMille, director of the first feature film made in Hollywood.

When she returned to Paris, Varda hosted an Oscar celebration at rue Daguerre. "It was very joyful," remembered Hélène Demy-McNulty, her sister-in-law. Apart from immediate family, the guests included François Hollande, former president of the Republic, actresses Isabelle Huppert and Jane Birkin, and artists Christian Boltanski and Annette Messager, all eager to congratulate her and pose for pictures with her new roommate, Oscar.

16

Over Varda's last fifteen months, her continued productivity shamed those a fraction of her age.

In a profile of the filmmaker, Holly Brubach wrote, "Retirement seems to be nowhere on Agnès's to-do list. She's editing a new film about her work, *Varda by Agnès*, intended to take the place of the many lectures she's been giving and relieve her of the need to travel so much. 'This film will be traveling . . . and I will stay home!' she said."

On January 23, 2018, while she was editing sequences of what would be her last film, *Varda by Agnès*, a phone call came in from the Academy: *Faces Places* had received a nomination for best documentary. At the time, she was the oldest nominee, in any category, in Oscar history.

Varda already had the honorary statuette, famously derided by Marlene Dietrich as "the deathbed Oscar." Here was the prospect of winning a competitive one, a tremendous honor—and one requiring a lot of intercontinental travel for an eighty-nine-year-old. Not only was she expected to attend the awards ceremony in March, but also the nominee lunch on February 5—just twelve days away. Eight days

later, she and JR learned that the film had won two César nominations, for best documentary and best score, by Matthieu Chedid.

Given the demands on Varda's time and energy, it was decided that
JR would attend the nominee lunch. His date was a cardboard cutout
of Varda. Other nominees included Greta Gerwig, Meryl Streep, and
Steven Spielberg, all thrilled to pose with Cardboard Varda.

Because Varda had committed to deliver one of the distinguished
Charles Eliot Norton Lectures at Harvard in late February—sharing
the honor that year with Frederick Wiseman and Wim Wenders—
Cardboard Varda was also JR's plus-one for the Césars on March 2.
The film failed to win in either category. JR then flew to Los Angeles
to join Varda at the Independent Spirit Awards on March 3, where
Faces Places won the best documentary prize. The following evening
was the Academy Awards.

Their film didn't win the Oscar. But in the age of social media,
when more people in 2018 had Instagram accounts (1 billion) than
watched the Oscars, Varda had more currency as the punk monk in
rose-patterned silk Gucci pajamas (a gift from designer Alessandro
Michele) than as a director with or without a statuette. She was now
a global meme.

For her April installation at Galerie Nathalie Obadia, Varda created her last structure using 35mm film, *The Greenhouse of Happiness*.
It used every frame from a mothballed print of her 1965 film *Le Bonheur*. Except for its iron armature and the pots of artificial sunflowers
inside (echoing images from the film), the greenhouse and accompanying ceremonial arch (an Arc de Triomphe created from old film
canisters) are created from recycled movie paraphernalia. Inside the
greenhouse, one gets the sensation of being inside film.

In her artist's statement, Varda said that she didn't know whether
this installation was a work of nostalgia or of recycling. It was a convergence of the two, works of vernacular architecture built of analog
film materials and containers, a place where cinephiles and civilians
both could find shelter and diversion.

During Varda's final year, Rosalie had to leave Paris and asked Nathalie Obadia to look in on her mother. Late one afternoon, the gallerist went to rue Daguerre for afternoon tea and a long chat in the courtyard. Shortly before 7 pm, the two women went inside and Obadia got the hint that Varda wanted to be alone when she arranged herself in a chair in front of the television and her cat, Nini, jumped into her lap. "She wanted to watch *Columbo*," said Obadia. "She was crazy for *Columbo*. She loved Peter Falk."

In fall 2018, Simon Hattenstone of the *Guardian* asked Varda if she ever found love after Demy. "No. Not a man or woman or anything," she said. "I never approached anybody's skin. I don't know if it was a decision. It just happened like this. I used to say my ability to love a man was dead."

As was their annual custom, in May 2019 before the Cannes Film Festival commenced, Varda welcomed journalists Manohla Dargis, Joan Dupont, and Amy Taubin to rue Daguerre for lunch in the courtyard. Taubin recalled that she was aware of Varda's precarious health. "But I think this was the first time I heard her talking directly about her cancer and that she knew she probably had only a year, at most, to live."

"She said that she wasn't afraid," remembered Taubin. Then she said, "It will be an ending." Her candor, Taubin said, "knocked me out. Because in her films, endings are very important and very thought-out."

All four women were headed to Cannes. Varda wasn't invited to screen a film or accept an award. She was there to lead the 2018 Women's March with actress Cate Blanchett, president of the festival jury. When Thiérry Fremaux, director of the festival, held a news conference on May 8, some in the press corps were mystified. What did he mean when he announced, "A large group of women were going to do something that affirmed their presence"?

Most of the female journalists knew that the international gender equality group 50/50 by 2020, in tandem with the French Directors

Guild, had planned a women's march for Saturday, May 13. Kristen Stewart, twenty-eight, was one of the youngest of the eighty protesters; Claudia Cardinale and Jane Fonda were among the elders in the actress contingent that included Marion Cotillard and Salma Hayek. Blanchett and Varda, who would turn ninety at month's end, jointly led the march. Rosalie marched as well.

The women's march did more than simply affirm the presence of female actors, directors, and producers, although it's understandable that Frémaux so carefully parsed his words. Those who marched that day demanded that all international film festivals take a three-point pledge: 1) To compile the gender and race of the directors of all films submitted; 2) To make public the gender and race of selection committee members and programming consultants; and 3) To make public the gender and race of executive boards and commit to a schedule of parity in all these bodies.

Five years later, the Berlin, Cannes, Toronto, and Venice film festivals had signed on to the pledge. Varda's last march had real political effect in helping to get films by women and minorities into the distribution pipeline.

Happily, Varda's presence at what would be her last Cannes enabled her to make meaningful connections with other female filmmakers. One was Ava DuVernay, director of *Selma*, who had crossed paths with Varda at the honorary Oscars, where the younger director had presented an award to Charles Burnett.

On the steps of the Palais du Festival during the women's march, the two women embraced. DuVernay knew Varda's work and was thrilled to learn that Varda knew hers. Their encounter was sealed with a kiss and a selfie—DuVernay smooching Varda as Blanchett photobombs the shot. The two filmmakers made a date for breakfast the following morning.

"We had a beautiful breakfast at her hotel," said DuVernay. "I had questions about how she managed family and work. It was a wide-ranging conversation, and yet while I was speaking with her, there was this acute awareness that this was her last time at the festival. She was fearless about aging. Not mournful, but matter-of-fact. I had never faced someone who was at the end."

"And then," DuVernay recalled, "she started talking about *Selma*. It wasn't a give-and-take conversation. I just listened." DuVernay doesn't remember the details of what Varda said. "Just the feeling. Warm and wonderful."

After breakfast, Rosalie told DuVernay that she was struggling to find finishing funds for *Varda by Agnès*. "I committed to it," DuVernay said, "and emailed other filmmakers who jumped in." Among them were Patty Jenkins (*Wonder Woman*), Nicole Kassell (*Watchmen*), and actress-director Eva Longoria. In the end, numerous institutions and individuals funded the film.

There were three more festivals on Varda's to-do list: Marrakech in early December, Berlin in February, if *Varda by Agnès* was accepted, and Qatar in March for a master class that would be moderated by Richard Peña, former head of the New York Film Festival.

During the fall of 2018, Varda's doctors discovered new cancerous foci and prescribed another cycle of chemotherapy. To a friend avid to see her in October, Varda explained by phone that it was "a little complicated." She received treatments in the mornings and returned home, fatigued and nauseous, to rest. She would wake from her nap by 4 pm. From 4 to 8 pm, she edited *Varda by Agnès*.

In early December, Mathieu and Rosalie accompanied their mother to Marrakech for its seventeenth annual film festival, where she was an honoree. She spent time with Martin Scorsese, there to give a masterclass and to introduce Robert De Niro, another honoree. When Varda received her award and accompanying swag, she reminded the audience of her aim to shine a light on those too rarely seen on-screen. "There are thousands of people who are fighting to survive, to find some work, to receive a decent salary, to get a little dignity, and a little bit of happiness. And millions of people are seeking refuge."

BY YEAR'S end, the Berlin Film Festival told the director that *Varda by Agnès* had been accepted for its February event. The first three months of 2019 were shaping up: Berlin in February, Doha in early March, and a group art installation at the Domaine de Chaumont-sur-Loire, near Tours, at the end of March.

According to Jane Birkin, Varda put a stop to her chemotherapy before she died. It is likely that this happened in November 2018, as she was finishing *Varda by Agnès*. Chemo would make it even more difficult for the ninety-year-old to speak on camera and to make public appearances.

At Berlin, female filmmakers directed 63 percent of the movies screened, a festival record, suggesting a positive result of the women's march. Agnieszka Holland, there with her Stalin-era film *Mr. Jones*, was asked if she had been inspired by a woman director. "Agnès Varda," she immediately replied. Isabel Coixet, accompanying her film *Elisa and Marcel*, got the same query. "Agnieszka Holland is my hero; Agnès Varda is my god," she said.

Varda and Rosalie conceived the director's final cinematic effort as a last word on her artistic tenets, focused on her four principles. Accordingly, it plays more like a TED talk than a film. She describes her mantra as "Inspiration, Creation, Sharing" and makes clear that the director must be electrified by an idea. The energy generated from that idea sparks the excitement of creating the film. And the film must engage others. Varda's first principle: *You don't make films to watch them alone.* Ideally, she suggests, the less time there is between inspiration and creation, the better. That way, the energy doesn't dissipate. If you don't have a digital camera, film it on your phone. Varda's second principle: *Film quickly with the means at hand.* Whether the filmmaker works in documentary or fiction, the director's attitude is key. Don't condescend to subjects or characters. Don't be afraid of the commonplace. Varda's third principle: *Nothing is banal if you film it with empathy and love.* Most critical, Varda's fourth principle: *You need a viewpoint to make a film.*

In Berlin, Varda's swan song was warmly embraced by festival audiences, as it was by critics. Unusually, she did not meet with individual journalists. Instead, most likely because she wanted to save time and energy, she held a press conference and told the audience that she was fed up with speaking about herself.

Maria Giovanna Vagena moderated the press conference, introducing Varda as "Director. Screenwriter. Legend." Varda balked. "No. No! It's enough! I'm not a religion. I'm still alive." Poised and articulate as was her custom, she appeared not to be thrown when a journalist asked, "Is this film a way of organizing yourself and saying goodbye?"

"Of course," she answered.

Most of the questions were expressions of thanks. Most of Varda's answers were expressions of gratitude. The last question, "What do you say to feminist filmmakers who want to direct?" came from a young Turkish woman who thanked Varda for her work, adding, "We are grateful to you because you make us think we can make films."

Later that day, the festival presented Varda with the Berlinale Camera, a tribute to "personalities and institutions that have made a unique contribution to film and to whom the festival feels especially close." Varda met all the prerequisites.

It was a long day for a nonagenarian. And then, to the accompaniment of triumphal music, festival director Dieter Kosslick escorted Varda to the podium. While she was fêted, she leaned on the podium. As she thanked the festival, it was with audible shortness of breath.

Two weeks later, as Richard Peña was preparing questions for the scheduled masterclass in Doha with Varda, he was interrupted by a phone call. It was Rosalie. Her mother's doctor forbade Varda to fly. Peña quickly rescripted the event as a two-session lecture, with movie clips, on Varda's mastery.

DESPITE HER failing health, Varda kept busy until the end.

March 23 was a mild spring day near Tours at the Domaine de Chaumont-sur-Loire, celebrated for its lush gardens and programs reinforcing the connection between art and nature. Varda was one of many artists invited to participate in a group exhibition at the UNESCO World Heritage Site. The opening would be March 28. Varda and Julia Fabry, her studio and camera assistant, were there to place, hang, and put the final touches on the filmmaker's three contributions.

There were unpublished photographs of the clasped hands of people she loved, including JR and Prune Nourry, and Christian Boltanski and Annette Messager, surrounded by potato hearts. They needed to be spaced and hung. There was *The Greenhouse of Happiness*, lately at the Galerie Nathalie Obadia; the artificial sunflowers needed to be just so. And finally, there was *The Tree of Nini*. When a storm uprooted a tree in the rue Daguerre courtyard that her cat liked to lounge on, Varda salvaged its trunk as a pedestal for a larger-than-life statue of Nini.

Still-life photos of clasped hands surrounded by gleaned potato hearts. An installation recycling 35mm film from the ironically titled *Le Bonheur* (Happiness). A dead tree recycled as a plinth for a cat sculpture. Together, they represented Varda's careers as photographer, filmmaker, and installation artist, as well as representing her practices of gleaning, recycling, and ailurophilia. Varda's last living artistic testament.

Their work done, Fabry drove Varda the two hours back to rue Daguerre, her home of sixty-eight years. She went to her bedroom to rest.

That week, Jane Birkin got a call from Rosalie. "She said that [Agnès] wanted to say goodbye to all the people she loved and who loved her, so we gathered at her home." It was March 28. One by one, family members and friends filed into her bedroom for a private audience.

News of Varda's death was on the *Le Monde* website by 1 pm on March 29. Even though Birkin had been at her friend's side the previous evening, she was in disbelief. She told *Paris Match* that she'd thought Varda was "immortal." Her death was international news, and in France, it was a national loss and a local tragedy.

Before long, the pavement in front of rue Daguerre came to resemble a shrine. The offerings to Varda's memory included flowers, postcards of cats, personal letters, and, of course, potatoes, heart-shaped and otherwise.

Inside the house, Julia Fabry was on the phone with a Canadian broadcaster, informing her that the mood at rue Daguerre was not mournful but "sweet." Rosalie, Mathieu, and their children greeted friends paying condolence calls. Family members brought glasses of water to strangers outside who were bearing floral and tuber gifts for the deceased.

French president Emmanuel Macron said it not with flowers but with words: "She taught us how to see again." On Instagram, Martin Scorsese likewise praised her work. "Movies big and small, playful and tough, generous and solitary, lyrical and unflinching, and *alive*." He exhorted his young followers to watch them.

Thunderstorms drenched Paris on the morning of April 2, the day of Varda's memorial at the Cinémathèque française. Her funeral at Montparnasse cemetery would follow; she would be buried next to Demy. By 10:30, mourners were crowding the entrance of the Cinémathèque, designed by Frank Gehry in 1992. There were Varda's family, her cinema family, art family, collaborators, government officials, and friends, so many friends. Cinephiles habitually come early to claim the best seats. Those were in the salle Henri Langlois where press and speakers already had assembled. It took three auditoriums at the Cinémathèque to accommodate the seven hundred mourners. Those arriving late sat in either the Franju or the Epstein room and watched the proceedings livestreamed from the Langlois.

In the large theater were three generations of French actresses, including Catherine Deneuve, Jane Birkin, Sandrine Bonnaire, and Marion Cotillard. The art world was represented by JR and his partner, Prune Nourry, Christian Boltanski and Annette Messager, and Dominique Païni, art critic and curator. Government officials included Franck Riester, the current minister of culture, his predecessor, Jack Lang, and Marlène Schiappa, minister of gender equity. Naturally, French film's administrative troika of Frédérique Bredin of the CNC, Thierry Frémaux of Cannes, and Serge Toubiana of Unifrance were present.

Because Varda hated tributes, Frédéric Bonnaud, president of the Cinémathèque, framed the event as a family reunion. It celebrated Varda's artistic, political, and lighthearted sides. Most of all, it emphasized her talent for friendship.

Sandrine Bonnaire and then JR each spoke of their special bond with Varda. Bonnaire gave thanks to the surrogate mother who rooted her in the profession; JR spoke of how he treasured their similarities, despite their differences in age and culture.

Then a montage of news clips on the theme of "women in cinema" played, highlighting Varda's variously brusque, biting, and tongue-in-cheek responses. This was followed by another montage, of Dancing Varda, which closed with her "dance of cinema" with Jolie.

The last three speakers struggled to hold back tears.

Thierry Frémaux gave thanks to Varda for her activism, her films, and herself.

A visibly overcome Deneuve recited Arthur Rimbaud's poem "Sensation," about losing oneself in nature. The imagery of wheat spikes swaying in the wind is reminiscent of many a Varda film.

The "family reunion" ended with Jane Birkin's a cappella rendition of "L'amour de moi," a traditional song about a friend's death: "To life she said, 'pause' / That's how she went."

Outside the Cinémathèque buses waited to take mourners to Montparnasse cemetery. There, a short walk from rue Daguerre, Varda would be interred next to Demy in the place where her friends Brassaï, Henri Langlois, Chris Marker, Philippe Noiret, Alain Resnais, Delphine Seyrig, and Susan Sontag had preceded her.

On the avenue leading to the gravesite, many noticed an improvised memorial to Varda's two-tone hair. The finials atop a row of metal bollards were painted red with white circles inside. It was the work of Corentin Vignet, Varda's grandson. Previously he had done this as a prank and been arrested, and his grandmother had to pick him up from the police station. That time, his handiwork was painted over. This time, it was treated as a gesture of love, and remains untouched.

At the gravesite where Varda had planted a tree and placed a wooden bench for her visits to Demy, Rosalie and Mathieu spoke. Rosalie talked of her adult years with her mother, quoting Varda's epigram that "all one needs in life is a computer, a camera, and a cat." With equal parts humor and incredulity, Mathieu recalled his mother's art world debut. "At seventy-five years old, strolling around the Venice Biennale dressed as a potato!" He celebrated her powers of persuasion: "She could convince you that the glass was full when it was only half empty. She could even convince you that it was full when there was no glass!"

She was survived by her two children, five grandchildren, three cats, forty-four films, 20,400 photographic negatives, and artworks in museums and private collections around the world.

Those numbers quantify personal and professional accomplishments. Beyond them were Varda's greatest legacy—her immeasurable catalytic effect on those she inspired to protest inequality, to recycle, to pick up a movie or still camera, to find new forms for art.

An Agnès Varda Filmography

1955   *La Pointe Courte* (FEATURE FILM)

1958   *L'opéra-mouffe / Diary of a Pregnant Woman* (SHORT FILM)

1958   *La cocotte d'azur* (SHORT FILM)

1958   *Du côté de la côte / Along the Coast / Coasting the Coast*
       (SHORT FILM)

1958   *Ô saisons, ô châteaux* (SHORT FILM)

1961   *Les fiancés du pont MacDonald*
       (MÉFIEZ-VOUS DES LUNETTES NOIRES) (SHORT FILM)

1962   *Cléo de 5 à 7 / Cléo from 5 to 7* (FEATURE FILM)

1963   *Salut les cubains* (SHORT FILM)

1965   *Le Bonheur* (FEATURE FILM)

1965   *Elsa la rose* (SHORT FILM)

1966   *Les Créatures / The Creatures* (FEATURE FILM)

1967   *Oncle Yanco / Uncle Yanco* (SHORT FILM)

1968   *Black Panthers* (SHORT FILM)

1969   *Lions Love . . . and Lies* (FEATURE FILM)

1970   *Nausicaa* (TV MOVIE, NEVER BROADCAST)

1975   *Daguerréotypes* (FEATURE FILM)

1975   *Réponse de femmes / Women Reply* (SHORT FILM)

1976   *Plaisir d'amour en Iran* (SHORT FILM)

1977   *L'une chante, l'autre pas / One Sings, the Other Doesn't*
           (FEATURE FILM)

1981   *Mur Murs* (FEATURE FILM)

1981   *Documenteur* (FEATURE FILM)

1982   *Ulysse* (SHORT FILM)

1983   *Une minute pour une image* (TV SERIES)

1984   *Les dites cariatides / The So-Called Caryatids* (SHORT FILM)

1984   *7p. cuis., s. de b., . . . à saisir* (SHORT FILM)

1985   *Sans toit ni loi / Vagabond* (FEATURE FILM)

1986   *T'as de beaux escaliers, tu sais / You've Got Beautiful Stairs,
           You Know* (SHORT FILM)

1988   *Jane B. par Agnès V. / Jane B. by Agnès V.* (FEATURE FILM)

1988   *Le petit amour / Kung Fu Master* (FEATURE FILM)

1991   *Jacquot de Nantes* (FEATURE FILM)

1993   *Les demoiselles ont eu 25 ans / The Young Girls Turn 25*
           (FEATURE FILM)

1994   *Les cent et une nuits de Simon Cinéma / A Hundred and
           One Nights* (FEATURE FILM)

1995   *L'univers de Jacques Demy / The World of Jacques Demy*
           (FEATURE FILM)

2000   *Les glaneurs et la glaneuse / The Gleaners and I*
           (FEATURE FILM)

2002   *Les glaneurs et la glaneuse . . . deux ans après / The Gleaners
           and I: Two Years Later* (FEATURE FILM)

2002   *Hommage à Zgougou* (ET SALUT À SABINE MAMOU) /
       TRIBUTE TO ZGOUGOU THE CAT (SHORT FILM)

2003   *Le lion volatil* (SHORT FILM)

2004   *Ydessa, les ours et etc. / Ydessa, the Bears and etc.*
       (SHORT FILM)

2004   *Viennale Walzer / Vienna International Film Festival
       2004 – Trailer* (SHORT FILM)

2005   *Les dites cariatides bis / The So-Called Caryatids 2*
       (SHORT FILM)

2005   *Cléo de 5 à 7: souvenirs et anecdotes / Cléo from 5 to 7:
       Remembrances and Anecdotes* (SHORT FILM)

2006   *Quelques veuves de Noirmoutier / Some Widows of
       Noirmoutier*

2008   *Les plages d'Agnès / The Beaches of Agnès* (FEATURE FILM)

2011   *Agnès de ci de là Varda* (TV SERIES, 5 EPISODES)

2015   *Les 3 boutons / The Three Buttons* (SHORT FILM)

2017   *Visages Villages / Faces Places* (FEATURE FILM)

2019   *Varda par Agnès / Varda by Agnès* (FEATURE FILM)

and her memoir in book form:

1994   *Agnès Varda, Varda par Agnès,* Paris: Editions Cahiers du
       cinéma et Ciné-Tamaris

Acknowledgments

THANK YOU to Rosalie Varda and Mathieu Demy for their help and their commitment to preserving the films and papers of their parents, and their care for their mother's extensive photographic work and art installations.

Hat tips to Glenn Kenny and Paul Bresnick, who suggested that a Varda biography was a good idea. Salutes to Matt Weiland and Huneeya Siddiqui for their judicious editing and enthusiasm. A curtsey to Allegra Huston, whom, among her other talents, is an ace copyeditor.

Gratitude to Bernard Bastide, film scholar, former Varda archivist, and *vrai gentilhomme*, for his sagacity, thoughtfulness, and research assistance.

I stand on the shoulders of Varda lovers, scholars, and writers, notably Sandy Flitterman-Lewis, Rebecca DeRoo, Alison Smith, Delphine Benezet, Kelley Conway, Larry Kardish, Richard Neupert, Richard Peña, and Ginette Vincendeau, and am indebted to them in so many ways.

For their help and their scholarship, observations, and translation assistance, my thanks to these cinephiles, film savants, and movie geeks: the late Gerald Ayres, Judy Baca, Cari Beauchamp, Peter

Becker, Jeanine Basinger, Lisa Blok-Linson, Meredith Brody, Mark Cousins, Hélène Demy-McNulty, Joan Dupont, Alonso Duralde, Ava DuVernay, David Ehrenstein, Andrew Ferrett, Nancy Gertsman, Alizee Gex, Bruce Goldstein, Marie Therese Guirgis, Piers Handling, Liz Helfgott, Agnieszka Holland, Julie Huntsinger, Noah Isenberg, Dave Kehr, Wendy Keys, Chloe King, Homay King, Jessica Lajard, Martha Lauzen, Gillian Lefkowitz, Lynne Littman, Adrian Martin, Louis Massiah, Patricia Mazuy, Annette Messager, Adeline Monzier, Nathalie Obadia, the late Max Raab, Toby Rafelson, B. Ruby Rich, Reid Rosefelt, Emily Russo, Wade Saunders, Martin Scorsese, Matt Severson, Girish Shambu, Melissa Silverstein, Joan Simon, Kira Simon-Kennedy, Alan Singer, Gillian Slonem, Helga Stephenson, Scout Tafoya, Anne Thompson, John Timpane, Marco Troietti, Laura Truffaut, and Patricia White.

It takes a village to raise a child, and it took friends and family from three states to get this book airborne. Love to Aunts Marion and Nina Barsky for their humor and wisdom. A hug for Laurence Dreiband, who instigated my film education at age sixteen with a gift of books by André Bazin, Georges Sadoul, and Andrew Sarris. Three more hugs for nephew Laurence Donahue-Greene, his wife Heather, and spiritual nephew Alfredo Lopez.

Concentric circles of professors, editors, colleagues, and friends have sustained me over the years. They are Pat Baxter, Diane Burko, Corinne Cacas, the late Vince Canby, the late Roger Ebert, the late Manny Farber, Ellen Ginsburg, Debra Goldstein, the late Stephen Harvey, Linda Hasert, Molly Haskell, Jan Hoffman, Kathleen Hall Jamieson, Joanna Kiernan, Ann Kolson, Robin Komita-Moussa, Jennifer Kotter, Joyce and Max Kozloff, Gary Kramer, Phillip Lopate, Lainey Moseley, Ligia Rave, Judith Stein, Jeff Weinstein, Signe Wilkinson, and Susan Zukin.

Notes

ABBREVIATIONS

AVI: *Agnes Varda Interviews*, edited by T. Jefferson Kline
    (Jackson: University of Mississippi Press, 2014)
HV: Hélène Varda d'Allens, "Histoire de Varda," unpublished
HDM: Hélène Demy-McNulty interview by the author,
    February 24, 2023
JV–BB: Jean Varda, interview by Bernard Bastide, April 2, 2021
RV: Rosalie Varda, interview by the author, April 11, 2021
VpA: Agnès Varda, *Varda par Agnès* (Paris: Éditions Cahiers du
    cinéma), 1994

EPIGRAPH

vii **"Talent is insignificant"**: James Baldwin, "James Baldwin: The Art
    of Fiction," interview by Jordan Elgrably, *Paris Review*, no. 78, issue 91
    (Spring 1984).

INTRODUCTION

xii **"Cléo is the cliché woman"**: Mireille Amiel, "Agnès Varda Talks about the
    Cinema," AVI, 73.
xii **Over more than sixty years**: Martha M. Lauzen, "The Celluloid Ceiling:
    Behind-the-Scenes Employment of Women on the Top 250 Films of 2009,"

Center for the Study of Women in Television and Film, San Diego State University, 2010.

xii **As Martin Scorsese put it**: Martin Scorsese, email interview by the author, March 27, 2023.

xiii **"a group of hot-headed noisy auteurs"**: Michel Capdenac, "Agnès Varda: The Hour of Truth," AVI, 17.

xiii **"a complicated passion"**: Agnès Varda to the author, Unifrance luncheon, Cannes, May 1988.

xiii **a 2018 march at the Cannes Film Festival**: Rebecca J. DeRoo, "Power and Protest at the Cannes Film Festival," *Camera Obscura* 106 (2021), 132–35.

xiv **"People often speak of how [Agnès] broke new ground"**: Thom Bettridge, "Angelina Jolie, Jane Birkin, Isabelle Huppert, and Others, Write Love Letters to Agnès Varda," *Interview*, September 6, 2018.

xiv **"she was more loved"**: Bettridge, "Angelina Jolie, Jane Birkin, Isabelle Huppert, and Others, Write Love Letters to Agnès Varda."

xiv **"can draw consolation from"**: Donald Clarke, "Agnès Varda's Death Is a Loss to French Cinema, but Her Legacy Lives On," *Irish Times*, March 29, 2019.

xv **"the first chime"**: Jean de Baroncelli, *Le Monde*, June 5, 1955.

CHAPTER I

3 **They had named her Arlette**: VpA, 10.

3 **an ethnic Greek born in 1890**: HV.

3 **Following Eugène's education**: HV.

3 **Eugène marched with the Belgian army**: JV–BB, April 2, 2021.

4 **At Verdun in 1916**: JV–BB.

4 **Born in 1898, she was**: HV.

4 **Her brother Jean was told**: JV–BB.

5 **"Did Mom, by naming me"**: VpA, 10.

5 **"My beloved daughter Christiane"**: HV.

6 **"Of my birth and my little entrance"**: VpA, 35.

7 **Varda's daughter, Rosalie, remembers**: RV.

9 **"What is certain is that I hated Snow White"**: Bernard Bastide, interview with Agnès Varda, in Carole Aurouet, "Contes et legends a l'ecran," *Cinemaction* no. 116, 2005, pp. 256–261.

9 **Varda would tell critic Amy Taubin**: Amy Taubin, interview by the author, January 15, 2021.

10 **"a minimum of effects for each child"**: VpA, 13.

12 **"The real times of my youth"**: VpA, 22.

13 **"What a godsend for me"**: VpA, 22.

13 **"wed around a crate of cherries"**: VpA, 22.

CHAPTER 2

15 **The only public place to see the French tricolor**: Larry Collins and Dominique Lapierre, *Is Paris Burning?* (New York: Warner, 1965), 8.

15 **Nearly two hundred bronze statues**: Collins and Lapierre, *Is Paris Burning?*, 7.

15 **The ersatz coffee**: Collins and Lapierre, *Is Paris Burning?*, 8.

15 **The Gaumont-Palace**: Collins and Lapierre, *Is Paris Burning?*, 10.

16 **"sacred activity"**: Collins and Lapierre, *Is Paris Burning?*, 11.

16 **"listened to a poem by Mallarmé"**: *The Beaches of Agnès.*

16 **"didn't climb the Eiffel Tower"**: *The Beaches of Agnès.*

16 **"we rarely talked about the war"**: *The Beaches of Agnès.*

16 **"excruciating," "grey, inhuman"**: John Wakeman, World Film Directors (New York: H. W. Wilson, 1988), 1142.

17 **Leslie Caron**: Leslie Caron, *Thank Heaven* (New York: Viking, 1009), 29–30.

17 **"of theater, painting and of craftsmen"**: VpA, 22.

19 **"the debris of a country in ruins"**: Michael Kelly, *The Cultural and Intellectual Rebuilding of France after the Second World War* (London: Palgrave Macmillan, 2004), 15.

19 **Between 1944 and 1947**: Transcript of grades, École du Louvre.

19 **"too abstract"**: VpA, 25.

19 **"she was happy"**: VpA, 25.

20 **"We were four girls"**: Kelley Conway, *Agnès Varda* (Urbana: University of Illinois Press, 2015), 134.

20 **She was drawn to Lautréamont**: Joan Simon, "Joan Simon in Conversation with Agnes Varda," *Cahiers d'Art*, no. 1 (2015).

20 **"I liked the arts"**: VpA, 8.

21 **She did not change her name legally**: Bernard Bastide, email to the author, January 14, 2023.

21 **"unambiguous cohabitation"**: *The Beaches of Agnès* (2008), Criterion.

21 **"curled on a small coil"**: *The Beaches of Agnès.*

21 **"One day the relationship took"**: VpA, 30.

22 **She liked being one of the guys**: VpA, 30.

CHAPTER 3

23 **"The good Gaston"**: VpA, 10.

23 **"had this dream of the *material*"**: Gordon Gow, "The Underground River," AVI, 42.

24 **"stupid, antiquated"**: quoted in John Wakeman, ed., *World Film Directors*, vol. 2 (New York: H. W. Wilson, 1988), 1142–48.

25   "At the time, you needed a CAP": VpA, 12.

25   "with tiny points of gray": VpA, 28.

25   During Christmastime in 1948 and 1949: VpA, 25.

26   "A bathroom where I rinsed photos": VpA, 13.

26   "What a pleasure when it was filled": VpA, 13.

28   "Who would want to live *there*?": VpA, 16–17.

28   "[Eugène and Agnès] weren't in the same universe": JV–BB, April 2, 2021.

29   "When you're a photographer": Nicole Jolivet, "Discover Paris with ... Agnès Varda: Rue Daguerre and the 14th," *France-Soir*, August 16, 1975.

29   "a work in progress": Nathalie Obadia, interview with the author, February 27, 2023.

30   "I don't live in Paris": Jolivet, "Discover Paris."

30   "Vilar was a teacher to me": VpA, 33–34.

31   "he eliminated all signs of privilege": Maria Shevtsova, "Jean Vilar," in *Fifty Key Theatre Directors*, edited by Shomit Mitter and Maria Shevtsova (New York: Routledge, 2005), 62.

31   "theater was as necessary": Shevtsova, "Jean Vilar," 63.

32   "smiled when sad": David Thomson, *The New Biographical Dictionary of Film* (New York: Alfred A. Knopf, 2002), 678.

32   "When Gérard Philipe": Jean Simon, "Agnès Varda in Conversation with Joan Simon," *Cahiers d'Art*, no. 1 (2015).

32   Vilar and Varda took Calder: Simon, interview with AV.

33   "Would you like me to make you a necklace?": Simon, interview with AV.

33   "all black, large flat leaves": VpA, 12.

33   "We would make paella": Simon, interview with AV.

34   "they were less erotic": VpA, 12.

35   made her movie debut in front of the camera: "Agnès Varda et Brassaï, rue Daguerre," YouTube video.

CHAPTER 4

39   "total ignorance of beautiful films": VpA, 38.

39   "I was struck": "Academy Visual History with Agnès Varda," Academy of Motion Picture Arts and Sciences, YouTube video.

40   "In the beginning": VpA, 38.

41   "charming projects": VpA, 39.

41   "like stashing away notebooks": VpA, 40.

42   "We therefore had more than ten times less money": VpA, 40.

43   "[Varda's] first film had all the markings of the avant-garde": Richard

Neupert, *A History of the French New Wave Cinema*, 2nd ed. (Madison: University of Wisconsin Press, 2007), 58.

44 **"It was clear"**: VpA, 42.

44 **"Your research is too close to mine . . . I collapsed"**: VpA, 46.

45 **"While I can't . . . rushes"**: VpA, 46.

45 **"This is a monk's job"**: VpA, 46.

45 **"I did what you said . . . Overtime, no"**: VpA, 46.

47 **"By scrupulously editing my film"**: VpA, 47.

48 **Varda would later admit to Jean-Luc Douin**: Jean-Luc Douin, "Agnès Varda, cinéaste et plasticienne," in *Alain Resnais* (Paris: Éditions de la Martinière, 2013), 251–53.

48 **And he was equally fond of her**: RV.

48 **If she expected to find him alone**: VpA, 13.

49 **"They quoted thousands of films"**: VpA, 13.

49 **Bazin wrote favorably**: André Bazin, "La Pointe Courte: Un Film Libre et Pur," *Le Parisien libéré*, January 7, 1956.

50 **"Main aspect of this film"**: Peter Debruge, "A Critic's Appreciation of Agnès Varda," *Variety*, November 10, 2017.

50 **"the first work of a talented young woman"**: Jean de Baroncelli, "La Pointe Courte," *Le Monde*, January 10, 1956.

51 **"the cream of the intellectual set"**: Kelley Conway, *Agnès Varda* (Urbana: University of Illinois Press, 2015), 142.

51 **"I'm sure she's hiding"**: Jean-Luc Cheray, director of Studio Parnasse, interviewed in the television documentary *Marchands d'images*, directed by Roger Boussinot and J. C. Bergeret, 1964.

51 **"Did anyone notice"**: Jean-Luc Cheray, director of Studio Parnasse, interviewed in the television documentary *Marchands d'images*, directed by Roger Boussinot and J. C. Bergeret, 1964.

51 **"earnest and intelligent work"**: François Truffaut, "La Pointe Courte," *Arts*, January 11, 1956.

52 **"is an admirable film"**: François Truffaut, interview broadcast on Radio-Television Belgique Francophone, 1961.

52 **"for a film that never received"**: Conway, *Agnès Varda*, 23–24.

52 **the term "New Wave" was demographic**: Françoise Giroud, "The New Wave Arrives!," *L'Express*, October 3–December 12, 1957.

52 **"to drop the notion of guaranteed subsidies"**: Neupert, *History of the French New Wave Cinema*, 38.

53 **"certainly the first film of the New Wave"**: Ginette Vincendeau, "*La Pointe Courte*: How Agnes Varda 'Invented' the New Wave," Criterion.com, January, 21, 2008.

CHAPTER 5

56   "collective behavior . . . civic sharing": VpA, 13–14.

56   "sublime juxtaposition": VpA, 13–14.

56   "in short, everything one finds": VpA, 13–14.

57   "tender friendship grew": Antoine Bourseiller, *Sans Relache* (Arles: Actes Sud, 2008), 23.

57   "the island where sand is blue": Bourseiller, *Sans Relache*, 24.

57   "I watched the Leica": Bourseiller, *Sans Relache*, 25.

57   "I stumbled into": VpA, 74–75.

59   Varda told Rosalie that: RV.

61   "The film won some notoriety": Laurence Kardish, "Agnès Varda's Long-Term Legacy," *Indiewire*, March 31, 2019.

61   "Justine": RV.

61   "The more I see [*Ô saisons*]": VpA, 229.

61   "irritated impatience . . . completely free style": Jacques Gerber, *Anatole Dauman: Pictures of a Producer* (London: British Film Institute, 1992), 31.

62   "to the part of her . . . brandishing a camera!": Gerber, *Anatole Dauman*, 31.

64   "Except for 30 seconds": Gerber, *Anatole Dauman*, 34.

64   "appalled . . . lacked any fizz": Gerber, *Anatole Dauman*, 33.

64   "I claim that [the film] does not exist": VpA, 232.

66   "invited me to the local café": VpA, 17.

66   "She personally requested me": Gerber, *Anatole Dauman*, 4.

66   "I gently called to her": Gerber, *Anatole Dauman*, 35.

66   "her usual aggressive manner": Michael Temple and Karen Smolens, eds., *A Richard Roud Anthology* (Basingstoke: Palgrave Macmillan, 2014), 230.

66   "chirping from her baby basket . . . biblically": VpA, 215.

CHAPTER 6

68   the term "New Wave" was first applied: Richard Neupert, *A History of the French New Wave Cinema*, 2nd ed. (Madison: University of Wisconsin Press, 2007), 5.

69   "Cinema and its function had changed": Richard Brody, *Everything Is Cinema* (New York: Holt, 2008), 56.

69   "I do not subsidize groceries": Neupert, *History of the French New Wave Cinema*, 38.

69   "When Jacques made me read": VpA, 4.

70   "are to cinema what drawing": VpA, 23.

70   "astonishing": Neupert, *History of the French New Wave Cinema*, 333.

70 "a triumph . . . innovated in everything": Jean Douchet, *Arts*, no. 726 (June 10, 1959).

72 "the story of a man": Jean Michaud and Raymond Bellour, *Cinéma 61*, no. 60 (October 1961).

72 "When we become, we do not cancel": Bernard Bastide, "La mélangite, le 'western mental,'" *Trafic*, no. 118 (Summer 2021).

72 "Agnès Varda has shot a sequence": Gilles Jacob and Claude de Givray, eds., *François Truffaut: Correspondence 1945–1984* (New York: Farrar, Straus and Giroux, 1990), 151.

73 "I wanted to try": Bastide, "La mélangite."

73 Varda was annoyed when a representative: VpA, 18.

73 "make a little film in black-and-white": VpA, 48.

74 "beautifully balanced": "Agnès Varda Tributes," *Deadline*, March 29, 2019.

74 "How could you refuse": Michel Legrand, *J'ai le regret de vous dire oui* (Paris: Éditions Liana Levi, 2020), 144.

75 "Agnès was the pragmatist . . . nurturer": Tom Luddy, interview by the author, January 22, 2020.

75 "Jacques really raised me": RV.

75 "What did Paris evoke for me?": VpA, 48.

75 "a portrait of a woman": Adrian Martin, "*Cléo from 5 to 7*: Passionate Time," Criterion.com, January 21, 2008.

76 "risked making a movie": Michel Capdenac, "Agnès Varda: The Hour of Truth," AVI, 21.

76 "turns Paris into a hall of mirrors": Molly Haskell, "*Cléo from 5 to 7*," Criterion.com, May 15, 2000.

77 "quite a shock . . . dramatic circumstances": Martin Scorsese, email interview by the author, March 27, 2023.

78 "woman seen to a woman seeing": Alison Smith, *Agnès Varda* (Manchester: Manchester University Press, 1998), 100.

78 "it was one of those films": Neupert, *History of the French New Wave Cinema*, 361.

78 "intimate and whispering . . . quite a stir": VpA, 59.

78 "*Cléo from 5 to 7* Is a Masterpiece": Jean-Louis Bory, *Arts*, April 1962.

78 "Varda's [film] is excellent": Jacob and Givray, *François Truffaut: Correspondence*, 167.

79 "Do you see a greater meaning": Conway, *Agnès Varda*, 46–56.

79 The two women appeared together: "Madonna c'est Madonna," television documentary broadcast October 14, 1993, on TeleFrance 1. Excerpted in "Madonna and Agnès," DVD extra, "The Complete Films of Agnes Varda," Criterion, 2020.

CHAPTER 7

80 **"was ecstatic"**: Bernard Bastide, interview with Agnès Varda, June 17, 1998.

80 **"Jacques and I weren't particularly keen"**: Bernard Bastide, interview with Agnès Varda, June 17, 1998.

82 **"I am surprised that three"**: VpA, 11.

84 **"They had totally different . . . swimming pool"**: Rodney F. Hill, "The Family Business," *Cineaste*, Spring 2020.

85 ***"bricoleuse"***: Philippe Martin, *Mag Bodard: Portrait d'une productrice* (Paris: La Tour Vert, 2013), 76.

86 **"very hesitant"**: Agnès Varda, "Un petit coin de parapluie," press kit for 1992 rerelease of *The Umbrellas of Cherbourg*, 16–17.

86 **"We are floating"**: Michel Legrand, *J'ai le regret de vous dire oui* (Paris: Éditions Liana Levi, 2020), 159.

87 **"Don't calm me down!"**: VpA, 65.

87 **"I never started to think . . . stencil"**: VpA, 65.

88 **"A ripe summer peach"**: "Agnès Varda on *Le Bonheur*," 1998. DVD extra, "The Complete Films of Agnès Varda," Criterion, 2020.

89 **"intended to make a pastoral?"**: Amy Taubin, "*Le Bonheur*: Splendor in the Grass," Criterion.com, January 21, 2008.

90 **"When we presented the film"**: Marie-France Boyer, "The Two Women of *Le Bonheur*," Criterion Channel.

90 **"The real scandal"**: Georges Sadoul, *Les Lettres françaises*, March 4–10, 1965.

90 **"perhaps with tongue in cheek"**: A. H. Weiler, " '*Le Bonheur*' at the Fine Arts: A Moving but Immature Treatment of Love," *New York Times*, May 24, 1966.

90 **"unforgivably cruel . . . women's cinema"**: Claire Johnston, "Women's Cinema as Counter-Cinema," in Bill Nichols, ed., *Movies and Methods*, vol. 1 (Berkeley: University of California Press, 1976), 208–17.

90 **"The idea is extraordinary"**: Nicole Brenez, "Chantal Akerman: The Pajama Interview," *LOLA*, no. 2 (June 2012).

90 **most misunderstood film**: Richard Neupert, *A History of the French New Wave Cinema*, 2nd ed. (Madison: University of Wisconsin Press, 2007).

90 **"profoundly feminist"**: Sandy Flitterman-Lewis, *To Desire Differently: Feminism and the French Cinema* (Urbana: University of Illinois Press, 1990), 227.

90 **"I can say that I am a feminist"**: Jacqueline Levitan, "Mother of the New Wave," AVI, 56.

91 **"Can we accept something painful"**: Boyer, "The Two Women of *Le Bonheur*."

91   *Paris Match* **celebrated Varda and Demy:** Georges Reyer, "Un *'Bonheur'* qui fait grincer des dents," *Paris Match*, no. 831 (March 13, 1965).

92   **"Oh, Gerry":** Gerald Ayres, *Everywhere Hollywood* (self-published, 2016), 54.

93   **"like a priest rushing through Mass":** VpA, 84.

94   **"Varda Film Bewilders Festival Audience":** *New York Times*, August 30, 1966.

94   **"Your film is as silly as Jean Renoir":** VpA, 243.

95   **"marvelous":** VpA, 18.

95   **"It made a lasting impression . . . my hero":** Agnieszka Holland, interview by the author, July 5, 2020.

95   **"Marguerite built up airs":** Brenez, "Chantal Akerman."

95   **"Agnès was a mother figure . . . absorbed":** Holland, interview by the author.

CHAPTER 8

97   **"each time the phone would ring":** quoted in Scott Feinberg, "Martin Scorsese Calls Agnès Varda 'One of the Film Gods' at Fest Tribute," *Hollywood Reporter*, August 31, 2019.

97   **"where people of all colors":** VpA, 92.

98   **"cliché house":** VpA, 93.

98   **"a modest cottage":** Gerald Ayres, *Everywhere Hollywood* (self-published, 2016), 76.

98   **"snorted in contempt . . . resented it":** Ayres, *Everywhere Hollywood*, 76.

98   **"by watching the dubbed version":** VpA, 92.

99   **Hélène Demy recalls that the disciplined Varda:** HDM.

99   **"Strong and intelligent personalities":** VpA, 93.

99   **"Some people get eaten up":** Sandy Flitterman-Lewis, interview by the author, February 16, 2022.

100 **"patchwork quilt of a houseboat":** Homay King, "Floating Roots," *Camera Obscura* 106 (2021), 12.

100 **"He instantly became the image":** Agnès Varda, introduction to *Uncle Yanco*, Criterion DVD.

102 **Varda hoped to cast Sharon Tate:** VpA, 103.

102 **"Agnès balked . . . End of deal":** Ayres, *Everywhere Hollywood*, 72.

103 **"brilliant, funny, and incredibly mean":** VpA, 94.

103 **Demy wrote a script for Hepburn and Jim Morrison:** Ayres, *Everywhere Hollywood*, 107.

103 **"a monument of platinum curls":** VpA, 101.

103 **"Mischievous as the devil":** VpA, 103.

103 **"received me in an Oriental dress"**: VpA, 103.

104 **an interview with Huey Newton**: Tom Luddy, interview by the author, January 22, 2020.

104 **"You can't say no to Agnès"**: Luddy, interview by the author.

104 **"the girls continued their joyful racket"**: VpA, 102.

105 **"Jacques Demy is as gentle"**: Lynne Littman, diary entry, September 20, 1968.

106 **"But the agency"**: Max Nelson, "The Intimate and the Collective," *The Nation*, January 23, 2020.

106 **"They say that filmmaking is a collaborative medium"**: Littman, diary entry, September 20, 1968.

107 **"too old to be hippies"**: Max Raab, interview by the author, 2005.

107 **"I gave her money because I loved *Le Bonheur*"**: Max Raab, interview by the author, 2005.

107 **Through Michel Legrand's agent**: Ayres, *Everywhere Hollywood*, 89.

107 **visited the Factory**: Hans Ulrich Obrist, "The Last Living Dinosaur of the New Wave," *Interview*, September 5, 2018.

107 **"[Warhol] was there, royal"**: VpA, 34.

109 **"There is so much so pleasant about *Lions Love*"**: Vincent Canby, "Film Fete: Viva, Ragni and Rado in *Lions Love*, Movie by Agnès Varda Is Set in Hollywood," *New York Times*, September 22, 1969.

109 **"touching on the grotesque"**: Seventh New York Film Festival, Jack Kroll interview with Susan Sontag and Agnès Varda, September 1969, YouTube video.

110 **"ironic that Miss Varda"**: Canby, "Film Fete."

CHAPTER 9

111 **"they were like Bedouins"**: Gerald Ayres, *Everywhere Hollywood* (self-published, 2016), 49.

111 **"introduced her to painting and cinema . . . intimidated"**: HDM.

113 **"France sold a lot of Mirage planes"**: Mireille Amiel, "Agnès Varda Talks about the Cinema," AVI, 72.

113 **She took solace in the memory**: VpA, 118.

113 **"Many had come to think of the New Wave"**: Richard Neupert, interview by the author, February 3, 2022.

115 **Varda had advocated for reproductive rights**: Ginette Vincendeau, "A Woman's Truth," Criterion.com, August 11, 2020.

115 **"One million women in France have abortions"**: Christine Delphy, "Beauvoir, l'héritage oublié," *Travail, genre et sociétés* 2, no. 20 (2008): 173–80.

116 **"I realize something has to be changed"**: Jacqueline Levitin, "Mother of the New Wave," AVI, 56–57.

117 **"Jim had developed a real fondness"**: Jerry Hopkins and Danny Sugerman, *No One Here Gets Out Alive* (New York: Grand Central, 2006), 362.

118 **Jim Morrison's death and funeral**: Hopkins and Sugerman, *No One Gets Out of Here Alive*; Stephen Davis, *Jim Morrison: Life, Death, Legend* (New York: Gotham, 2004); Clément Mathieu, "Les dernières heures de Jim Morrison," *Paris Match,* April 25 1991; and *The Last Days of Jim Morrison*, documentary film, directed by Michaëlle Gagnet, 2006.

118 **"I saw him dead"**: Mathieu, "Les dernières heures de Jim Morrison."

119 **as Morrison biographer Stephen Davis suggests**: Davis, *Jim Morrison*, 458.

CHAPTER 10

120 **"discouraged . . . between 1966 and 1975"**: Mireille Amiel, "Agnès Varda Talks about the Cinema," AVl, 76–77.

120 **"There are two problems"**: Jacqueline Levitin, "Mother of the New Wave," AVI, 60.

121 **"dreaded being thought. . . have to understand"**: Gerald Ayres, *Everywhere Hollywood* (self-published, 2016), 216.

122 **"Give birth! . . . We'll make the front page!"**: Giovanni Marchini Camia, "A Filmmaker's Joy," *Fireflies*, no. 5 (April 8, 2019).

122 **"Despite my joy, I couldn't help"**: Amiel, "Agnès Varda Talks Cinema," 76–77.

123 **"began as a joke"**: Rodney Hill, "Demy Monde: Jacques Demy and the French New Wave," PhD dissertation, University of Kansas, 2006, 115–16.

124 **"the heart of the problem . . . finally awake"**: Agnès Varda, "Notes sur Toronto," *La Revue du Cinéma: Image et Son*, no. 283 (April 1974): 63–66.

125 **"I learned a lot"**: HDM.

125 **"Tamaris went dormant"**: Kelley Conway, "Agnès Varda, Producer," *Camera Obscura* 106 (2021), 111.

126 **"Little by little the feminist movement"**: Levitin, "Mother of the New Wave," 55.

126 **"felt a bit stuck"**: Mireille Amiel, "Agnès Varda Talks about the Cinema," AVI, 65.

127 **"affectionate anthropology"**: Richard Brody, "Daguerreotypes," *New Yorker*, April 14, 2015.

127 **Varda was disappointed that the closer she got to her neighbors**: Agnès Varda in conversation with the author, Cannes Film Festival, 1988.

128 **"What does it mean"**: VpA, 252.

128 **"as an affirmation"**: VpA, 252.

129 **"Demy and Varda were always together"**: Laura Truffaut, interview by the author, September 30, 2022.

130 **"It was a venue beloved"**: Laurence Kardish, interview by the author, August 18, 2021.

132 **"In a woman's life"**: Ruth McCormick, *One Sings, the Other Doesn't,* AVI, 97.

132 **"does for the spirit of sorority"**: Molly Haskell, "Agnès Varda's Ode to Female Friendship Returns to Theaters," quoted in "In Theaters," Criterion.com, May 31, 2018.

132 **"At key moments"**: Vincent Canby, "Varda's 'One Sings,'" *New York Times,* September 23, 1977.

133 **"Look, for once you have a film"**: McCormick, *One Sings,* 97.

133 **"Agnès was one of the Gods"**: Martin Scorsese, email interview by the author, March 27, 2023.

133 **"feminist men . . . anxiety onto men"**: McCormick, *One Sings,* 99.

133 **who observed that Bergman**: Molly Haskell in conversation with the author.

134 **"That really hurt"**: Françoise Aude and Jean-Pierre Jeancolas, "Interview with Agnès Varda," AVI, 117.

134 **"seemed to have unlimited means"**: Gilbert Adair, "Journals: Gilbert Adair from Paris," *Film Comment,* March/April 1979, 2–4.

134 **"somehow got on Demy's radar"**: Gillian Lefkowitz, interview by the author, September 20, 2022.

134 **"Agnès was no-bullshit"**: Lefkowitz, interview by the author.

135 **"She scared the shit out of me"**: Chloe King, interview by the author, August 6, 2022.

135 **"the target of the film's critique"**: Darren Waldron, *Jacques Demy* (Manchester: Manchester University Press, 2014), 138.

137 **"Agnès spent her time doing"**: Lynne Littman, interview by the author, September 6, 2022.

137 **"At this moment in our lives"**: VpA, 216.

137 **"Colette reminds me"**: Tom Luddy, interview by the author, March 25, 2020.

CHAPTER 11

138 **"I had a car and spoke French"**: Lisa Blok-Linson, interview by the author, September 10, 2022.

139 **"The pun is a mistake"**: Mireille Amiel, "Review of *Mur Murs,*" *Cinéma 82,* no. 277 (January 1982).

139 **"Agnès ended up on my doorstep"**: Judy Baca, interview by the author, July 11, 2020.

141 **"a shadow of *Mur Murs*"**: VpA, 166.

141 **"If it was sunny"**: Blok-Linson, interview by the author.

142 **"Sabine listened"**: Jean Darrigol, "Playing with Tarot Cards," AVI, 150–51.

142 **"said to me ... process of creating"**: Interview with Sabine Mamou, Jukola Art Community website.

142 **"Our core crew on *Documenteur*"**: Blok-Linson, interview by the author.

142 **"is the only time Agnès opened the door"**: Matt Severson, ed., *Agnès Varda: Director's Inspiration* (Los Angeles and New York: DelMonico Books / Academy Museum of Motion Pictures, 2023), 104.

142 **"Agnès processed her life"**: Blok-Linson, interview by the author.

143 **"Solitude in California"**: VpA, 151.

143 **the odds against finding money for feature films**: Agnès Varda and Sandrine Bonnaire, "Un lion d'or pour *Sans toit ni loi*," radio interview, Oroleis Paris/EVB-FR3, December 1985.

144 **"The evening conceived by Agnès Varda"**: Hervé Guibert, "Photographie Sonore," *Le Monde*, July 14, 1982.

145 **"Rather than fix a meaning"**: Ari J. Blatt, "Thinking Photography in Film, or the Suspended Cinema of Agnès Varda and Jean Eustache," *French Forum* 36, no. 2/3 (2011): 181–200.

146 **"is both educational and supremely fun"**: Joseph Pomp, "Photo Playing: The Archival Journey of *Une minute pour une image*," in *Cleo: A Journal of Film and Feminism* 6, no. 1 (Summer 2019).

149 **"The experience of improvising"**: Kelley Conway, *Agnès Varda* (Urbana: University of Illinois Press, 2015), 63.

149 **"I felt it worked for me"**: Conway, *Agnès Varda*, 64.

150 **"To a degree, Agnès was her own archivist"**: Richard Neupert, interview by the author, February 3, 2022.

151 **"The New Poor are growing"**: "Les 'nouveaux pauvres' sont de plus en plus nombreux," *Le Monde*, May 10, 1982.

151 **"Characters began to exist"**: VpA, 166.

152 **"She was such an extraordinary character"**: Françoise Wera, "Interview with Agnès Varda," AVI, 120.

152 **"It must be said that when"**: Conway, *Agnès Varda*, 68.

153 **"Varda took a red pen"**: Patricia Mazuy, interview by the author, November 18, 2022.

153 **He had discretionary funds**: René Prédal, *50 ans de cinéma français* (Paris: Nathan, 1996), 455.

153 **influence of Nathalie Sarraute**: Fabian Gastellier, "Agnès Varda, une cinéaste état d'urgence," *L'Unité*, no. 627 (December 14, 1985).

153 **"Because she talks about what"**: Gastellier, "Agnès Varda, une cinéaste état d'urgence."

155 **"that walking is the central, defining fact"**: Conway, *Agnès Varda*, 62.

155 **"[Mona] smells, she's contemptuous"**: *"Vagabond* Remembrances," DVD extra with *Vagabond,* directed by Agnès Varda, Criterion Collection, 2020.

156 **"You should probably take"**: Conway, *Agnès Varda*, 69.

156 **"Did you really make this film"**: VpA, 181.

156 **"The choice for the top prize"**: E. J. Dionne, "Venice Awards Top Prize to Varda Film," *New York Times*, September 7, 1985.

157 **"When I met you, I was a flower"**: Sandrine Bonnaire, "Goodbye to Agnès Varda, Not a Tribute but a Family Reunion," *Le Parisien*, April 2, 2019.

CHAPTER 12

159 **"Jacques enjoyed his partnership"**: Gerald Ayres, *Everywhere Hollywood* (self-published, 2016), 216.

159 **"crossing the Nile"**: VpA, 215.

160 **"A slightly grotesque happiness"**: VpA, 215.

162 **"At the time, I was like"**: Anne Diatkine, "Un film à la patte," *Libération*, July 6, 2000.

162 **"[Varda] sort of camped in our living room"**: Sam Adams, interview with Charlotte Gainsbourg, *AV Club*, November 3, 2009.

162 **"Oedipal wink"**: "Le clin d'oeil d'Oedipe à la comédie musicale" (interview with Yves Montand), *Le Monde*, November 24, 1988.

163 **"For the next two years"**: Michel Legrand, *J'ai le regret de vous dire oui* (Paris: Éditions Liana Levi, 2020), 184.

163 **"He's sick, but I didn't know it"**: Legrand, *J'ai le regret*.

163 **"We all went together"**: Clarence Tsui, "French Film Legend Agnès Varda on *Faces Places*, Her Feminist Vision, and Visits to Hong Kong and China," *South China Morning Post*, June 5, 2018.

163 **"a shady producer"**: VpA, 20.

163 **"Jacques was tired"**: Jean Decock, "Entretien avec Agnès Varda sur 'Jacquot de Nantes,'" *French Review* 66, no. 6 (May 1993).

164 **"You should make it"**: Academy of Motion Pictures Arts and Sciences Visual History, Agnès Varda interview by Manouchka Labouba, November 9, 2017.

165 **"little flashes, like premonitions"**: Academy Visual History, Varda interview.

165 **"The making of this film"**: Kelley Conway, *Agnès Varda* (Urbana: University of Illinois Press, 2015), 72.

166 **"Jacques hasn't been to the cinema"**: Agnès Varda, "Vers le visage de Jacques," *Cahiers du cinéma*, no. 438 (December 1990): 30–33.

167 **"He thought he could hide it"**: Simon Hattenstone, "Agnès Varda: 'I am still alive. I am still curious. I am not a piece of rotting flesh,'" *Guardian*, September 12, 2018.

167 **"We had the same idea"**: Reid Rosefelt, interview by the author, June 28, 2020.

169 **"When Alice Guy-Blaché died"**: Joan Simon, interview by the author, June 10, 2021.

169 **"compelled to put things in order"**: Bernard Bastide, email to the author, October 13, 2022.

170 **"seriously joking and joyfully precise"**: "Le jardin de Madame V," *Le Monde*, March 25, 1994.

170 **"opened most of the paths"**: "Le jardin de Madame V"

171 **"The evocations of great moments in film history"**: Jean-Michel Frodon, "Bric-à-brac," *Le Monde*, January 26, 1995.

172 **"there never have been so many women"**: Agnès Varda to the author, Unifrance luncheon, Cannes, May 1988.

172 **In 1998, when Varda turned seventy**: Martha M. Lauzen, "The Celluloid Ceiling: Behind-the-Scenes Employment of Women on the Top 250 Films of 2009," Center for the Study of Women in Television and Film, San Diego State University, 2010.

CHAPTER 13

174 **Bruce Goldstein . . . visited rue Daguerre**: Bruce Goldstein, interview by the author, October 3, 2022.

174 **reported Henri Béhar**: Henri Béhar, "Lettre d'Amerique," *Le Monde*, April 18, 1996.

174 **"Agnès came to New York"**: Laurence Kardish, "Agnès Varda's Long-Term Legacy: Why It Took Decades for American Audiences to Appreciate Her Work," *Indiewire*, March 30, 2019.

175 **"Initially it was intimidating"**: Marie-Therese Guirgis, interview by the author, October 25, 2022.

175 **"In practice, she was opposed"**: Guirgis, interview by the author.

175 **"And practiced with it throughout the summer"**: Rodney F. Hill, "The Family Business," *Cineaste*, Spring 2020.

177 **"was the discovery of the digital camera"**: Melissa Anderson, "The Modest Gesture of the Filmmaker," *Cineaste*, Fall 2001.

177 **"This is the camera"**: Anderson, "The Modest Gesture."

178 **"The film suggests that our culture is too quick"**: Kelley Conway, *Agnès Varda* (Urbana: University of Illinois Press, 2015), 78–79.

178 **"waste is related to not knowing"**: Anderson, "The Modest Gesture."

179 **"coincided . . . with a convergence of concerns"**: Ruth Cruickshank, "The Work of Art in the Age of Global Consumption: Agnès Varda's *Les Glaneurs et la glaneuse*," *L'Esprit Créateur* 47, no. 3 (Fall 2007): 119–32.

180 **"I think she may have been surprised"**: Emily Russo, interview by the author, October 28, 2022.

180 **"It really opened up the personal essay film"**: Richard Peña, interview by the author, July 31, 2020.

CHAPTER 14

183 **"A writer does a poem"**: James Adams, "Seven Questions: Agnès Varda," *Toronto Globe and Mail*, February 18, 2005.

183 **"in France, the *court métrage*"**: Tom Luddy, interview by the author, January 22, 2020.

183 **"to collapse the time"**: Jean-Michel Frodon, "La caméra numérique force les cinéastes à ouvrir l'oeil," *Le Monde*, August 14, 2001.

186 **"a heterogeneous, multiform"**: Linda Nochlin, "Pictures from an Exhibition: The Venice Biennale," *Artforum*, September 2003.

187 **"Before the Biennale opened"**: Annette Messager, interview by the author, March 8, 2023.

188 **"At first, tired eyes"**: A'dora Phillips, "Agnès Varda's Third Life as a Visual Artist: Interview with Rosalie Varda," *Vision and Art Project*, July 13, 2021.

188 **"just to deal with the urgency to create"**: Eric Kohn, "Agnès Varda's Daughter on Her Mother's Death and the Future of Her Archive," *Indiewire*, September 5, 2019.

189 **"were in the main theater"**: Serge Toubiana, "Unifrance Pays Tribute to Agnès Varda," Unifrance press release, March 29, 2019.

190 **described as a void**: Dominique Bluher, "Varda's Third Life," *Camera Obscura* 106 (2021), 194.

190 **"give shape to an emotion . . . offered"**: Jean-Luc Douin, "Varda donne forme à l'émotion," *Le Monde*, June 28, 2006.

190 **"to have the funereal exaltation"**: Douin, "Varda donne forme à l'émotion."

192 **"the couple of Agnès Varda and Jacques Demy"**: Nathalie Obadia, interview by the author, February 27, 2023.

192 **"We were at a table of about sixteen . . . confident"**: Obadia, interview by the author.

194 **"Because the sound mix . . . film history"**: Piers Handling, interview by the author, September 25, 2022.

194 **"Tender, playful, maliciously inventive"**: Jean-Luc Douin, "'Les Plages d'Agnés': Between modesty and display of intimacy, Agnès Varda pieces together the puzzle of her life," *Le Monde*, December 16, 2008.

194 **"elegant, eccentric, and distinctly literary"**: Peter Bradshaw, "A Witty and Engaging Cine-Autobiography," *Guardian*, October 1, 2009.

194 **"a rapturous tribute to life itself"**: Richard Brody, *The New Yorker*, April 25, 2016.

195 **"conceals as much as it reveals"**: Bradshaw, "A Witty and Engaging Cine-Autobiography."

195 **As Claire Denis . . . remembered**: Brooke Huseby, "Claire Denis Is in No Hurry to Make Films for You – or Anyone, Besides Herself," *Interview*, April 16, 2019.

196 **greater visibility . . . for female filmmakers**: Rebecca DeRoo, "Le Collectif 50/50 en 2020," *Camera Obscura* 106 (2021), 138; Tim Palmer, "Women Crash the Millionaire's Club," *Studies in French Cinema* 12 (2012).

197 **In the U.S. during the 2000s**: Martha M. Lauzen, "The Celluloid Ceiling: Behind-the-Scenes Employment of Women on the Top 250 Films of 2009," Center for the Study of Women in Television and Film, San Diego State University, 2010.

197 **"In spite of illness"**: Edith Wharton, *A Backward Glance* (New York: Touchstone, 1988), xix.

197 **"surprised by the flurry of young people"**: Reid Rosefelt, interview by the author, June 30, 2020.

197 **"database of images"**: Conway, *Agnès Varda*, 118.

197 **"Her standard working method now"**: Conway, *Agnès Varda*, 118.

199 **"effectively risen to state-sponsored canonization"**: Palmer, "Women Crash the Millionaire's Club."

CHAPTER 15

201 **"Sixty years of creation"**: Agnès Varda, TEDx Venice Beach, October 15, 2017.

201 **"In the ten years between when Agnès was eighty and ninety"**: Susan Kouguell, "Academy-Award-Nominated Producer Rosalie Varda Discusses Her Documentary Film, *Varda by Agnès*," *Script*, November 19, 2019.

201 **"This is shaping up to be the Year of Agnès Varda"**: Peter Debruge, "Locarno Honor Marks the Latest of Agnès Varda's Lifetime Achievements," *Variety*, August 10, 2014.

202 **"More women should be chosen"**: European Film Awards, "Agnieszka Holland Pays Tribute to Agnès Varda," December 2014, YouTube video.

203 **"It sounds crazy"**: Jada Yuan, "Agnès Varda and JR Talk Aging, *Faces Places*, and Road Trips Over Afternoon Tea," *Vulture*, October 11, 2017.

203 **"Our aims . . . meet in villages"**: Yuan, "Agnès Varda and JR Talk."

203 **"It's not a short film, but a documentary"**: Eric Kohn, "Agnès Varda's Daughter on Her Mother's Death and the Future of Her Archive," *Indiewire*, September 5, 2019.

204 **"Many filmmakers have taught me"**: Alonso Duralde, "Agnès Varda Appreciation: She Had Endless Curiosity About People and Filmmaking, And It Shows," *The Wrap*, March 29, 2019.

204 **"moving along with her gut"**: Julia Fabry, "It Was All about Life," *Exberliner*, July 18, 2022.

205 **Fabry recalled**: Fabry, "It Was All about Life."

205 **"But *their* films made money"**: Michael Rosser, "Agnès Varda to Receive Honorary Palme d'or," *Screen Daily*, May 9, 2015.

205 **"all the inventive and courageous filmmakers"**: Rebecca J. DeRoo, *Agnès Varda between Film, Photography, and Art* (Oakland: University of California Press, 2017), 5.

206 **"I have a few words to say"**: "Agnès Varda at the Logan Center Discussing Chantal Akerman," October 2015, video.

208 **"Agnès spoke and then said"**: Piers Handling, interview by the author, September 25, 2022.

208 **"As the only woman of the French New Wave"**: Agnés Varda, *Women in Film*, September 9, 2016, YouTube video.

208 **At Lincoln Center**: New York Film Festival, *Faces Places* Q & A, October 20, 2017, YouTube video.

208 **"that she could not have made this film alone"**: Amy Taubin, interview by the author, March 18, 2023.

209 **"She had a talent for seeing things"**: Patricia Mazuy, interview by the author, November 18, 2022.

210 **When Le Monde's Laurent Charpentier**: Laurent Charpentier, "Agnès Varda: Les féministes ont raison de gueuler!," *Le Monde*, November 10, 2017.

210 **Academy Governors Awards**: November 11, 2017, YouTube video.

213 **"It was very joyful"**: HDM.

CHAPTER 16

214 **"Retirement seems to be nowhere"**: Holly Brubach, "Agnès Varda," *Gentlewoman*, no. 18 (Autumn/Winter 2018).

216 **"She wanted to watch *Columbo*"**: Nathalie Obadia, interview by the author, February 27, 2023.

216 **"No. Not a man or a woman"**: Simon Hattenstone, "Agnès Varda: 'I am still alive, I am still curious. I am not a piece of rotting flesh,'" *Guardian*, September 21, 2018.

216 **"But I think this was the first time"**: Amy Taubin, interview by the author, March 18, 2023.

216 **"A large group of women"**: Gwilym Mumford, "Cannes 2018," *Guardian*, May 8, 2018.

217 **"We had a beautiful breakfast"**: Ava DuVernay, interview by the author, March 17, 2021.

218 **"And then . . . Warm and wonderful"**: Ava DuVernay, text message to the author, November 17, 2022.

218 **"I committed to it"**: DuVernay, text message.

218 **"There are thousands of people"**: Elsa Keslassy, "Agnès Varda Receives Honorary Award at Marrakech Film Festival," *Variety*, December 3, 2018.

219 **Varda put a stop to her chemotherapy**: Jane Birkin, "Agnès Varda Remembered by Jane Birkin," *Guardian*, December 16, 2018.

219 **Agnieszka Holland . . . was asked**: Laura Berger, "Berlinale, 2019: Meet Agnieszka Holland," WomenandHollywood.com, February 8, 2019.

219 **"Agnieszka Holland is my hero"**: Isabel Coixet at Berlinale press conference, February 14, 2019.

220 **"Director. Screenwriter. Legend"**: Agnès Varda at Berlinale press conference, February 13, 2019.

221 **"She said that [Agnès] wanted to say goodbye"**: Birkin, "Agnès Varda Remembered."

222 **thought Varda was "immortal"**: Agence France-Presse, "Mort d'Agnès Varda: l'hommage ému des stars et du septième arts," *Paris Match*, March 29, 2019.

222 **not mournful but "sweet"**: Canadian Broadcasting Company, "Agnès Varda's Art Will 'Live Forever,' Says Friend and Collaborator," March 29, 2019.

222 **"She taught us how to see again"**: Andreas Wiseman, "Agnès Varda Tributes," *Deadline*, March 29, 2019.

222 **"Movies big and small"**: Wiseman, "Agnès Varda Tributes."

222 **Varda's funeral and interment**: Bernard Bastide, "Funerailles d'Agnès V," unpublished notes taken at the time. All quotes and descriptions are taken from this document.

Bibliography

"Agnès Varda at the Rencontres d'Arles, 1982." *L'Œil de la photographie*, May 15, 2015.

Archibald, Sasha. "End of the End of the End: Agnès Varda in Los Angeles." *East of Borneo*, March 7, 2020.

Bear, Liza. "Agnès Varda." *Interview*, May 22, 2009.

Beauchamp, Cari, and Henri Béhar. *Hollywood on the Riviera*. New York: William Morrow, 1992.

Bénézet, Delphine. *The Cinema of Agnès Varda: Resistance and Eclecticism*. London and New York: Wallflower Press, 2014.

Bluher, Dominique, and Julia Fabry. *The Third Life of Agnès Varda*. Leipzig: Spector, 2022.

Bourg, Julian. *From Revolution to Ethics: May 1968 and Contemporary French Thought*. Montreal and Kingston, Ont.: McGill–Queens University Press, 2017.

Butler, Cornelia, and Alexandra Schwartz, eds. *Modern Women: Women Artists in the Museum of Modern Art*. New York: Museum of Modern Art, 2010.

Campany, David, ed. *The Cinematic*. London and Cambridge, MA: Whitechapel Gallery and MIT Press, 2007.

Criterion Collection. *The Complete Films of Agnès Varda*. DVD box set. New York, 2020.

Criterion Collection. *The Essential Jacques Demy*. DVD box set. New York, 2014.

de Baecque, Antoine, and Serge Toubiana. *Truffaut*. New York: Alfred A. Knopf, 1999.

De Beauvoir, Simone, *The Second Sex*. Translated by Constance Borde and Sheila Malovany-Chevallier. New York: Vintage, 2011.

Decock, Jean. "Entretien avec Agnès Varda sur 'Jacquot de Nantes.'" *French Review* 66, no. 6 (May 1993).

DeRoo, Rebecca J. *Agnès Varda between Film, Photography, and Art*. Oakland: University of California Press, 2017.

Des Femmes de Musidora. *Paroles . . . elles tournent!* Artigues-près-Bordeaux: La Société Nouvelle des Imprimeries Delmas, 1976.

Dossin, Catherine, ed. *France and the Visual Arts since 1945*. New York: Bloomsbury Visual Arts, 2019.

Études cinématographiques. Editions 179–86. Paris: Lettres Modernes, 1991.

Fishman, Sarah. *From Vichy to the Sexual Revolution*. New York: Oxford University Press, 2017.

Flitterman-Lewis, Sandy. *To Desire Differently: Feminism and the French Cinema*. Urbana: University of Illinois Press, 1990.

Fondation Cartier. *"Agnès Varda, L'ÎLE et ELLE*: Regards sur l'exposition." Arles: Actes Sud, 2006.

Frodon, Jean-Michel. "Godard et Varda dans l'espace." *Cahiers du cinéma*, September 2006.

Gauvin, Jean-Baptiste. "Agnès Varda at the Palais idéal." *L'Œil de la photographie*, November 8, 2021.

Goetschel, Pascale, and Emmanuelle Loyer. *Histoire culturelle de la France*. Paris: Armand Colin, 2014.

Insdorf, Annette. *François Truffaut*. Cambridge and New York: Cambridge University Press, 1994.

Leblanc, Claire, ed. *Agnès Varda: Patates et compagnie*. Milan: Silvana Editoriale, 2016.

Menand, Louis. *The Free World*. New York: Farrar, Straus and Giroux, 2021.

Nelson, Max. "The Intimate and the Collective." *Nation*, April 14, 2020.

Picq, Françoise. *Libération des femmes, quarante ans de mouvement*. Paris: Editions du Seuil, 1991.

Quandt, James. "James Quandt on *Cinevardaphoto*." *Artforum*, April 2005.

Rich, B. Ruby. "Gleaners Over Gladiators." *Nation*, March 22, 2001.

Sadoul, Georges. *Dictionary of Film Makers*. Berkeley: University of California Press, 1972.

Singh-Kurtz, Sangeeta. "The Joy of Agnès Varda." *The Cut*, September 1, 2020.

Smith, Alison. *Agnès Varda*. Manchester, UK, and New York: Manchester University Press, 1998.

Taubin, Amy. "Passages: Agnès Varda." *Artforum*, Summer 2019.

Unger, Steven. *Cléo de 5 a 7*. Basingstoke: BFI/Palgrave Macmillan, 2008.

White, Patricia. *Women's Cinema, World Cinema*. Durham, NC: Duke University Press, 2015.

Williams, Conor. "Rosalie Varda on the Enduring Legacy of Her Mother, Agnès." *Interview*, November 20, 2019.

Index